Game Theory

Game Theory

Introduction and Applications

GRAHAM ROMP

OXFORD
UNIVERSITY PRESS

OXFORD

UNIVERSITY PRESS

Great Clarendon Street, Oxford OX2 6DP

Oxford University Press is a department of the University of Oxford.
It furthers the University's objective of excellence in research, scholarship,
and education by publishing worldwide in

Oxford New York

Athens Auckland Bangkok Bogotá Buenos Aires Calcutta
Cape Town Chennai Dar es Salaam Delhi Florence Hong Kong Istanbul
Karachi Kuala Lumpur Madrid Melbourne Mexico City Mumbai
Nairobi Paris São Paulo Singapore Taipei Tokyo Toronto Warsaw

with associated companies in Berlin Ibadan

Oxford is a registered trade mark of Oxford University Press
in the UK and in certain other countries

Published in the United States
by Oxford University Press Inc., New York

© Graham Romp 1997

British Library Cataloguing in Publication Data

Data available

Library of Congress Cataloging in Publication Data
Romp, Graham.
Game theory : introduction and applications / Graham Romp.
p.   cm.
Includes bibliographical references and index.
1. Game theory.   2. Economics, Mathematical.   I. Title.
HB144.R66   1997   330'.01'5193—dc21   97–475

ISBN 0-19-877501-6
ISBN 0-19-877502-4 (Pbk.)

5 7 9 10 8 6 4

Printed in Great Britain
on acid-free paper by
Alden Press, Osney Mead, Oxford

PREFACE

This textbook is primarily aimed at students undertaking advanced undergraduate courses or introductory postgraduate courses, which incorporate economic applications of game theory. Following the widespread use of game theory in economics such courses are now common in many universities. Although quite a number of textbooks have recently been published on game theory, few place extensive emphasis on the economic applications of this theory. Furthermore these textbooks often present the material using high-level mathematics, which many students find over difficult. This text seeks to remedy these shortcomings. In particular we illustrate how game theory can be used to help us gain a deeper understanding of many issues economists are interested in. To do this we analyse a broad range of topics taken from both macroeconomics and microeconomics. This is done without the use of advanced-level mathematics. Instead, all that is required is a level of mathematics taught on most introductory undergraduate courses. This is achieved by the extensive use of examples and diagrams to illustrate arguments presented in the text. The book avoids deriving highly complex proofs used in game theory. Instead, general results are derived as extensions to more specific problems.

In order to further aid student learning, each of the main chapters incorporates a number of exercises. These exercises are an integral part of the text. They seek to develop previous ideas and often provide the basis for subsequent discussion. Students are, therefore, strongly recommended to attempt these exercises before continuing with the text. None the less full solutions to these exercises are provided at the end of each chapter, which can then be used as worked examples for future reference. Although we have attempted to maintain a constant level of difficulty with these exercises, some are necessarily more complex than others. These have been marked with an asterisk (*). Finally, to guide further reading a selective list of relevant books and articles is provided at the end of each chapter.

My thanks go to colleagues at UCE for their help and support in writing this book. Thanks also go to current and past students for undertaking many of the exercises and offering helpful suggestions. Finally, my thanks go to Jacky for her patience and love. This book is dedicated to her.

G.R.

University of Central England
Birmingham

CONTENTS

Contents

Contents

1

What is Game Theory?

GAME theory is concerned with how rational individuals make decisions when they are mutually interdependent. In recent years this theory has been increasingly applied to various branches of economics. Often this synthesis has significantly improved our understanding of economic issues and led to important new insights being developed. In many instances the application of game theory has transformed the way economists think about both microeconomic and macroeconomic problems. This is evidenced by the frequent use of the adjective 'new' when game theory is applied to different branches of economics. For example, it is now common for economists to refer to New Industrial and New International Economics. Both of these areas have developed as game theory has been applied to traditional disciplines within economics. Also, while not uniquely defined by their use of game theory, much of New Classical and New Keynesian Macroeconomics has incorporated game theoretical analysis. Indeed, so widespread is the use of game theory in economics that it is difficult to find an area where such an approach has not yielded new insights and challenged traditional theory. The aim of this book is to provide an introduction to basic game theory concepts and to illustrate how these have been applied to a diverse range of economic issues. In the first section of this chapter we discuss the broad characteristics of game theory. These, in turn, delimit the range of economic issues for which game theoretical analysis is applicable. In the second section we provide an outline of subsequent chapters.

1.1 Basic Assumptions of Game Theory

As stated above game theory is concerned with how rational individuals make decisions when they are interdependent. To understand this definition more fully we discuss what is meant by individualism, rationality, and mutual interdependence.

1

1.1.1 Individualism

It is usual to distinguish two separate branches of game theory. These are co-operative and non-cooperative game theory. Strictly speaking the previous definition of game theory only applies to non-cooperative game theory. In *non-cooperative game theory* the individuals, or players, in a game are unable to enter into binding and enforceable agreements with one another. Due to this assumption non-cooperative game theory is inherently individualistic. In contrast, *co-operative game theory* analyses situations where such agreements are possible. The focus of co-operative game theory is therefore on how groups of individuals committed to each other formulate rational decisions. This distinction does not mean that non-cooperative game theory precludes individuals working together. However, it does state that this will only happen if individuals perceive such co-operation to be in their own self-interest. From this perspective individuals work together not because they have to, but because they voluntarily choose to do so. This individualistic approach is clearly consistent with the dominant emphasis within neoclassical economics. For this reason it is non-cooperative game theory that has had the greatest impact within mainstream economics. Given this prominence we restrict ourselves in this book to economic applications of non-cooperative game theory. None the less it should be realized that in many cases we consider the co-operative and non-cooperative approaches are not clearly distinguished. For example, in many instances complex organizations such as firms, governments, and indeed countries are considered to act as individual decision-makers. Clearly this is an extreme simplification and one that ignores how decisions are formulated within these institutions. The value of such a simplification is to make the resulting models more tractable. As in other areas the skill of the economist is to select the level of aggregation most appropriate for the problem being analysed.

1.1.2 Rationality

The second characteristic of game theory is that individuals are assumed to be instrumentally rational. This means that individuals are assumed to act in their own self-interest. This presupposes that individuals are able to determine, at least probabilistically, the outcome of their actions, and have preferences over these outcomes. As with individualism this characteristic dominates neoclassical economics and its justification has been attempted in a number of ways.

The *first* justification is to argue that individuals are indeed rational. However, given the complexity of many decisions, and the amount of information that often needs to be analysed, this seems unrealistic. Indeed evidence from many experimental studies suggests that individuals are not fully rational but instead solve complex decisions by adopting simplistic rules that are generally suboptimal. A *second* justification for rationality is that due to some process of natural selection the economy eventually converges on the fully rational outcome. From this perspective the assumption of rationality is consistent with focusing on the long-run equilibrium of the economy. For example, it is argued that if firms suboptimize then the competitive process will eventually force them to leave the industry. The result of this is that in long-run equilibrium all remaining firms must be optimizing and fully rational. One problem with this argument, however, is that although such an evolutionary process may be considered relevant for competition between firms, it is not always clear how it applies in other contexts. For example, there seems to be no evolutionary process whereby rational consumers can eliminate non-rational consumers. Without such a process of selection the economy will not necessarily converge on the rational outcome. The *final* justification for rationality is that it is not intended to describe how individuals actually solve complex decisions, but rather it is only assumed that individuals act *as if* they were fully rational. Once again the assumption of rationality is used to make the resulting models more tractable. As noted by Friedman (1953) all theories must involve some simplification, as none can include all the possible features of reality. According to this positive methodology the assumption of rationality should not be dismissed merely because it is believed to be unrealistic. This is because all simplifying assumptions are necessarily unrealistic. Instead rationality should only be rejected if the results based on this assumption are found to be unhelpful. This will be true if the theory either gives rise to no relevant predictions or these predictions are falsified by empirical evidence. With this methodology a theory should be judged on its usefulness rather than on the supposed realism of its assumptions. In this book it is argued that game theory based on rationality can be extremely useful in helping us understand a diverse range of economic issues. This, however, does not imply that departures from complete rationality will not also provide useful insights and predictions. Indeed, a major theme of this book is that minor departures from full rationality are often required in order to derive meaningful results from game theory, and that further research incorporating these modifications is warranted. An alternative justification for analysing models that incorporate departures from full rationality is that as economists we may not only be interested in finding *useful* theories, but also interested in discovering theories that are true. If this is our aim, then the positivist methodology fails. If a theory's assumptions are falsified, then these need to be modified so that they conform to reality. As discussed in this book this is an ongoing process in the development of game theory and its application to economics.

1.1.3 Mutual interdependence

The final characteristic of game theory is that it considers situations where individuals are mutually interdependent. In this situation the welfare of any one individual in a game is, at least partially, determined by the actions of other players in the game.

Significantly with mutual interdependence individuals may now have the incentive to act strategically. With strategic decision-making individuals seek to anticipate the effect their own actions will have on the behaviour of others. Given this expectation each individual then determines his/her optimal response in order to achieve the most desirable outcome. In contrast to individualism and rationality this characteristic of mutual interdependence is less prominent within neoclassical economics. For example, in General Equilibrium Theory all agents are assumed to be atomistic. This ensures that the actions of agents taken in isolation have no effect on market outcomes or the welfare of others. This is assumed true for both firms and consumers. With this, and other assumptions it can be demonstrated that the competitive equilibrium is Pareto efficient. This means that no one individual can be made better off without making someone else worse off. In contrast once interdependence is introduced, so that an individual's welfare depends on the actions of others, there is the possibility of market failure and Pareto inefficiency. In this situation at least one individual can be made better off without any other agent being made worse off. The possibility of such inefficiency has been confirmed in numerous economic applications of game theory. Examples of mutual interdependence considered in this book include those between different firms, between firms and their employees, between the government of a country and the private sector, and between different governments.

1.2 Outline of Subsequent Chapters

The purpose of this book is to introduce readers to the main concepts of non-cooperative game theory, and to examine how these concepts have been applied within economics. These general aims are reflected in the structure of the book. The first two chapters focus on game theory itself, with little economic analysis except by way of illustration. In contrast Chapters 3 to 11 focus much more on various economic issues that have been analysed using game theory. In the final chapter we review the current state of game theory by discussing a number of criticisms levelled against recent models. From these criticisms we make some recommendations concerning the direction of future research.

In Chapter 2 we examine static games. These are one-off games where the players are considered to determine their actions simultaneously. In this context we examine two alternative ways in which games can be represented. These are the normal form and the extensive form. We also discuss various techniques commonly used to solve static games. These solutions correspond to predictions for what each player will do in the game, and are based on the concepts of dominance or equilibrium. It is here that we introduce the commonly used solution technique of Nash equilibrium, and discuss how this may be found for both pure and mixed strategies.

Chapter 3 continues our analysis of game theory by examining dynamic games.

These games conform more closely to real world examples where individuals and organizations repeatedly interact with each other. In these games players are often able to condition their actions on past events. This greatly enhances the set of strategies available to players. Once more this chapter discusses how dynamic games can be analysed and predictions made. In this context the key concept of credibility is introduced, and various refinements of Nash equilibrium, such as subgame perfection and sequential equilibrium, are presented.

In Chapters 4 and 5 we begin to focus more exclusively on the economic applications of game theory by considering two topics taken from industrial economics. The first is concerned with oligopoly, and examines the consequences of strategic interdependence between currently competing firms. Initially we consider one-off games between oligopolies, and discuss the now classic models of Cournot, Stackelberg, and Bertrand competition. The results from these one-off games are then contrasted with the results derived when firms are assumed to repeatedly interact. In particular, it is demonstrated that repeated interaction may enable firms to co-ordinate on the collusive outcome where joint profits are maximized. The second application taken from industrial economics is that of entry deterrence. Here the interdependence is between firms already in the market and potential entrants. To illustrate this type of strategic interdependence we examine the situation where a monopolist has the incentive to try and deter other firms from entering the market and competing against it. Initially this involves a critical discussion of Bain's (1956) Theory of Limit Pricing. Subsequent to this we present more recent models of entry deterrence based on non-cooperative game theory. These models serve to highlight the important roles of predatory pricing, precommitment, and incomplete information in oligopolistic markets.

Whilst the games considered in Chapters 4 and 5 are primarily microeconomic, Chapters 6 and 7 focus on macroeconomic games. In Chapter 6 we analyse New Classical results and give them a game theory interpretation. In the first two sections we illustrate how New Classical Macroeconomics has challenged earlier results related to the effectiveness of government policy. This discussion naturally raises the issue of time inconsistency. This occurs when the government has a short-run incentive to deviate from its long-run optimal policy. With the private sector perceiving such an incentive the final equilibrium is Pareto inefficient. In the third section of this chapter we evaluate various suggestions for how governments might avoid the problem of time inconsistency.

In Chapter 7 our attention turns to New Keynesian Macroeconomics. Specifically we examine a number of game theory models that attempt to explain the occurrence of involuntary unemployment and the effectiveness of government demand policy, whilst assuming that all agents are rational. Three separate, though related, strands of New Keynesian Macroeconomics are presented. The first focuses on efficiency wage models, where unemployment is due to real rigidities. The second examines how unemployment can result when agents do not fully adjust nominal wages and prices to an adverse demand shock. Finally, we examine models that exhibit multiple equilibria and co-ordination failure. This occurs when agents within the economy co-ordinate on a Pareto-dominated equilibrium. Significantly it is argued that this possibility may arise even in the absence of real or nominal rigidities.

Chapters 8, 9, and 10 analyse game theory models set in an international context. In Chapter 8 we examine the role of international policy co-ordination. This chapter argues that given the presence of spillover effects between countries uncoordinated policy is likely to lead to an inefficient outcome. This provides the incentive for countries to try and co-ordinate their domestic policies. Despite potential gains there are a number of problems associated with policy co-ordination. These are also discussed. Finally, this chapter seeks to assess the likely magnitude of such gains by reviewing a number of empirical studies.

Chapter 9 considers the possibility that a government may improve domestic welfare with the appropriate use of strategic trade policy. This possibility is discussed in two separate contexts. The first context is where all markets are perfect, but the country itself has some degree of market power. This occurs when the country in question is large, and gives rise to the 'optimal tariff argument'. With two or more countries pursuing such a policy, however, all countries can be made worse off. Various mechanisms for avoiding this outcome are discussed. The second context that provides some justification for strategic trade policy is when domestic industries engaged in international trade have some degree of market power. Faced with oligopolistic competition we analyse how government trade policy can be welfare enhancing and review some of the problems associated with such a policy.

The final chapter set in an international context is concerned with environmental economics. In Chapter 10 we analyse the incentives for countries to enter into international environmental agreements (IEAs). Initially we consider bilateral agreements and then analyse multilateral agreements. In each case we highlight the costs of countries failing to reach agreement over environmental control, and discuss various ways co-ordination can be achieved. In particular we examine the use of side payments between countries, the prospect of punishing countries that break environmental agreements, and how the number of countries signing IEAs might be expanded.

Chapter 11 is somewhat different from the previous chapters. In this chapter we focus on a recent branch of economics known as Experimental Economics. Instead of analysing the theoretical implications of game theory, we discuss a number of experiments that have been designed to test the predictions of this theory. This is done by testing whether they are confirmed by the behaviour of individuals in a controlled environment. Given how rapidly the literature within experimental economics is expanding we focus on studies concerned with testing three of the more important game theory concepts widely used in economics. These are the concepts of Nash equilibrium, sequential equilibrium, and the possibility of co-ordination failure in games with Pareto-ranked multiple equilibria. From a review of such experiments we conclude that the predictions of game theory often perform remarkably well. None the less it is clear that not all relevant game theory predictions are confirmed by experimental evidence. Despite the inherent problems with interpreting such results we argue that greater research is needed on how individuals seek to solve complex decisions under conditions of uncertainty, and how they seek to learn and co-ordinate appropriate strategies over time. Similar conclusions are reached in Chapter 12. In this final chapter we focus on a number of theoretical criticisms levelled at recent game theory models. These specifically relate to assumptions concerning the rationality of individuals. It is argued that models based purely on instrumental rationality are either self-defeating, incomplete, or inconsistent. However, rather than being purely destructive these criticisms can be viewed as a stimulus to further research. We predict that this will involve a re-evaluation of what is meant by rationality, and a greater emphasis given to factors such as the role of institutions, culture, and the previous experience of agents. Such research is an ongoing process, and it is confidently expected that it will lead to further fruitful applications to economics.

2
Static Game Theory

I N this chapter we will look at how static games can be represented, and examine some ways that have been suggested how they might be solved. A solution to a game is a prediction of what each player in that game will do. In static games the players make their moves in isolation without knowing what other players have done. This does not necessarily mean that all decisions are made at the same time, but rather only *as if* the decisions were made at the same time. An example of a static game is a one-off sealed bid auction. In this type of auction each player submits only one bid, without knowing what any of the other players has bid. The highest bid is then accepted as the purchase price. In contrast to static games, dynamic games have a sequence to the order of play and players observe some, if not all, of one another's moves as the game progresses. An example of a dynamic game is a so-called English auction. Here players openly bid up the price of an object. The final and highest bid is accepted as the purchase price.

2.1 Normal Form and Extensive Form Games

In non-cooperative game theory there are two ways in which a game can be represented. The first type is called a *normal form game* or *strategic form game*. The second type is called an *extensive form game*. Both are widely used in economics and we examine each in turn.

2.1.1 Normal form games

A normal form game is any game where we can identify the following three things:

(1) The players
The players in a game are the individuals who make the relevant decisions. For there to be interdependence we need to have at least two players in the game. In most of the applications we look at there will be only two players. In some games 'Nature' is consid-

ered a further player, whose function is to determine the outcome of certain random events, such as the weather or the 'type' of players in the game.

(2) The strategies available to each player

A strategy is a complete description of how a player could play a game. This does not necessarily just list the player's alternative actions. Instead it describes how the player's actions are dependent on what he or she observes other players in the game to have done. For example, if I am thinking about selling my car, then my actions are limited to selling it or keeping it. My chosen strategy, however, tells me how these possible actions are dependent on what other people do. If someone offers me £5,000 or more for my car, I will certainly sell it. If they offer me less than £5,000 I will keep the car. In dynamic games such as this a player's strategy set will be much larger than his or her possible actions. In static games, however, the two are the same. This is because in static games decisions are taken in isolation and so players cannot make their actions dependent on what other players do. In the example where I try to sell my car, this would correspond to the very strange game where I have to accept or reject someone's offer without knowing what it is! In this case my strategies are the same as my actions: to sell or not to sell. (In this discussion we have ignored the possibility of players adopting mixed strategies. These are discussed later in this chapter.)

(3) The pay-offs

A pay-off is what a player will receive at the end of the game contingent upon the actions of all the players in the game. A normal form game shows the pay-offs for every player, except Nature, for every possible combination of available strategies. These are then represented in the form of a matrix or matrices. The pay-offs are defined so that the players in the game always prefer higher to smaller pay-offs. For example, the pay-offs may correspond to monetary rewards, such as profits, or the utility each player obtains at the end of the game. Players are said to be rational when they seek to maximize their pay-off. Players who do not have this objective are said to be irrational, because they are not acting in their own self-interest.

To make the ideas discussed more specific we will look at one well-known static game called 'the *Prisoners' Dilemma*'. In this game the police have arrested two suspects of a crime. However, they lack sufficient evidence to convict either of them unless at least one of them confesses. The police hold the two suspects in separate cells and explain the consequences of their possible actions. If neither confesses, then both will be convicted of a minor offence and sentenced to one month in prison. If both confess, they will be sent to prison for six months. Finally, if only one of them confesses, then that prisoner will be released immediately while the other one will be sentenced to nine months in prison—six months for the crime and a further three months for obstructing the course of justice.

The above description of the game satisfies the three requirements of a normal form game. We have two players, each of whom has two strategies (which in this static game are the same as the prisoners' actions, to confess or not confess), and pay-offs for each possible combination of strategies. The normal form for this game is shown in Fig. 2.1. The pay-offs are shown as the negative number of months in prison for each outcome and for each prisoner. This assumes that each suspect, if rational, seeks to minimize the amount of time spent in prison. By convention the first pay-off listed in each cell refers to the row player, prisoner 1, and the second pay-off refers to the column player, prisoner 2.

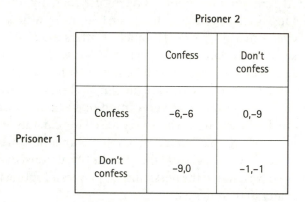

Fig. 2.1 The Prisoners' Dilemma in Normal Form

2.1.2 Extensive form games

In extensive form games greater attention is placed on the *timing* of the decisions to be made, as well as on the amount of *information* available to each player when a decision has to be made. This type of game is represented not with a matrix but with a decision, or game, tree. The extensive form for the prisoners' dilemma is shown in Fig. 2.2.

Starting at the left of the diagram the open circle represents the first decision to be made in the game. It is labelled 1 to show that it is prisoner 1 that makes this decision. The branches coming out of this initial node represent the actions available to the player at that point in the game. Prisoner 1 can either confess to the crime or not confess. At the end of these branches there is a node representing prisoner 2's decision. Again this prisoner can either confess to the crime or not confess, as given by the branches coming from his decision nodes. However, prisoner 2 makes this decision without knowing what prisoner 1 has done. This is shown by joining prisoner 2's decision nodes with a dotted line. This dotted line shows that the connected nodes are in the same information set. This means that prisoner 2 is unable to distinguish which of the two nodes he is at, at the time this decision is made. This is because he does not know if prisoner 1 has confessed or not confessed to the crime. Finally, at the end of the game we have the pay-offs for each player. These are again dependent on what each pris-

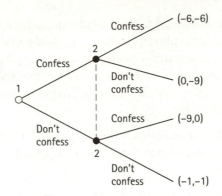

Fig. 2.2 The Prisoners' Dilemma Game in Extensive Form

oner has done in the game, and they are listed in the order of the players in the game, i.e. prisoner 1's pay-off is first, and prisoner 2's pay-off is second.

Generalizing from Fig. 2.2 we can state that extensive form games have the following four elements in common:

Nodes   This is a position in the game where one of the players must make a decision. The first position, called the initial node, is an open dot, all the rest are filled in. Each node is labelled so as to identify who is making the decision.

Branches   These represent the alternative choices that the person faces, and so correspond to available actions.

Vectors   These represent the pay-offs for each player, with the pay-offs listed in the order of players. When we reach a pay-off vector the game ends. When these pay-off vectors are common knowledge the game is said to be one of complete information. (Information is *common knowledge* if it is known by all players, and each player knows it is known by all players, and each player knows that it is known that all players know it, and so on *ad infinitum*.) If, however, players are unsure of the pay-offs other players can receive, then it is an incomplete information game.

Information Sets   When two or more nodes are joined together by a dashed line this means that the player whose decision it is does not know which node he or she is at. When this occurs the game is characterized as one of imperfect information. When each decision node is its own information set the game is said to be one of perfect information, as all players know the outcome of previous decisions.

A fundamental assumption of game theory is that the structure of the game is common knowledge. This places three specific requirements on information sets. The *first* is that players always remember whether they have moved previously in the game. This does not, however, mean that they always remember what decision they previously made, only that a decision was made. The *second* requirement is that nodes in the same information set have the same player moving. The *final* condition is that nodes in the same information set have the same possible actions coming from them. If this were not true, players could differentiate between the nodes by examining the available actions. Again generalizing from Fig. 2.2 we can state one further requirement that is always satisfied for extensive form games :

> **Each node has at least one branch pointing out of it (some action is available to the player) and at most one branch pointing into it. (The initial node has no branch pointing to it.)**

This means that at whatever node we begin at there is only one possible path back to the initial node and we never cycle back to the node we started from. For this reason extensive form games always look like trees. From the initial node we always branch out and a branch never grows back into itself.

We have now seen that there are two different ways of representing the same game, either as a normal form game or as an extensive form game. The normal form gives the minimum amount of information necessary to describe a game. It lists the players, the strategies available to each player, and the resulting pay-offs to each player. The extensive form gives additional details about the game concerning the timing of the decisions to be made and the amount of information available to each player when each decision has to be made. Clearly the two forms are closely related and we can state the following two results:

> **For every extensive form game there is one and only one corresponding normal form game.**

> **For every normal form game there are, in general, several corresponding extensive form games.**

The reason for this lack of one-to-one correspondence between a normal form game and an extensive form game is that, as described above, the extensive form game

---

EXERCISE 2.1

Depict the following situation as both a normal form game and an extensive form game:

Two rival firms are thinking of launching a similar product at the same time. If both firms launch the product, then they will each make a profit of £40,000. If only one firm launches its product, then it can act as a monopolist and will make a profit of £100,000. If either firm decides not to launch the product that firm makes a loss of £50,000, due to costs already incurred in developing the product.

includes additional information. This implies that different extensive forms can be drawn from the same normal form game, depending on what is assumed about these additional details of the game.

EXERCISE 2.2.

Interpret the following diagrams and discuss whether they represent valid extensive form games.

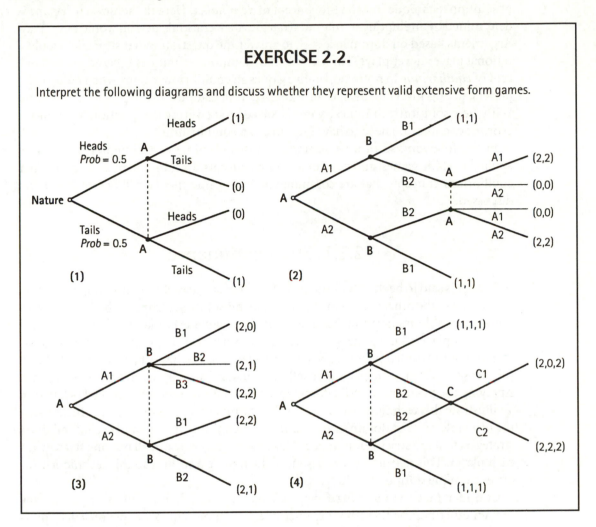

2.2 Solution Techniques for Solving Static Games

As stated at the beginning of this chapter a solution to a game is a prediction of what each player in that game will do. This may be a very precise prediction, where the solution gives one optimal strategy for each player. When this occurs the solution is said to be unique. However, it is often the case that the solution to a particular game is less precise, even to the extent that none of the available strategies are ruled out. As may be expected many different solution techniques have been proposed for different types of games. For static games two broad solution techniques have been applied. The first set of solution techniques rely on the concept of *dominance*. Here the solution to a game is determined by attempting to rule out strategies that a rational person would never play. Arguments based on dominance seek to answer the question 'What strategies would a rational player never play?' The second set of solution techniques is based on the concept of *equilibrium*. In non-cooperative games an equilibrium occurs when none of the players, acting individually, has an incentive to deviate from the predicted solution. With these solution techniques a game is solved by answering the question 'What properties does a solution need to have for it to be an equilibrium?'

In the following section we examine various dominance techniques that can be applied to static games, and two equilibrium concepts. In subsequent chapters further equilibrium concepts that are commonly used in game theory will be presented and discussed.

2.2.1 Strict dominance

A strategy is said to be strictly dominated if another strategy always gives improved pay-offs whatever the other players in the game do. This solution technique makes the seemingly reasonable assumption that a rational player will never play a strictly dominated strategy. If players knowingly play a strictly dominated strategy, they cannot be maximizing their expected pay-off, given their beliefs about what other players will do. In this sense a player who plays a strictly dominated strategy is said to be irrational. Applying the principle of strict dominance rules out this type of irrational behaviour. To illustrate this technique we use it to solve the prisoners' dilemma game. In applying the principle of strict dominance we examine each player in turn and exclude all those strategies that are strictly dominated. This process may rule out all but one strategy for each player. This is true for the prisoners' dilemma game, and so this technique produces a unique solution for this game.

Consider first the dilemma facing prisoner 1. Should she confess or should she remain quiet hoping the other prisoner does the same. The principle of strict dominance argues that prisoner 1 should confess. The reason for this is that whatever prisoner 2 decides to do prisoner 1 is always better off confessing. This means not confessing is strictly dominated and so it seems reasonable to suppose it will not be played. The same logic applies equally to prisoner 2 and so strict dominance predicts that he will also confess. The solution to this game based on strict dominance is that both prisoners confess even though both would be better off if neither confessed. As at least one of the players in this game can, with a different outcome, be made better off without the other player being made worse off this solution is said to be Pareto inefficient. (In fact if neither player confesses, both would be better off.) This is a very common feature of many games used in economics, and it will be illustrated in many contexts throughout this book.

It should be noted here that the cause of Pareto inefficiency is not that the players cannot communicate, but rather that they cannot commit themselves to the Pareto-efficient outcome. Even if both prisoners agreed before being arrested that neither of them will confess, once in custody it is in their individual self-interest to do the opposite. This illustrates the difference between non-cooperative and co-operative game theory. In co-operative game theory the two prisoners could enter into a binding and enforceable agreement not to confess and so be made better off. This is not possible in non-cooperative game theory.

EXERCISE 2.3

Solve the previous product launch game described in Exercise 2.1 using the principle of strict dominance.

2.2.2 Weak dominance

A strategy is said to be weakly dominated if another strategy makes the person better off in some situations and leaves them indifferent in all others. Again it seems reasonable to assume that a rational player will not play a weakly dominated strategy, as he or she could do at least as well, and possibly even better, by playing the dominant strategy. Consider the normal form game shown in Fig. 2.3. In this game there are two players each with two possible strategies. Player 1 can move either 'up' or 'down', and player 2 can move either 'left' or 'right'. The pay-offs are given in the matrix, where the first figure is the pay-off for player 1 and the second figure is the pay-off for player 2. For this game none of the available strategies is ruled out using the principle of strict dominance. This is because no strategy makes that player worse off in all circumstances. For example, if player 1 plays 'up', then player 2 is indifferent between 'left' and 'right'. Similarly if player 2 plays 'left', player 1 is indifferent between 'up' and 'down'. Although we cannot appeal to the principle of strict dominance to rule out any of the available strategies, we can apply the principle of weak dominance.

According to the principle of weak dominance player 1 will never play 'down' and so this can be ruled out. Similarly player 2 will never play 'right', and so this can also be ruled out. This leaves only one remaining strategy for each player. The predicted outcome is that player 1 will move 'up' and player 2 will move 'left'. Again this is a Pareto-inefficient solution. This is because the outcome 'down/left' makes player 2 better off

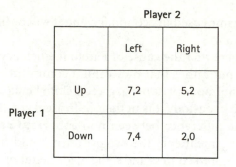

Fig. 2.3 An Application of Weak Dominance

and player 1 no worse off. The reason player 1 does not switch to playing 'down', even though this leads to a Pareto improvement, is that it entails greater risk for this player. If player 2 were to play 'right', then player 1 is definitely worse off moving 'down' instead of 'up'. This element of avoiding unnecessary risk is reflected in the principle of weak dominance.

2.2.3 Iterated strict dominance

Iterated strict dominance assumes that strict dominance can be applied successively to different players in a game. For example, if one player rules out a particular strategy, because it is strictly dominated by another, then it is assumed other players recognize this and that they also believe the other player will not play this dominated strategy. This in turn may lead them to exclude dominated strategies, and so on. In this way it may be possible to exclude all but one strategy for each player, and so make a unique prediction for the game being analysed. Consider the game shown in Fig. 2.4.

In this game player 1 has two possible strategies, 'up' and 'down', and player 2 has three possible strategies, 'left', 'middle', and 'right'. Initially neither 'up' nor 'down' is strictly dominated by the other for player 1. However, for player 2 'right' is strictly dom-

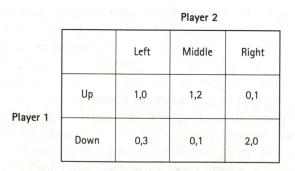

Fig. 2.4 An Application of Iterated Strict Dominance

inated by 'middle'. Appealing to strict dominance we can reason that player 2 will never play 'right'. If player 1 also knows that player 2 is rational and will not play 'right', then 'up' now strictly dominates 'down' for player 1. Iterated strict dominance now predicts that 'down' will not be played. Finally, if player 2 knows that player 1 will never move 'down', then iterated strict dominance predicts that player 2 will play 'middle'. The unique solution to this game based on successive or iterated strict dominance is therefore 'up/middle'.

2.2.4 Iterated weak dominance

The final dominance technique is iterated weak dominance. This is the same as iterated strict dominance except here it is weak dominance that is applied successively to different players in the game. Again it is possible that this technique can produce a unique solution to a particular game.

One problem with iterated weak dominance, which is not shared by iterated strict dominance, is that the predicted solution can depend on the order in which players' strategies are eliminated. This is true for the game shown in Fig. 2.5. If we start by applying weak dominance to player 1, then we predict that the players will choose the unique solution 'up/middle'. If we first apply weak dominance to player 2, then all we can conclude is that player 2 will not play 'right'. Clearly the order in which we apply weak dominance significantly affects the predicted outcome of the game. Unfortunately for most games this choice is totally arbitrary.

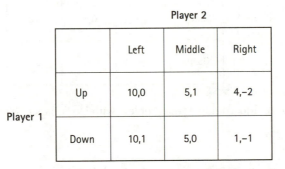

		Player 2		
		Left	Middle	Right
Player 1	Up	10,0	5,1	4,−2
	Down	10,1	5,0	1,−1

Fig. 2.5 An Application of Iterated Weak Dominance

It should be noted that in applying iterated-dominance arguments we are assuming a stronger version of rationality than we did with mere dominance. With dominance we assumed that rational players will not play dominated strategies. With iterated dominance we assume that rational players will not play dominated strategies, and also that players assume that other players are rational and will not do this. For iterated dominance to predict accurately people must not only be rational but assume that others are rational as well, and this requirement needs to be strengthened with each iteration. (For example, I need to assume that you believe that I believe that you believe that I am rational, and so on. When this sequence of reasoning continues *ad infinitum* we have the frequently used assumption of *common knowledge of rationality*.) As the number of iterations becomes large these additional assumptions become increasingly more dubious. An example of a game where the principle of iterated strict dominance is taken to extreme lengths is Rosenthal's (1981) centipede game. This dynamic game is discussed at the end of Chapter 3.

If a game yields a unique solution by applying either strict, weak, or iterated dominance, then that game is said to be dominance solvable. The main problem with all these solution techniques is that often they give very imprecise predictions about a game. Consider the game shown in Fig. 2.6. In this game arguments based on dominance lead to the very imprecise prediction that anything can happen! If a more specific solution to this type of game is needed, then a stronger solution technique must be applied. This leads us on to solution techniques based not on dominance but on the concept of equilibrium.

Player 2

Player 1		Left	Middle	Right
	Up	0,4	4,0	5,3
	Centre	4,0	0,4	5,3
	Down	3,5	3,5	6,6

Fig. 2.6 An Illustration of the Problem with Dominance Techniques

2.2.5 Nash equilibrium

As stated in the introduction to this section arguments based on dominance ask the question 'What strategies would a rational player never play?' In contrast the concept of Nash equilibrium is motivated by the question 'What properties must an equilibrium have?' The answer to this question from John Nash (1951), based on much earlier work by Cournot (1838), was that in equilibrium each player's chosen strategy is optimal given that every other player chooses the equilibrium strategy. If this were not the case, then at least one player would wish to choose a different strategy and so we could not be in an equilibrium. Again this concept seeks to apply the economist's assumption that individuals are rational in the sense that they seek to maximize their own self-interest.

Finding the Nash equilibrium for any game involves two stages. *First*, we identify each player's optimal strategy in response to what the other players might do. This involves working through each player in turn and determining their optimal strategies. This is done for every combination of strategies by the other players. *Second*, a Nash equilibrium is identified when all players are playing their optimal strategies simultaneously.

Strictly speaking, the above methodology only identifies pure-strategy Nash equilibria. It does not identify mixed-strategy Nash equilibria. A pure-strategy equilibrium is where each player plays one specific strategy. A mixed-strategy equilibrium is where at least one player in the game randomizes over some or all of their pure strategies. This means that players place a probability distribution over alternative strategies. For example, players might decide to play each of two available pure strategies with a probability of 0.5, and never play any other strategy. A pure strategy is therefore a restricted mixed strategy with a probability of one given to the chosen strategy, and zero to all the others. The concept of mixed-strategy Nash equilibrium is discussed later in this section.

To illustrate the two-stage methodology for finding a (pure-strategy) Nash equilibrium we apply it to the prisoners' dilemma game. This is shown in Fig. 2.7.

Prisoner 2

		Confess	Don't confess
	Confess	<u>−6</u>,<u>−6</u>	<u>0</u>,−9
Prisoner 1			
	Don't confess	−9,<u>0</u>	−1,−1

Fig. 2.7 The Nash Equilibrium of the Prisoners' Dilemma Game

Stage One.

We first need to identify the optimal strategies for each prisoner, dependent upon what the other prisoner might do. If prisoner 1 expects prisoner 2 to confess, then prisoner 1's best strategy is also to confess (−6 is better than −9). This is shown in Fig. 2.7 by underlining this pay-off element for prisoner 1 in the cell corresponding to both prisoners confessing. If prisoner 1 expects prisoner 2 not to confess, then prisoner 1's best strategy is still to confess (this time 0 is better than −1). Again we show this by underlining this pay-off element for prisoner 1. The same analysis is undertaken for prisoner 2 and his best strategy pay-offs are underlined.

Stage Two.

Next we determine whether a Nash equilibrium exists by examining the occurrence of the previously identified optimal strategies. If all the pay-offs in a cell are underlined, then that cell corresponds to a Nash equilibrium. This is true by definition, since in a Nash equilibrium all players are playing their optimal strategy given that other players also play their optimal strategies. In the prisoners' dilemma game only one cell has all its elements underlined. This corresponds to both prisoners confessing, and so this is the unique Nash equilibrium for this game.

This prediction for the prisoners' dilemma game is the same as that derived using strict dominance. In fact it is always true that a unique strict dominance solution is the unique Nash equilibrium. The reverse of this statement is, however, not always true. A unique Nash equilibrium is not always a unique strict dominant solution. In this sense the Nash equilibrium is a stronger solution concept than strict dominance. For this reason the Nash equilibrium concept may predict a unique solution to a game where strict dominance does not. This is illustrated in the game used previously to demonstrate that a game may not be dominance solvable. This game shown in Fig. 2.6 is reproduced in Fig. 2.8. As stated before, arguments based on dominance applied to this game predict that anything can happen. Using the two-stage methodology of finding a (pure-strategy) Nash equilibrium, however, yields the unique prediction that player 1 will choose 'down' and player 2 will choose 'right'. The concept of Nash equilibrium may therefore be particularly useful when dominance arguments do not provide a unique solution.

One important result from game theory is that for any finite game (i.e. games with a finite number of players and strategies) there always exists at least one Nash equilibrium. Before thinking that this result means that we can always make a definite predic-

Player 2

		Left	Middle	Right
	Top	0,<u>4</u>	<u>4</u>,0	5,3
Player 1	Centre	<u>4</u>,0	0,<u>4</u>	5,3
	Bottom	3,5	3,5	<u>6,6</u>

Fig. 2.8 A Further Application of Nash Equilibrium

tion about what people will do in any game the following two qualifications need to be stated.

First, the above result is only true if we include mixed strategies, as well as pure strategies. This means that we cannot always state for certain what all players in a game will do, but instead we may only be able to give the probabilities for various outcomes occurring. This possibility is discussed below.

Second, the above result does not rule out the possibility of multiple Nash equilibria. Indeed, many games do exhibit multiple Nash equilibria. With multiple equilibria the problem is how to select one equilibrium from many. In answer to this question

---

EXERCISE 2.4.

State whether the following games have unique pure strategy solutions, and if so what they are and how they can be found.

(1)

Player 2

Player 1		Left	Middle	Right
	Up	4, 3	2, 7	0, 4
	Down	5, 5	5, −1	−4, −2

(2)

Player 2

Player 1		Left	Middle	Right
	Up	4, 10	3, 0	1, 3
	Down	0, 0	2, 10	1, 3

(3)

Player 2

Player 1		Left	Middle	Right
	Up	10, 10	4, 3	7, 2
	Down	5, 6	8, 10	6, 12

numerous refinements of Nash equilibrium have been proposed to try and restrict the set of possible equilibria. Some of these refinements are discussed in later chapters.

2.2.6 Mixed strategy Nash equilibrium

To illustrate that there may be multiple Nash equilibria to a particular game, and also the idea of mixed strategies, we look at another classic game called the '*Battle of the Sexes*'. In this game a husband and wife are trying to decide where to go for an evening out. Whilst apart they must choose either to go to a boxing match, or to the ballet. Both players would rather go anywhere together, but given this the man prefers the boxing and the woman the ballet. (This game was proposed in the 1950s, which partly explains its stereotypical views.) These preferences are represented in the normal form game shown in Fig. 2.9.

Husband

		Go to boxing	Go to ballet
Wife	Go to boxing	<u>1,2</u>	0,0
	Go to ballet	0,0	<u>2,1</u>

Fig. 2.9 The Battle of the Sexes Games in Normal Form

Applying the two-stage method of identifying a pure-strategy Nash equilibrium we can see that the above game has two such equilibria. These are that either both will go to the boxing or both will go to the ballet. This means that each person will go wherever they think the other person will go. This is not very helpful, as it tells neither player what the other person is likely to do. As there is no unique pure-strategy Nash equilibrium neither player can confidently predict what the other person will do. Playing a mixed strategy is a response to this uncertainty. A mixed strategy is when a player randomizes over some or all of his or her available pure strategies. This means that the player places a probability distribution over their alternative strategies. A mixed-strategy equilibrium is where at least one player plays a mixed strategy and no one has the incentive to deviate unilaterally from that position.

The key feature of a mixed-strategy Nash equilibrium is that every pure strategy played as part of the mixed strategy has the same expected value. If this were not true, a player would play the strategy that yields the highest expected value to the exclusion of all others. This means the initial situation could not have been an equilibrium. Here we show how to identify the mixed-strategy Nash equilibrium for the battle of the sexes game.

Let $Prob(\text{boxing})_H$ be the probability that the husband goes to the boxing match, and $Prob(\text{boxing})_W$ the probability that the wife goes to the boxing match. Similarly let $Prob(\text{ballet})_H$ be the probability that the man goes to the ballet, and $Prob(\text{ballet})_W$ the probability that the woman goes to the ballet. As these are the only two alternatives it must be true that $Prob(\text{boxing}) + Prob(\text{ballet}) = 1$ for both the husband and wife. Given these probabilities we can calculate the expected value of each person's possible action.

From the normal form game the expected pay-off value for the wife if she chooses to go to the boxing match is given as

$$\pi(\text{boxing})_W = Prob(\text{boxing})_H(1) + Prob(\text{ballet})_H(0)$$

$$= Prob(\text{boxing})_H.$$

Similarly the expected pay-off value if she goes to the ballet is

$$\pi(\text{ballet})_W = Prob(\text{boxing})_H(0) + Prob(\text{ballet})_H(2)$$

$$= 2\,Prob(\text{ballet})_H.$$

In equilibrium the expected value of these two strategies must be the same and so we get

$$\pi(\text{boxing})_W = \pi(\text{ballet})_W$$

$$\therefore\ Prob(\text{boxing})_H = 2\,Prob(\text{ballet})_H$$

$$\therefore\ 1 - Prob(\text{ballet})_H = 2\,Prob(\text{ballet})_H$$

$$\therefore\ 1 = 3\,Prob(\text{ballet})_H$$

$$\therefore\ Prob(\text{ballet})_H = \tfrac{1}{3} \text{ and } Prob(\text{boxing})_H = \tfrac{2}{3}.$$

This means that in the mixed-strategy equilibrium the husband will go to the ballet with a 1/3 probability and the boxing with a 2/3 probability. We can perform the same calculations for the husband's expected pay-off and derive the similar result that in equilibrium his wife will go to the ballet with a probability of 2/3 and the boxing with a probability of 1/3. With these individual probabilities we can calculate that they will both go to the boxing with a probability of 2/9, both go to the ballet with a probability of 2/9, and go to separate events with a probability of 5/9.

This combination of mixed strategies constitutes a third Nash equilibrium for this game. Intuitively this seems the most reasonable Nash equilibrium of the three, as it explicitly takes into account the inherent uncertainty in the game. It should be noted that playing a mixed strategy does not mean that players flip a coin or roll a dice to make their decisions. Rather playing a mixed strategy is a rational response to uncertainty about what other players will do.

One curious aspect of a mixed-strategy equilibrium is that because each of the chosen pure strategies in the mixed strategy has the same expected pay-off value, each player is indifferent as to which strategy he or she actually plays. A mixed-strategy equilibrium is, therefore, said to be a weak equilibrium because none of the players is made worse off if they abandon their mixed strategy, and play any one of the pure strategy components of their mixed strategy. This feature of a mixed-strategy Nash equilibrium has caused its application within economics to be controversial. In particular this solution technique has been criticized as imposing unacceptable constraints on players' beliefs. Some of these criticisms are discussed in Chapter 12.

EXERCISE 2.5.

Draw the normal form game for the following game and identify both the pure- and mixed-strategy equilibria. In the mixed-strategy Nash equilibrium determine each firm's expected profit level if it enters the market.

There are two firms that are considering entering a new market, and must make their decision without knowing what the other firm has done. Unfortunately the market is only big enough to support one of the two firms. If both firms enter the market, then they will each make a loss of £10m. If only one firm enters the market, that firm will earn a profit of £50m., and the other firm will just break even.

2.3 Conclusions

Static games are where players make decisions in isolation. Each decision is made without knowing what the other players have done. These games can be represented as either normal or extensive form games. Normal form games give the minimum amount of information necessary to describe a game. They list the players in the game, the strategies available to each player, and the pay-offs dependent on the outcome of the game. Extensive form games give additional details on the timing of decisions and the amount of information players have when making these decisions. Static games are predominantly represented as normal form games. This is because in such games the amount of information available to players does not vary within the game, and the timing of decisions has no effect on players' choices. In the next chapter we examine dynamic games where the timing of decisions and information constraints critically determine the outcome of the game.

In attempting to predict the outcome of static games various solution techniques have been suggested. These are either based on the concept of dominance or equilibrium. These solution techniques try and predict what rational players will do in specified games. Sometimes they yield a definite prediction of what each player will do. Often, however, the solution is less precise. These solution techniques can also be applied to dynamic games, but as we will see in the next chapter additional assumptions are typically needed so that reasonable predications are generated.

2.4 Solutions to Exercises

Exercise 2.1

The normal and extensive forms for this static game are shown in Figs. 2.10 and 2.11 respectively:

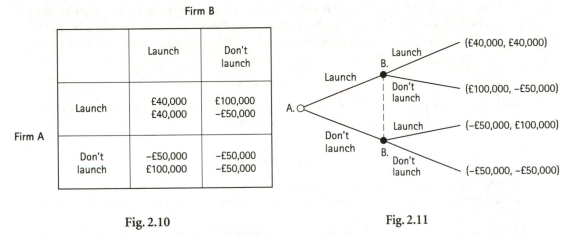

Fig. 2.10   Fig. 2.11

Exercise 2.2.

(1) This is a one-player static game against nature with imperfect information. Nature determines the outcome of the toss of an unbiased coin. Without knowing whether the outcome is heads or tails, player A calls either heads or tails. If the call is correct, the player wins a pay-off of 1. If the call is wrong, the player receives nothing. This diagram is a valid extensive form game. In such games we assume that players simply maximize their expected pay-off. In particular there are no strategic considerations in one-player games. For this reason this book only analyses games with two or more (rational) players.

(2) This is a dynamic game with imperfect recall. Player A initially decides between A1 and A2. This is observed by player B who then decides between B1 and B2. If B1 is chosen, the game ends. If B2 is chosen, player A moves again, playing either A1 or A2. Significantly these two final decision nodes are in the same information set, which means that player A does know which one she is at. However, the only difference in the paths to these nodes is player A's initial move. This means that player A must have forgotten what her first move was! This is a

25

valid extensive form game, and indeed some economic models have assumed that agents have imperfect recall. In this book, however, we limit ourselves to games where all players have perfect recall. This means that players do not forget any information that has been previously revealed to them.

(3) This is not a valid extensive form game as it entails a logical contradiction. In the diagram player B's decision nodes are in the same information set, which means that they cannot be distinguished. However, at the decision node following A1 there are three possible actions, while at the node following A2 there are only two options. Player B must know the actions available to him and so based on this information he will be able to distinguish between his decision nodes. This contradicts the fact they are shown as being in the same information set. To avoid such logical contradictions it is required that the set of possible actions from nodes in the same information set must be identical.

(4) This is not a valid extensive form game, as it violates one of the previous assumptions. This is the requirement that each node has at most one branch pointing to it. This is not true for player C's decision node. The reason this assumption is made is to guarantee a unique path from any decision node back to the initial node. (This is important for the application of backward induction discussed in the next chapter.) This diagram does not satisfy this feature, as there are two possible paths back to the initial node from player C's decision node.

Exercise 2.3

Strict dominance predicts that both firms will launch their respective products because this gives each firm a higher pay-off whatever the other firm does.

Exercise 2.4

(1) The unique pure-strategy equilibrium is 'down/left'. This is both a Nash equilibrium and an iterated strict dominant solution. The process of elimination for the dominant solution is 'right', 'up', 'middle'.

(2) The unique pure-strategy Nash equilibrium this time is 'up/left', and is both a Nash equilibrium and an iterated weak dominant solution. The process of elimination in the latter case is 'down', 'middle', 'right'.

(3) This game is not dominance solvable, but 'up/left' is a Nash equilibrium.

Exercise 2.5

The normal form for this static entry game is given in Fig. 2.12. Using the two-stage method for finding a pure-strategy Nash equilibrium we can see that there are two such equilibria. Both involve one firm entering the market, and the other firm staying out.

We can determine the mixed-strategy Nash equilibrium in the following way. Let $Prob(\text{enter})_1$ and $Prob(\text{enter})_2$ be the probabilities of firm 1 and firm 2 entering the market respectively. And let $Prob(\text{stay out})_1$ and $Prob(\text{stay out})_2$ be the probabilities of the two firms staying out of the market.

Expected profits for firm 1 if it enters the market are therefore

$$\pi(\text{enter})_1 = -10 \cdot Prob(\text{enter})_2 + 50 \cdot Prob(\text{stay out})_2$$

Firm 2

	Enters	Stays out
Enters	−£10m., −£10m.	£50m., <u>0</u>
Stays out	<u>0</u>, £50m.	0, 0

Firm 1

Fig. 2.12

and its expected profit if it stays out of the market is 0. In equilibrium these expected values must equal each other and so we get

$$-10 \cdot Prob(\text{enter})_2 + 50 \cdot Prob(\text{stay out})_2 = 0$$

$$\therefore 50 \cdot Prob(\text{stay out})_2 = 10 \cdot Prob(\text{enter})_2$$

$$\therefore 5 \cdot Prob(\text{stay out})_2 = Prob(\text{enter})_2$$

$$\therefore 5 \cdot Prob(\text{stay out})_2 = 1 - Prob(\text{stay out})_2$$

$$\therefore 6 \cdot Prob(\text{stay out})_2 = 1$$

$$\therefore Prob(\text{stay out})_2 = \tfrac{1}{6} \text{ and } Prob(\text{enter})_2 = \tfrac{5}{6}.$$

We could do the same calculations to find the same probabilities of firm 1 entering and staying out of the market.

Substituting these probabilities back into the equation for $\pi(\text{enter})_1$ we can find the expected value for firm 1 of entering the market.

$$\pi(\text{enter})_1 = -10 \cdot Prob(\text{enter})_2 + 50 \cdot Prob(\text{stay out})_2$$

$$\therefore \pi(\text{enter})_1 = -10 \cdot \tfrac{5}{6} + 50 \cdot \tfrac{1}{6}$$

$$\therefore \pi(\text{enter})_1 = 0.$$

The same result holds for firm 2. In the mixed-strategy Nash equilibrium the expected value for both firms if they enter the market is zero. This could have been found by noting that this equals the expected value of not entering which equals zero.

Further Reading

Aumann, R., and S. Hart (1992), *Handbook of Game Theory with Economic Applications*, New York: North-Holland.

Bierman, H. S., and L. Fernandez (1993), *Game Theory with Economic Applications*, Reading, Mass.: Addison-Wesley.

Static Game Theory

Dixit, A., and B. J. Nalebuff (1991), *Thinking Strategically: The Competitive Edge in Business, Politics, and Everyday Life*, New York: Norton.

Eatwell, J., M. Milgate, and P. Newman (1989), *The New Palgrave: Game Theory*, New York: W. W. Norton.

Gibbons, R. (1992), *Game Theory for Applied Economists*, Princeton: Princeton University Press.

Kreps, D. (1990), *A Course in Microeconomic Theory*, New York: Harvester Wheatsheaf.

Kreps, D. (1990), *Game Theory and Economic Modelling*, Oxford: Clarendon Press.

Rasmusen, E. (1993), *Games and Information*, Oxford: Blackwell.

Varian, H. (1992), *Microeconomic Analysis*, New York: Norton.

3
Dynamic Game Theory

IN the previous chapter we focused on static games. However, for many important economic applications we need to think of the game as being played over a number of time-periods, making it dynamic. A game can be dynamic for two reasons. *First*, the interaction between players may itself be inherently dynamic. In this situation players are able to observe the actions of other players before deciding upon their optimal response. In contrast, static games are ones where we can think of players making their moves simultaneously. *Second*, a game is dynamic if a one-off game is repeated a number of times, and players observe the outcome of previous games before playing later games. In section 3.1 we consider one-off dynamic games, and in section 3.2 we analyse repeated games.

3.1 Dynamic One-Off Games

An essential feature of all dynamic games is that some of the players can condition their optimal actions on what other players have done in the past. This greatly enhances the strategies available to such players in that these are no longer equivalent to their possible actions. To illustrate this we examine the following two-period dynamic entry game, which is a modified version of the static game used in Exercise 2.4.

There are two firms (A and B) that are considering whether or not to enter a new market. Unfortunately the market is only big enough to support one of the two firms. If both firms enter the market, then they will both make a loss of £10m. If only one firm enters the market, that firm will earn a profit of £50m., and the other firm will just break even. To make this game dynamic we assume that firm B observes whether firm A has entered the market before it decides what to do. This game can be represented by the extensive form diagram shown in Fig. 3.1.

In time-period 1 firm A makes its decision. This is observed by firm B which decides to enter or stay out of the market in period 2. In this extensive form game firm B's decision nodes are separate information sets. (If they were in the same information set, they would be connected by a dashed line.) This means that firm B observes firm A's action before making its own decision. If the two firms were to make their moves

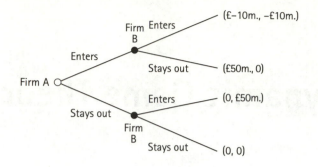

Fig. 3.1 The Dynamic Entry Game in Extensive Form

simultaneously, then firm B would have only two strategies. These would be either to enter or stay out of the market. However, because firm B initially observes firm A's decision it can make its decision conditional upon what firm A does. As firm A has two possible actions, and so does firm B, this means that firm B has four (2 × 2) strategies. We can list these as

> **Always enter the market whatever firm A does.**
> **Always stay out of the market whatever firm A does.**
> **Do the same as firm A.**
> **Do the opposite of firm A.**

Recognizing that firm B now has these four strategies we can represent the above game in normal form. This is shown in Fig. 3.2. Having converted the extensive form game into a normal form game we can apply the two-stage method for finding pure-strategy Nash equilibria, as explained in the previous chapter. *First*, we identify what each player's optimal strategy is in response to what the other players might do. This involves working through each player in turn and determining their optimal strategies. This is illustrated in the normal form game by underlining the relevant pay-off. *Second*, a Nash equilibrium is identified when all players are playing their optimal strategies simultaneously.

As shown in Fig. 3.2 this dynamic entry game has three pure-strategy Nash equilibria. In these three situations each firm is acting rationally given its belief about what the other firm might do. Both firms are maximizing their profits dependent upon what they believe the other firm's strategy is. One way to understand these possible outcomes is to think of firm B making various threats or promises, and firm A acting accordingly. We can therefore interpret the three Nash equilibria as follows:

1. Firm B threatens always to enter the market irrespective of what firm A does. If firm A believes this threat, it will stay out of the market.

2. Firm B promises always to stay out of the market irrespective of what firm A does. If firm A believes this promise, it will certainly enter the market.

Firm B

Firm A		Always enters	Always stays out	Same as firm A	Opposite of firm A
	Enters	−£10m. −£10m.	£50m. 0	−£10m. −£10m.	£50m. 0
	Stays out	0 £50m.	0 0	0 0	0 £50m.

Fig. 3.2 The Dynamic Entry Game in Normal Form

3. Firm B promises always to do the opposite of what firm A does. If firm A believes this promise, it will again enter the market.

In the first two Nash equilibria firm B's actions are not conditional on what the other firm does. In the third Nash equilibrium firm B does adopt a conditional strategy. A *conditional strategy* is where one player conditions his or her actions upon the actions of at least one other player in the game. This concept is particularly important in repeated games, and is considered in more detail in the next section.

In each of the equilibria firm A is acting rationally in accordance with its beliefs. However, this analysis does not consider which of its beliefs are themselves rational. This raises the interesting question 'Could firm A not dismiss some of firm B's threats or promises as mere bluff?' This raises the important issue of *credibility*. The concept of credibility comes down to the question 'Is a threat or promise believable?' In game theory a threat or promise is only credible if it is in that player's interest to carry it out at the appropriate time. In this sense some of firm B's statements are not credible. For example, firm B may threaten always to enter the market irrespective of what firm A does, but this is not credible. It is not credible because if firm A enters the market, then it is in firm B's interest to stay out. Similarly the promise always to stay out of the market is not credible because if firm A does not enter, then it is in firm B's interest to do so. Assuming that players are rational, and that this is common knowledge, it seems reasonable to suppose that players only believe credible statements. This implies that incredible statements will have no effect on other players' behaviour. These ideas are incorporated into an alternative equilibrium concept to Nash equilibrium (or a refinement of it) called subgame perfect Nash equilibrium.

3.1.1 Subgame perfect Nash equilibrium

In many dynamic games there are multiple Nash equilibria. Often, however, these equilibria involve incredible threats or promises that are not in the interests of the players making them to carry out. The concept of subgame perfect Nash equilibrium rules out these situations by saying that a reasonable solution to a game cannot involve players believing and acting upon incredible threats or promises. More formally a subgame perfect Nash equilibrium requires that the predicted solution to a game be a Nash equilibrium in every subgame. A *subgame*, in turn, is defined as a smaller part of the whole game starting from any one node and continuing to the end of the entire game, with the qualification that no information set is subdivided. A subgame is therefore a game in its own right that may be played in the future, and is a relevant part of the overall game. By requiring that a solution to a dynamic game must be a Nash equilibrium in every subgame amounts to saying that each player must act in his or her own self-interest in every period of the game. This means that incredible threats or promises will not be believed or acted upon.

To see how this equilibrium concept is applied, we continue to examine the dynamic entry game discussed above. From the extensive form of this game, given in Fig. 3.1, we can observe that there are two subgames, one starting from each of firm B's decision nodes. For the predicted solution to be a subgame perfect Nash equilibrium it must comprise a Nash equilibrium in each of these subgames. We now consider each of the Nash equilibria identified for the entire game to see which, if any, is also a subgame perfect Nash equilibrium.

1. In the first Nash equilibrium firm B threatens always to enter the market irrespective of what firm A does. This strategy is, however, only a Nash equilibrium for one of the two subgames. It is optimal in the subgame beginning after firm A has stayed out but not in the one where firm A has entered. If firm A enters the market, it is not in firm B's interest to carry out the threat and so it will not enter. This threat is not credible and so should not be believed by firm A. This Nash equilibrium is not subgame perfect.

2. In the second Nash equilibrium firm B promises always to stay out of the market irrespective of what firm A does. Again this is only a Nash equilibrium for one of the two subgames. It is optimal in the subgame beginning after firm A has entered but not in the one when firm A has stayed out . If firm A stays out of the market, it is not in the interest of firm B to keep its promise, and so it will enter. This promise is not credible, and so should not be believed by firm A. Once more this Nash equilibrium is not subgame perfect.

3. The third Nash equilibrium is characterized by firm B promising to do the opposite of whatever firm A does. This is a Nash equilibrium for both subgames. If firm A enters, it is optimal for firm B to stay out, and if firm A stays out, it is optimal for firm B to enter. This is a credible promise because it is always in firm B's interest to carry it out at the appropriate time in the future. This promise is therefore believable, and with this belief it is rational for firm A to enter the market.

The only subgame perfect Nash equilibrium for this game is that firm A will enter and firm B will stay out. This seems entirely reasonable given that firm A has the ability to enter the market first. Once firm B observes this decision it will not want to enter the market, and so firm A maintains its monopoly position. The way we solved this dynamic game has been rather time-consuming. This was done so that the concept of subgame perfection may be better understood. Fortunately, there is often a quicker way of finding the subgame perfect Nash equilibrium of a dynamic game. This is by using the principle of backward induction.

3.1.2 Backward induction

Backward induction is the principle of iterated strict dominance applied to dynamic games in extensive form. However, this principle involves ruling out the actions, rather than strategies, that players would not play because other actions give higher pay-offs. In applying this principle to dynamic games we start with the last period first and work backwards through successive nodes until we reach the beginning of the game. Assuming perfect and complete information, and that no player is indifferent between two possible actions at any point in the game, then this method will give a unique prediction which is the subgame perfect Nash equilibrium. Once more this principle is illustrated using the dynamic entry game examined above. The extensive form for this game is reproduced in Fig. 3.3.

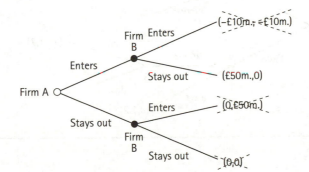

Fig. 3.3 The Dyanmic Entry Game and Backward Induction

Starting with the last period of the game first, we have two nodes. At each of these nodes firm B decides whether or not to enter the market based on what firm A has already done. At the first node firm A has already entered and so firm B will either make a loss of £10m. if it enters, or break even if it stays out. In this situation firm B will stay out, and so we can rule out the possibility of both firms entering. This is shown by crossing out the corresponding pay-off vector (−£10m., −£10m.). At the second node firm A has not entered the market, and so firm B will earn either £50m. if it enters or nothing if it stays out. In this situation firm B will enter the market, and we can rule out the possibility of both firms staying out. Once more we cross out the corresponding pay-off vector $(0,0)$. We can now move back to the preceding nodes, which in this game is the initial node. Here firm A decides whether or not to enter. However, if firm A assumes that firm B is rational, then it knows the game will never reach the previously excluded strategies and pay-offs. Firm A can reason therefore that it will either receive £50m. if it enters or nothing if it stays out. Given this reasoning we can rule out the possibility that firm A will stay out of the market, and so cross out the corresponding pay-off vector $(0, £50m.)$. This leaves only one pay-off vector remaining, corresponding to firm A entering the market and firm B staying out. This, as shown before, is the subgame perfect Nash equilibrium.

EXERCISE 3.1

Using the principle of backward induction find the subgame perfect Nash equilibrium for the following three-player extensive form game. State all the assumptions you make.

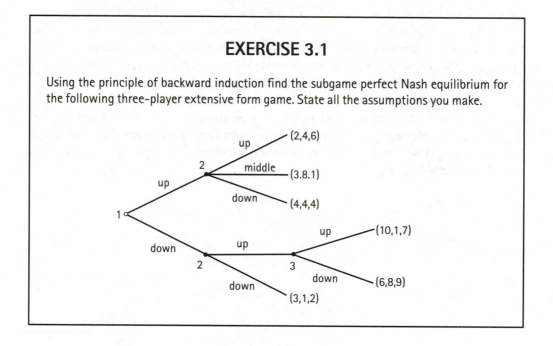

3.2 Repeated Games

The previous section considered one-off dynamic games. However, many games that economists are interested in involve repeated interaction between agents. Intuitively it would seem that repeated interaction between agents should have an effect on the predicted outcome of the game. For example, it would seem reasonable to assume that in repeated games players have more opportunity to learn to co-ordinate their actions so as to avoid the prisoners' dilemma discussed in the previous chapter. This section focuses on this issue and examines how repetition affects the predicted outcome of a game, and examines the conditions under which non-cooperative collusion is possible. This is undertaken in a number of contexts. *First*, we examine games where the one-off

EXERCISE 3.2

Convert the following extensive form game into a normal form game, and identify the Nash equilibria and subgame perfect Nash equilibrium. Finally, what is the Nash equilibrium if both players make their moves simultaneously?

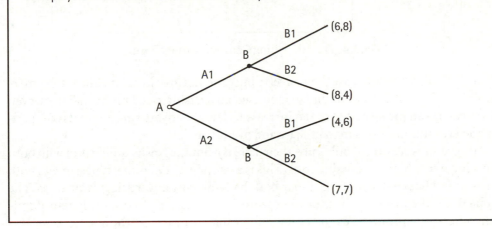

game (called the stage game) is repeated an infinite number of times. *Second*, we look at games where the stage game is repeated only a finite number of times and where the one-off game has a unique Nash equilibrium. In this context we discuss the so called 'paradox of backward induction'. This paradox is that while co-ordination may be possible in infinitely repeated games it is not possible in certain situations with finitely repeated games. This is true no matter how large the number of repetitions. *Finally*, we examine ways in which this paradox of backward induction may be avoided.

3.2.1 Infinitely repeated games

To illustrate some of the issues involved with repeated games we will consider the following situation between two competing firms. Assume that two firms, A and B, dominate a specific market. The marketing departments of both companies have discovered that increased advertising expenditure, all other things remaining the same, has a positive effect on that firm's sales. However, total sales also depends negatively on how much the other company spends on advertising. This is because it adversely affects the market share of the first company. If we assume there are only two levels of advertising (high or low expenditure) which each firm can carry out, then the pay-off matrix in terms of profits (£m. per year) for the two companies is given in Fig. 3.4.

From this normal form game both firms are better off if they each maintain low advertising expenditure compared to both incurring high advertising costs. This is

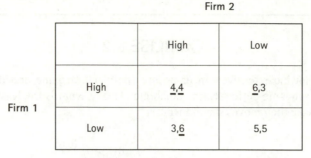

Fig. 3.4 The Advertising Game in Normal Form

because if both firms increase their advertising expenditure simultaneously, then market shares are unaffected, but due to increased advertising costs profits fall. However, each firm has an incentive to try and increase its level of advertising above its competitor's level as this increases market share and overall profits.

If this game were played only once, then there is a unique Nash equilibrium with both firms incurring high advertising costs. This is a prisoners'-dilemma-type game as both firms would be made better off if they both had low-cost advertising campaigns. The problem for the firms is how they can co-ordinate their actions on this Pareto-dominant outcome without the use of legally enforceable contracts. In the one-off game this would not seem to be possible as there is a clear incentive to increase advertising expenditure. However, if the interaction between the firms is infinitely repeated, then it is possible for the two firms to co-ordinate their actions on the Pareto-optimal outcome. This will occur if both firms adopt an appropriate conditional strategy and do not discount the future too much.

As stated previously a conditional strategy is where a player conditions what he or she does on the actions of at least one other player in the game. This allows the possibility for one or more players, in effect, to punish other players if they deviate from the Pareto-efficient outcome. This is known as a *punishment strategy*. If the prospect of punishment is sufficiently severe, players will be deterred from deviation. In this way the Pareto-efficient outcome can be maintained indefinitely. Once more the issue of credibility is important. For example, threatened punishment of deviant behaviour will only maintain the co-operative outcome if the threat is credible. This will only happen if it is in the interests of the person threatening punishment to exact it when deviation is observed. This implies that a punishment strategy will only be effective in maintaining the co-operative solution if it is part of a subgame perfect Nash equilibrium for the entire game. To illustrate how these ideas can work in practice consider the following specific punishment strategy for the previous advertising game.

> **Each firm starts off with low-cost advertising, and this is maintained provided the other firm has always done the same in previous periods. If, however, the other firm has undertaken a high-cost advertising campaign in the past, then the firm undertakes a high-cost advertising campaign thereafter.**

This particular type of punishment strategy is frequently used in infinitely repeated games and is known as a *trigger strategy*.

A trigger strategy is where the actions of one player in a game causes other players permanently to switch to another course of action. The above trigger strategy implies an infinite punishment period if either of the firms incurs high-cost advertising. Once one firm increases its level of advertising, the other firm does the same ever after. This rules out the possibility of ever returning to the Pareto-efficient outcome. A firm that undertakes a high-cost advertising campaign will see profits rise from £5m. to £6m. in the first year of deviation, but then fall to at most only £4m. per year thereafter. For this trigger strategy to maintain the Pareto-efficient outcome two conditions must be satisfied. *First*, the punishment itself must be credible. *Second*, the promise to maintain low-cost advertising, given the prospect of future punishment, must also be credible. We consider each of these issues in turn.

With the above trigger strategy the threat of punishment is credible because if one firm switches to high-cost advertising, then it is rational for the other firm to also switch to high-cost advertising. This punishment strategy is credible because it corresponds to the Nash equilibrium of the stage game. Playing the Nash equilibrium is always a credible strategy because, by definition, it is the optimal response to the other players' expected strategies. The remaining issue is whether the promise to continue with low-cost advertising is also credible. Assuming that firms attempt to maximize total discounted profits then the co-operative outcome, where both firms have low-cost advertising campaigns, will be maintained indefinitely if the present value of co-operation is greater than the present value of deviating. This will be the case if firms do not discount the future too much. This is demonstrated as follows.

As this is an infinitely repeated game we will have to assume that future pay-offs are discounted, so as to obtain a present value of future profits. Let $\delta = 1/(1 + r)$ equal each firm's rate of discount, where r is the rate of interest or the firm's rate of time preference. This represents the fact that a pound received today is worth more than a pound received in the future, because it can be invested at the rate of interest r. The further in the future a pound is received the less is its present value. With this rate of discount the present value of maintaining a low-cost advertising campaign, $PV(\text{low})$, is equal to

$$PV(\text{low}) = 5 + 5\delta + 5\delta^2 + \ldots$$
$$\therefore \delta\, PV(\text{low}) = 5\delta + 5\delta^2 + 5\delta^3 + \ldots$$
$$\therefore (1 - \delta)\, PV(\text{low}) = 5$$
$$\therefore PV(\text{low}) = \frac{5}{1 - \delta}.$$

Alternatively the present value of deviating from this co-operative outcome and engaging in a high-cost advertising campaign, $PV(\text{high})$, is equal to

$$PV(\text{high}) = 6 + 4\delta + 4\delta^2 + \dots$$
$$\therefore \; \delta PV(\text{high}) = 6\delta + 4\delta^2 + 4\delta^3 + \dots$$
$$\therefore \; (1-\delta)PV(\text{high}) = 6 + 4\delta - 6\delta$$
$$\therefore \; (1-\delta)PV(\text{high}) = 6(1-\delta) + 4\delta$$
$$\therefore \; PV(\text{high}) = 6 + \frac{4\delta}{1-\delta}.$$

Therefore the co-operative outcome will be maintained indefinitely if

$$PV(\text{low}) \geq PV(\text{high})$$

$$\therefore \; \frac{5}{1-\delta} \geq 6 + \frac{4\delta}{1-\delta}$$

$$\therefore \; \delta \geq 1/2.$$

This tells us that with infinite interaction, and the given trigger strategy, both firms will maintain low-cost advertising if their rate of discount is greater than one-half. Given that this condition is satisfied, this means that the promise to continue with low-cost advertising is credible. With both the threat of punishment and the promise to maintain low advertising being credible this corresponds to a subgame perfect Nash equilibrium for this game. (This outcome, however, is now only one of many subgame perfect equilibria. For example, another subgame perfect equilibrium is where both firms have high-cost advertising every period. The problem now becomes how firms co-ordinate upon one of the many equilibria. This problem is discussed in later chapters.) If the firms' rate of discount is less than one-half, then each firm will immediately deviate to high-cost advertising. The co-operative outcome cannot be maintained with the assumed trigger strategy because the future threat of punishment is not sufficient to deter deviation. This is because the firms place too great a weight on current profits, and not enough on future profits. The promise to maintain low-cost advertising is not credible, and so both firms will undertake high-cost advertising campaigns.

3.2.2 Finitely repeated games

In the previous section on infinitely repeated games it was shown that players may be able to maintain a non-cooperative collusive outcome, (co-operative outcome for short), which is different from the Nash equilibrium of the stage game. This was shown to be the case if the players adopt an appropriate punishment strategy and do not discount the future too much. Here we examine under what conditions this result continues to hold in the context of finitely repeated games.

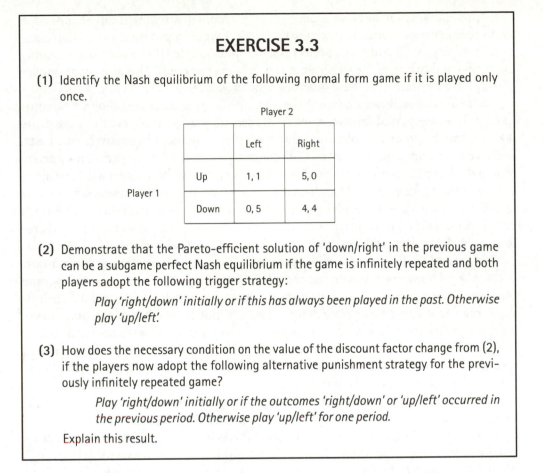

EXERCISE 3.3

(1) Identify the Nash equilibrium of the following normal form game if it is played only once.

Player 2

		Left	Right
	Up	1, 1	5, 0
Player 1			
	Down	0, 5	4, 4

(2) Demonstrate that the Pareto-efficient solution of 'down/right' in the previous game can be a subgame perfect Nash equilibrium if the game is infinitely repeated and both players adopt the following trigger strategy:

Play 'right/down' initially or if this has always been played in the past. Otherwise play 'up/left'.

(3) How does the necessary condition on the value of the discount factor change from (2), if the players now adopt the following alternative punishment strategy for the previously infinitely repeated game?

Play 'right/down' initially or if the outcomes 'right/down' or 'up/left' occurred in the previous period. Otherwise play 'up/left' for one period.

Explain this result.

The paradox of backward induction

One result obtained from applying the logic of backward induction to finitely repeated games is that if the one-off stage game has a unique Nash equilibrium, then the subgame perfect Nash equilibrium for the entire game is this Nash equilibrium played in every time-period. This is true however large the number of repetitions.

To understand this result consider the following argument. Suppose that a game having a unique Nash equilibrium is played a prespecified finite number of times. To find the subgame perfect Nash equilibrium for this game we start with the last period first. As the last period is just the one-off stage game itself, the predicted outcome in this period is the unique Nash equilibrium of the stage game. Now consider the penultimate period. Players using the principle of backward induction know that in the last period the Nash equilibrium will be played irrespective of what happens this period. This implies there is no credible threat of future punishment that could induce a player to play other than the unique Nash equilibrium in this penultimate period. All players know this and so again the Nash equilibrium is played. This argument can be applied to all preceding periods until we reach the first period, where again the unique Nash equilibrium is played. The subgame perfect Nash equilibrium for the entire game is simply the Nash equilibrium of the stage game played in every period. This argument implies that a non-cooperative collusive outcome is not possible.

This result can be illustrated using the advertising game described above, by assuming that it is only played for two years. In the second year we just have the stage game itself and so the predicted solution is that both firms will incur high advertising costs, and receive an annual profit of £4m. With the outcome in the second period fully determined the Nash equilibrium for the first period is again that both firms will have high-cost advertising campaigns. Similar analysis could have been undertaken for any number of finite repetitions giving the same result that the unique stage game Nash equilibrium will be played in every time-period. The subgame perfect solution, therefore, is that both firms will have high-cost advertising in both periods.

This general result is known as the paradox of backward induction. It is a paradox because of its stark contrast with infinitely repeated games. No matter how many finite number of times we repeat the stage game we never get the same result as if it were infinitely repeated. There is a discontinuity between infinitely repeated games and finitely repeated games, even if the number of repetitions is very large. This is counter-intuitive. It is also considered paradoxical because with many repetitions it seems reasonable to assume that players will find some way of co-ordinating on the Pareto-efficient outcome, at least in early periods of the game.

The reason for this paradox is that a finite game is qualitatively different from an infinite game. In a finite game the structure of the remaining game changes over time, as we approach the final period. In an infinite game this is not the case. Instead its structure always remains the same wherever we are in the game. In such a game there is no endpoint from which to begin the logic of backward induction. A number of ways have been suggested in which the paradox of backward induction may be overcome. These include the introduction of bounded rationality, multiple Nash equilibria in the stage game, uncertainty about the future, and uncertainty about other players in the game. These are each examined below.

Bounded rationality

One suggested way of avoiding the paradox of backward induction is to allow people to be rational but only within certain limits. This is called bounded, or near, rationality. One specific suggestion as to how this possibility might be introduced into games is by Radner (1980). Radner allows players to play suboptimal strategies as long as the payoff per period is within epsilon, $\varepsilon \geq 0$, of their optimal strategy. This is called an ε-best reply. An ε-equilibrium is correspondingly when all players play ε-best replies. If the number of repetitions is large enough, then playing the co-operative outcome, even if it is not a subgame perfect Nash equilibrium, can still be an ε-equilibrium given appropriate trigger strategies. This is demonstrated for the repeated advertising game described above. Assume that both firms adopt the punishment strategy given when considering infinite repetitions, but now the game is only played a finite number of times. If we assume that there is no discounting, then the pay-off for continuing to play according to this strategy, if the other firm undertakes high-cost advertising, is $3 + 4(t-1)$, where t is the remaining number of periods the firms interact. The pay-off for initiating a high-cost advertising campaign is at most $6 + 4(t-1)$. Deviating from the punishment strategy therefore yields a net benefit of 3. This is equal to $3/t$ per period. If players are boundedly rational as defined by Radner, then the co-operative outcome is an ε-equilibrium if $\varepsilon > 3/t$. This will be satisfied for any value of ε, provided the remaining number of periods is great enough. Given a large number of repetitions co-operation, which in this example means low-cost advertising, will be observed in the initial periods of the game.

Although interesting to analyse the effects of bounded rationality in repeated games, it is not clear that Radner's suggestion is the best way of doing this. For example, Friedman (1986) argues that bounded rationality might imply that people only calculate optimal strategies for a limited number of periods. If this is true, then the game becomes shorter, and the result of backward induction more likely. Furthermore if people do not fully rationalize we should consider why. If it is due to calculation costs, then these costs should be added to the structure of the game itself. This is an area of ongoing research.

Multiple Nash equilibria

The paradox of backward induction can be avoided if there are multiple Nash equilibrium in the stage game. With multiple Nash equilibria there is no unique prediction concerning the last period of play. This may give the players in the game a credible threat concerning future play which induces other players to play the co-operative solution. This is illustrated for the hypothetical game shown in Fig. 3.5 which we assume is played twice.

Player 2

		Left	Middle	Right
	Up	1,1	5,0	0,0
Player 1	Centre	0,5	4,4	0,0
	Down	0,0	0,0	3,3

Fig. 3.5 A Normal Form Stage Game with Multiple Nash Equilibria

This one-off stage game has two Nash equilibria 'up/left' and 'right/down'. These are both Pareto inefficient. If the players could co-ordinate on 'middle/centre', then both players would be better off. In the repeated game suppose that both players adopt the following punishment strategy:

**In the first period play 'middle/centre'. In the second period play 'right/down'
if 'middle/centre' was the outcome in the first round, otherwise play 'up/left'.**

Assuming the two periods are sufficiently close to each other we can ignore any discounting of pay-offs and so the matrix for the entire game is now that shown in Fig. 3.6.

Player 2

		Left	Middle	Right
	Up	2,2	6,1	1,1
Player 1	Centre	1,6	7,7	1,1
	Down	1,1	1,1	4,4

Fig. 3.6 The Pay-off Matrix with No Discounting and Appropriate Punishment Strategy

The choices shown in this matrix correspond to each player's first-period move, dependent on them adopting the previous punishment strategy. The pay-offs in this matrix were obtained by adding 3 to the player's second-round pay-off, when 'middle/centre' is the first-round outcome, but only 1 to all other first-round outcomes. This game now has three Nash equilibria, the previous two and now 'middle/centre'. Playing 'middle/centre' in the first round and 'right/down' in the second is a subgame perfect Nash equilibrium. Players thus avoid the paradox of backward induction, and achieve Pareto efficiency in the first period.

Uncertainty about the future

Another way of avoiding the paradox of backward induction is to introduce uncertainty about when the game might end. One way of doing this is to suppose there is a constant probability that the game will end after any one period. In this situation, although the game is finite, the exact timing of when the game will end is unknown. The implication of this is that, as with an infinitely repeated game, the structure of the remaining game does not change the more periods are played. As no one period can be classified as the last period of the game, we have no certain point from which to begin the process of backward induction and so the paradox is avoided. Backward induction is, therefore, only applicable to games which have a definite known end. If the final period is indefinite, credible threats and promises can be made that result in non-cooperative collusion in every time-period. This analysis is the same as with the infinite game except that the rate of discount, δ, has to be redefined. Instead of this depending only on the rate of interest, *r*, it will also depend on the probability that the game will end after any time-period. In effect players discount the future more heavily, as now there is a positive probability that future returns will not be received as the game will have ended by then. The rate of discount is now equal to

$$\delta = \frac{1 - Prob}{1 + r}$$

where *Prob* is the probability that the game ends at the end of any one period.

Uncertainty about other players

So far we have only considered games of complete information. A game is said to have *complete* information if all players' pay-off functions are common knowledge. This means that everyone knows everyones' pay-off function, and everyone knows everyone knows this, and so on *ad infinitum*. In contrast *incomplete* information means that players are not sure what the other players in the game are like, as defined by their pay-off functions, or what they know about other players. (Incomplete information should not be confused with imperfect information. Imperfect information is where at least one player does not know all the moves other players have made in either past or current periods. We have already examined games of imperfect information, indeed static games with more than one player are always, by definition, imperfect information games.) Clearly in many real-world situations people do not have complete information about everyone they interact with. For example, I may know that you are rational, but I may not know that you know that I am rational. This lack of common knowledge can greatly add to the complexity of a game, and the possible strategies that players might adopt. This is particularly true in repeated games.

To introduce some of these issues we examine an amended version of the advertising game previously analysed. Suppose that the game is played only once, but now Firm 1 can be one of two types (type A or type B) represented by different pay-offs. Firm 1 knows which type it is but Firm 2 does not. This is therefore a game of incomplete information as Firm 2 does not know the type of firm it is competing against. This situation can be illustrated by two separate extensive form games, one for each type of Firm 1. We assume that the pay-offs are as shown in Fig. 3.7 where L represents low-cost advertising and H high-cost advertising.

There are two changes to the firms' pay offs as compared to the previous advertising game represented in Fig. 3.4.

1. Firm 1 has the same pay-offs as before if it is type A, but type B receives £4m. less per year if it undertakes a high-cost advertising campaign. This can reflect either a

genuine cost differential between the two types of firm, or a difference in preferences, i.e. type B might have moral objections against high-powered advertising.

2. Firm 2 now receives £2m. per year less than before if it undertakes a high-cost advertising campaign, and firm 1 has a low-cost campaign. This might, for example, be due to a production constraint that precludes the firm benefiting from higher demand for its goods. Its other pay-offs remain the same. The effect of this change, and the reason it was made, is that Firm 2 no longer has the strictly dominant strategy of high-cost advertising. This implies that its behaviour can depend on which type of competitor it thinks it is playing against. This is the result we wish to show.

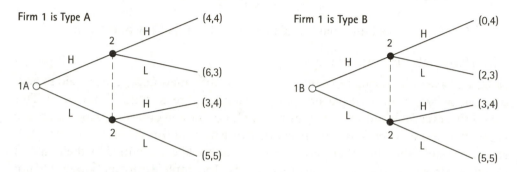

Fig. 3.7 The Modified Advertising Game with Incomplete Information

One immediate problem of solving games with incomplete information is that the techniques so far discussed cannot be directly applied to these situations. This is because they all make the fundamental assumption that players know which game they are playing. This is not the case if players are unsure what their opponents are like. As Fig. 3.7 illustrates Firm 2 does not know which of the two extensive form games it is playing. Fortunately Harsanyi (1967,1968) showed that games with incomplete information, can be transformed into games of complete but imperfect information. As we have already examined such games the previous solution techniques can be applied to these transformed games. The transformation is done by assuming that Nature determines each player's type, and hence pay-off function, according to a probability distribution. This probability distribution is assumed to be common knowledge. Each player is assumed to know his or her own type but not always the type of other players in the game. This is now a game of complete but imperfect information as not all players observe Nature's initial moves. If we assume that Nature assigns Type A to Firm 1 with probability *Prob* and Type B with probability 1 − *Prob*, then this situation can now be represented by just the one extensive form game. This is shown in Fig. 3.8.

As this is a game of complete information we can use the solution techniques used for solving static games. This specific game can be solved using the principle of iterated strict dominance which gives us a unique Nash equilibrium. If Firm 1 is of Type A, then

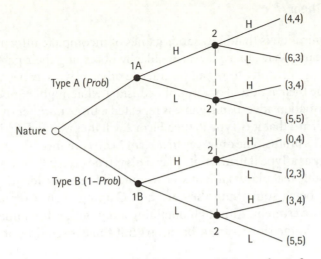

Fig. 3.8 The Modified Advertising Game with Imperfect Information

having a high-cost advertising campaign strictly dominates a low-cost campaign. If, however, it is of Type B, then low-cost advertising dominates. If Firm B assumes Firm 1 is rational, whatever its type, then it knows that it will see Firm 1 incurring a high-cost campaign with probability *Prob*, and a low-cost campaign with probability $1 - Prob$. With these probabilities it can calculate its own expected profit conditional on its level of advertising. If Firm 2 decides on high-cost advertising then its expected profit level is

$$(\Pi_B \mid H) = 4Prob + 4(1 - Prob).$$

If it decides on low-cost advertising then its expected profit level is

$$(\Pi_B \mid L) = 3Prob + 5(1 - Prob).$$

Assuming Firm 2 wishes to maximize expected profit it will undertake a high-cost advertising campaign if $(\Pi_B \mid H) > (\Pi_B \mid L)$. This gives us the following condition:

$$4Prob + 4 - 4Prob > 3Prob + 5 - 5Prob$$

$$\therefore Prob > 1/2.$$

Firm 2 will play H if *Prob* > 1/2 and will play L if *Prob* < 1/2. If *Prob* = 1/2, then it is indifferent between these two options. The optimal strategy for Firm 2, therefore, depends on the probability that its competitor is a particular type. In this game the firms will achieve a Pareto-efficient solution, with both firms playing L and receiving £5m., if Firm 1 is of Type B and *Prob* < 1/2.

The above illustration has shown that incomplete information can lead to player's achieving a Pareto-efficient outcome. However, in this one-off game, this only happened if Firm 1 was of a type that always undertakes a low-cost advertising campaign. If the game is repeated a finite number of times, this restriction need not always apply for the outcome to be Pareto efficient. Unfortunately, solving such repeated games is far from straightforward. This is because of two added complications.

The *first* complication is that in dynamic games of incomplete information, players may be able to learn what other players are like by observing their past actions. This gives players the opportunity to try and influence other players' expectations of their type by modifying their actions. For example, consider what might happen if the above incomplete information advertising game is repeated a finite number of times. If Firm 1 can convince Firm 2 that it is Type B, then Firm 2 will incur low advertising costs and so increase Firm 1's profits. The only way that Firm 1 can convince the other firm that it is Type B is to play as a Type B firm would play. This is true even if firm 1 is actually Type A. Thus it is possible that players might seek to conceal their true identity, so as to gain a reputation for being something they are not. Gaining such a reputation can be thought of as an investment. Although obtaining a reputation for something you are not will be costly in the short-run, it brings with it the expectation of higher future returns.

The *second* complication is that players know that other players might have this incentive to conceal their true identity. This will influence how they update their probability assessment of the other player's type conditional on observing his or her actions. The other player will in turn take this into account when determining their behaviour, and so on.

Only recently have such games been explicitly solved by game theorists and applied to economic situations. The equilibrium concept often used in such games is *Bayesian Subgame Perfect Nash Equilibrium*, or Bayesian Perfect for short. This type of equilibrium satisfies two conditions:

(1) It is subgame perfect in that no incredible threats or promises are made or believed.

(2) The players update their beliefs rationally in accordance with Bayes' Theorem.

(An alternative equilibrium concept used is *sequential equilibrium*. This was developed by Kreps and Wilson (1982*b*) and is a slightly stronger condition than Bayesian perfect equilibrium with regard to the consistency of the solution. In many cases, however, the two concepts yield the same solution.)

Bayes' Theorem is explained in Appendix 3.1. The relevance of Bayesian perfect equilibrium is that even very small amounts of uncertainty concerning the type of player you are playing against can be greatly magnified in repeated games. This alters the incentives faced by players in the game, and often leads to the prediction that the Pareto-optimal solution is played in early stages of the game. In this way the paradox of backward induction is overcome. To illustrate this possibility we discuss the *centipede game* developed by Rosenthal (1981). Consider the extensive form game shown in Fig. 3.9.

In this game there are two players each with two possible moves. They can either move across (A) or down (D). The resulting pay-offs are as shown in the diagram. Solving this game by backwards induction gives the result that person 1 will immediately play down and so both players receive the same pay-off of 1. This is clearly a Pareto-inefficient outcome because if both players play across they both receive poten-

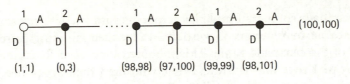

Fig. 3.9 Rosenthal's Centipede Game

tially much greater pay-offs. In this sense the game is very much like a repeated prisoner's dilemma game, where initial co-operation can make everyone better off. There are two specific points to notice about this subgame perfect prediction.

First, the prediction that the first player will immediately play down is based on 200 rounds of iterated strict dominance. In reality it is often hard to believe that players are so sure of their opponents' rationality, and that their opponents are sure of their opponents' rationality etc.

Second, what effect will player 1 have on player 2 if instead of playing downs he plays along? Player 2 now has direct evidence that player 1 is not rational. Based on this evidence, player 2 may decide that it is best to also play along, and take player 1 for a ride. In this situation we move out along the tree and both players are made better off. This reasoning suggests that it may be rational to initially pretend to be irrational! (We return to some of these issues in Chapter 12.)

Each of these points suggests that for this game the assumption of common knowledge of rationality may be inappropriate. An alternative assumption is to introduce incomplete information. With this assumption players are unsure if their opponent is rational. This has a dramatic effect on the equilibrium behaviour of a rational player. Even if there is only a very small probability that your opponent is co-operative, in that he or she always plays across, then it is rational for players to play across in the initial periods of the game. In this way each player builds up a reputation for being co-operative. It can be shown that the sequential equilibrium of this incomplete information game involves both players initially playing across, and then to randomize over their actions as they approach the end of the game. In fact the number of periods for which the players will adopt mixed strategies does not depend on the number of periods the game is played. In consequence as the number of periods increases the proportion of the game characterized as co-operative also increases. This equilibrium strategy is depicted in Fig. 3.10.

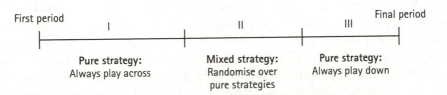

Fig. 3.10 Bayesian Subgame Perfect Nash Equilibrium for Rosenthal's Centipede Game with Incomplete Information

As players initially co-operate and play across the paradox of backward induction is partially overcome. In Appendix 3.2 we derive the sequential equilibrium for a simplified version of the centipede game. This modified version of Rosenthal's game was developed by McKelvey and Palfrey (1992), who used their simplified game to test whether experimental subjects actually played according to the sequential equilibrium hypothesis. This experiment, among others, is reviewed in Chapter 11.

EXERCISE 3.4

Assume that two players are faced with Rosenthal's centipede game. Use Bayes' theorem to calculate the players' reputation for being co-operative in the following situations if they play across.

(1) At the beginning of the game each player believes that there is a 50/50 chance that the other player is rational or co-operative. It is assumed that a co-operative player always plays across. Furthermore suppose that a rational player will play across with a probability of 0.2

(2) At their second move the players again move across. (Continue to assume that the probability that a rational player plays across remains equal to 0.2).

(3) How would the players' reputation have changed after the first move had the other player believed that rational players always play across. (Assume all other probabilities remain the same.)

(4) Finally, how would the players' reputation have changed after the first move had the other player believed that rational players never play across. (Again assume all other probabilities remain the same.)

3.3 Conclusions

Most interaction between people and organizations are not one-off events, but rather take place within the context of an ongoing relationship. This makes them dynamic. In dynamic games players observe the moves of other players before making their own optimal responses. This possibility greatly enriches the strategies that players might adopt. This chapter has examined how dynamic games can be analysed and predictions made. A key concept in all dynamic games is credibility. For a threat or promise to be credible it must be in that players interest to carry it out at the appropriate time. If a threat or promise is not credible, then it would seem reasonable to suppose that it will not be believed. Subgame perfection applies this insight to dynamic games. In games of perfect and complete information, where players are not indifferent between various actions, backward induction generates a unique prediction. This prediction is the subgame perfect Nash equilibrium.

When a game is repeated it might be supposed that the players will learn over time to co-ordinate their actions so as to avoid Pareto-inefficient outcomes. This possibility was examined in section 3.2. Initially we examined infinitely repeated games where the stage game had a unique Nash equilibrium. It was demonstrated that, provided players do not discount future returns too much, a non-cooperative collusive outcome can indeed be maintained. This result breaks down, however, if the game is only finitely repeated. This is the paradox of backward induction. As this paradox is counter-intuitive many explanations have been proposed as to how it might be avoided. This chapter examined four ways in which the paradox of backward induction is overcome. These were the introduction of bounded rationality, multiple Nash equilibria, uncertainty about the future, and incomplete information. These concepts have become central to many recent developments in game theory.

This and the previous chapter have presented many of the basic concepts needed to understand non-cooperative game theory models. All of these basic ideas are employed in subsequent chapters where we analyse, in greater depth, recent economic applications of game theory.

3.4 Solutions to Exercises

Exercise 3.1

Using the principle of backward induction we start at the end of the game and work backwards ruling out strategies that rational players would not play. If the game reaches player 3's decision node, then she receives with certainty a pay-off of 7 if she plays 'up' or 9 if she plays 'down'. Assuming this player is rational she will play 'down', and so we can exclude her strategy of 'up'.

Moving back along this branch we reach player 2's node after player 1 has moved 'down'. If we assume player 2 believes player 3 is rational then he anticipates receiving a pay-off of 8 if he moves 'up', and 1 if he moves 'down'. If player 2 is also assumed to be rational, then at this decision node he will play 'up' and we can exclude 'down' from this node.

Player 2 also has a decision node following player 1 moving 'up'. By considering player 2's certain pay-off's following this decision we can exclude 'up' and 'down' as we have already assumed this player is rational.

We now only have to solve player 1's move at the start of the game. There are now only two remaining pay-offs for the game as a whole. If we assume player 1 believes player 2 is rational then she will anticipate a pay-off of 3 if she moves 'up'. Further, if we assume that player 1 believes that player 2 believes that player 3 is rational then she will anticipate a pay-off of 6 if she moves 'down'. With these assumptions we can exclude player 1 moving 'up'.

With the above assumptions we are left with one remaining pay-off vector corresponding to the subgame perfect Nash equilibrium. This equilibrium is that player 1 moves 'down' followed by player 2 moving 'up', and finally player 3 choosing to play 'down'. We derive the same solution if we assume all players in the game are rational and that this is common knowledge. This assumption is stronger than absolutely necessary, but for convenience it is typically made when applying the principle of backward induction.

Exercise 3.2

For the extensive form game given in this exercise there are two Nash equilibria, but only one is perfect. To identify these Nash equilibria we first convert the game into a normal form game. Player A has only two strategies, A1 or A2. However, player 2 has four available strategies because he can condition his actions on what he observes player A does. Player 2's strategies are, therefore, to always play B1, to always play B2, do the same as player A, or do the opposite. This gives us the normal form game shown in Fig. 3.11.

Player B

		Always B1	Always B2	Same as A	Opposite to A
Player A	A1	<u>6</u>,<u>8</u>	<u>8</u>,4	<u>6</u>,<u>8</u>	<u>8</u>,4
	A2	4,6	7,<u>7</u>	<u>7</u>,<u>7</u>	4,6

Fig. 3.11

Using the two-stage procedure for finding pure-strategy Nash equilibria we can identify that 'A1/Always B1' and 'A2/Same as A' are both Nash equilibria. The concept of subgame perfect Nash equilibrium, however, rules out 'A1/Always B1' because it is not a Nash equilibrium for the subgame beginning at B's choice node following 'A2'. This is because player B threatening to always play 'B1', irrespective of what player A does, is not credible. If player A plays 'A2', then player B has the incentive to play 'B2'. The only subgame perfect equilibrium for this game is 'A2/Same as A'. This subgame perfect equilibrium could also have been found by using backward induction.

If the players take their actions simultaneously rather than sequentially, then we get the normal form game illustrated in Fig. 3.12.

In this new game we have a unique Nash equilibrium of 'A1/B1'. All that we have changed between the two games is the amount of information that player B has available to him when he makes his decision. None the less the predicted outcome and corresponding pay-offs are very different. Indeed, in this game giving player B less information, now he cannot observe player A's move, actually makes him better off!

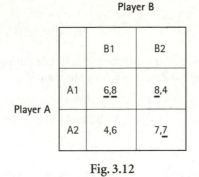

Fig. 3.12

Exercise 3.3

(1) Applying the two-stage methodology for finding pure-strategy Nash equilibria it can be shown that this game has the unique Nash equilibrium of 'up/left'. It should be confirmed by the reader that there is no mixed-strategy Nash equilibrium for this prisoners' dilemma game.

(2) With infinite repetitions the co-operative outcome can result in 'right/down' being played indefinitely if the players adopt the suggested trigger strategy and players do not discount the future too much. This is demonstrated as follows.

Let the player's rate of discount be δ. The present value of always playing 'right/down' to each player is therefore

$$4 + 4\delta + 4\delta^2 + 4\delta^3 + \ldots = \frac{4}{1-\delta}.$$

The present value of deviating to each player is

$$5 + \delta + \delta^2 + \delta^3 \ldots = 5 + \frac{\delta}{1-\delta}.$$

Thus we can predict that the two players will continue to collude as long as

$$\frac{4}{1-\delta} \geq 5 + \frac{\delta}{1-\delta}$$

$$\therefore \delta \geq 1/4.$$

The threat of punishment is credible since having observed the other player's defection from the co-operative solution it is rational to play the static Nash equilibrium. Furthermore, if the above condition holds, then the promise to play 'right/down' is also credible, because the loss incurred as a result of deviating outweighs the possible gains.

(3) With the players adopting this alternative one-period punishment strategy, each player has the option of deviating from the Pareto-efficient outcome every other period. Indeed, if it is rational to deviate initially this is what they will do. The present value of deviating this period is therefore equal to

$$5 + \delta + 5\delta^2 + \delta^3 + \ldots = \frac{5+\delta}{(1-\delta)(1+\delta)}.$$

Comparing this with the present value pay-off of not deviating we get the result that both players will continually play the Pareto-efficient outcome if

$$\frac{4}{1-\delta} \geq \frac{5+\delta}{(1-\delta)(1+\delta)}$$

$$\therefore \delta \geq 1/3.$$

As future punishment is less severe, lasting for only one period following each deviation, players are less likely to be deterred from deviating from the Pareto-optimal outcome. This is shown by the smaller subset of discount values which maintain Pareto efficiency.

Exercise 3.4

From Bayes' Theorem we can write

$$Prob(A \mid B) = \frac{Prob(B \mid A)Prob(A)}{Prob(B \mid A)Prob(A) + Prob(B \mid \text{not } A)Prob(\text{not } A)}.$$

where A corresponds to the statement that 'the other player is co-operative', and B to the observation that 'the other player has just played across'. The probabilities in the equation, therefore have the following interpretation.

$Prob(A \mid B)$ = the probability that the other player is co-operative, given that he or she has just played across. This corresponds to that player's reputation for being co-operative.

$Prob(A)$ = the prior probability that the other player is co-operative.

$Prob(\text{not } A)$ = the prior probability that the other player is rational
= $1 - Prob(A)$

$Prob(B \mid A)$ = the probability that the other player will play across if he or she is co-operative. In our example this equals 1 by definition

$Prob(B \mid \text{not } A)$ = the probability that the other player will play across if he or she is rational.

(1) From the above equation we can calculate the probability that players are co-operative if they initially play across. This equals $Prob(A \mid B) = (1 \times 0.5)/((1 \times 0.5) + (0.2 \times 0.5)) = 0.833$. From this we can see that the player's reputation for being co-operative has increased as a result of playing across.

(2) If the players play across with their second move, then the other player assigns an even greater probability to the belief that the player is co-operative. Using the result derived in (1) as the new prior probability that the player is co-operative we get: $Prob(A \mid B) = (1 \times 0.833)/((1 \times 0.833) + (0.2 \times 0.167)) = 0.961$.

(3) If rational players always play across then we have $Prob(B \mid \text{not } A) = 1$. Substituting this into Bayes' Theorem we get $Prob(A \mid B) = (1 \times 0.5)/((1 \times 0.5) + (1 \times 0.5)) = 0.5$. In this situation there is no useful information learnt from observing a player's move across. This is because

both rational and co-operative players are predicted to act alike. With no new information available the players' reputations remain unchanged.

(4) In this final example we have $Prob(\text{B} \mid \text{not A}) = 0$, and so $Prob(\text{A} \mid \text{B}) = (1 \times 0.5)/((1 \times 0.5) + (0 \times 0.5)) = 1$. In this example the players learn for certain that both are co-operative. This occurs because the prior belief was that a rational player would always play down. The only consistent explanation of observing the other player move across, therefore, is that they are co-operative.

From the results derived in (3) and (4) we can note that players' reputations can only be improved if they adopt a mixed strategy. Otherwise their reputation remains unchanged, or their identity is fully revealed.

Appendix 3.1 Bayes' Theorem

Bayes' Theorem, named after the Reverend Thomas Bayes (1702–61), shows how probabilities can be updated as additional information is received. It answers the question 'Given that event B has occurred what is the probability that event A has or will occur?' This revised probability is written as $Prob(\text{A} \mid \text{B})$. It is the conditional probability of event A given the occurrence of event B. For example in games of incomplete information a player can use Bayes' Theorem to update their probability assessment that another player is of a certain type, by observing what he or she does. The Theorem can be written as follows:

Suppose that event B has a non-zero probability of occurring, then for each event A_i, of which there are N possibilities,

$$Prob(\text{A}_i \mid \text{B}) = \frac{Prob(\text{B} \mid \text{A}_i) \cdot Prob(\text{A}_i)}{\sum_{i=1}^{N} Prob(\text{B} \mid \text{A}_i) \cdot Prob(\text{A}_i)}.$$

For example, if there are only two possible types of a certain player, A_1 and A_2, the updated probability for each type, given that this player has undertaken an action B is:

$$Prob(\text{A}_1 \mid \text{B}) = \frac{Prob(\text{B} \mid \text{A}_1) \cdot Prob(\text{A}_1)}{Prob(\text{B} \mid \text{A}_1) \cdot Prob(\text{A}_1) + Prob(\text{B} \mid \text{A}_2) \cdot Prob(\text{A}_2)}$$

and

$$Prob(\text{A}_2 \mid \text{B}) = \frac{Prob(\text{B} \mid \text{A}_2) \cdot Prob(\text{A}_2)}{Prob(\text{B} \mid \text{A}_1) \cdot Prob(\text{A}_1) + Prob(\text{B} \mid \text{A}_2) \cdot Prob(\text{A}_2)}.$$

The probabilities used on the right-hand side of these expressions are called 'prior probabilities', and are determined before event B occurs. The updated probabilities $Prob(\text{A}_i \mid \text{B})$ are called 'posterior probabilities'. In repeated games these posterior probabilities would then be used as the prior probabilities of $Prob(\text{A}_i)$ in subsequent periods.

Proof of Bayes' Theorem

From the nature of conditional probabilities it is true that

$$Prob(A_i \text{ and } B) = Prob(B \mid A_i) \cdot Prob(A_i) \tag{1}$$

and

$$Prob(A_i \text{ and } B) = Prob(A_i \mid B) \cdot Prob(B). \tag{2}$$

From (2) we get

$$Prob(A_i \mid B) = \frac{Prob(A_i \text{ and } B)}{Prob(B)}. \tag{3}$$

Substituting in for $Prob(A_i \text{ and } B)$ from equation (1) gives

$$Prob(A_i \mid B) = \frac{Prob(B \mid A_i)Prob(A_i)}{Prob(B)}. \tag{4}$$

Multiplying through by $Prob(B)$ yields

$$Prob(B) \cdot Prob(A_i \mid B) = Prob(B \mid A_i) \cdot Prob(A_i). \tag{5}$$

Summing both sides over the index i gives

$$Prob(B) \cdot \sum_{i=1}^{N} Prob(A_i \mid B) = \sum_{i=1}^{N} Prob(B \mid A_i) \cdot Prob(A_i). \tag{6}$$

Since the events $\{A_1, \ldots, A_N\}$ are mutually exclusive and exhaustive we know that

$$\sum_{i=1}^{N} Prob(A_i \mid B) = 1. \tag{7}$$

Substituting (7) into (6) we have

$$Prob(B) = \sum_{i=1}^{N} Prob(B \mid A_i) \cdot Prob(A_i). \tag{8}$$

Substituting (8) into (4) gives us Bayes' Theorem. This completes the proof.

Appendix 3.2 Sequential Equilibrium In A Modified Centipede Game

In this appendix we demonstrate how a sequential equilibrium may be identified for a modified version of Rosenthal's centipede game. This version of the game is due to McKelvey and Palfrey (1992). The extensive form of this game, assuming complete information, is shown in Fig. 3.13.

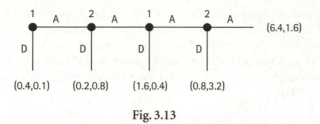

Fig. 3.13

With complete information the unique subgame perfect Nash equilibrium for this game is for player 1 to play down (D) at the first decision node. This solution can be confirmed using the principle of backward induction. With this outcome the pay-offs are 0.4 and 0.1 for players 1 and 2 respectively. Clearly this is a Pareto-inefficient outcome as both players can be made better off if they initially co-operate and play across (A). With incomplete information, however, sequential equilibrium will generally involve some degree of co-operation by both players. To illustrate this we will assume there is a small probability of either player in the game being co-operative in the sense that they always play across. This may be because they are either altruistic, and care about their opponent's final pay-off, or because they are irrational. Each player is assumed to know he or she is rational or co-operative, but not the type of the opponent. It is assumed that the prior probability that a player is co-operative is 0.05. As a 'co-operative' player always plays across we need only derive the equilibrium predictions for a 'rational' player. With this degree of uncertainty it is rational for player 1 to always play across at the first decision node, thus partially offsetting the paradox of backward induction. At the next two nodes the players will adopt a mixed strategy. If the game reaches the final node player 2 will always play down.

To derive this equilibrium we start from the last period first and work back to the beginning of the game. We will use the following notation. Let $\prod_j^k$ be the expected final pay-off for player $k = 1, 2$, if the game is at decision node $j = 1, \ldots, 4$. ($j = 1$ is the first node, $j = 2$ the second etc.). This will be conditional on whether player k plays down (D) or across (A) at that node. Similarly $Prob_j^k(A)$ and $Prob_j^k(D)$ are the probabilities of player k, if he or she is rational, playing A or D at decision node j. Finally, r_j^k is the probability assessment by the other player that player k is 'co-operative' if the game has reached decision node j. This corresponds to player k's reputation for being 'co-operative'. Initially, by assumption, $r_1^1 = r_1^2 = r_2^2 = 0.05$. This final probability is based on the fact that player 2 can do nothing to affect his reputation prior to node 2, as this is player 2's first decision node.

4th node ($j = 4$) If the game reaches player 2's final decision node, then the expected pay-offs for that player are $\prod_4^2(D) = 3.2$ and $\prod_4^2(A) = 1.6$. As down strictly dominates across it is clear that if player 2 is rational he will always play down. This pure-strategy prediction implies that $Prob_4^2(A) = 0$ and $Prob_4^2(D) = 1$ for a rational player.

3rd node ($j = 3$) Based on the results derived for node 4 the expected pay-offs for player 1 if the game reaches node 3 are $\prod_3^1(D) = 1.6$ and $\prod_3^1(A) = 0.8(1 - r_3^2) + 6.4r_3^2$. If one of these expected pay-offs is greater than the other, then player 1 will play a pure strategy at this node. If, however, these expected values are equal, then player 1 (if rational) is indifferent between playing across or down. In this situation player 1 can play a mixed strategy at this node. This will occur when $r_3^2 = 1/7$. Player 1 will only play a mixed strategy at this node if player 2 has previously enhanced his reputation for being 'co-operative'. This, in turn, can only happen if player 2 has played a mixed strategy at decision node 2. Specifically using Bayes' Theorem we can calculate the implied probability of player 2 playing down at node 2 in order to induce player 1 to play a mixed strategy at node 3. Thus

$$r_3^2 = \frac{r_2^2}{r_2^2 + [1 - Prob_2^2(D)](1 - r_2^2)} = 1/7$$

$$\therefore \frac{0.05}{0.05 + [1 - Prob_2^2(D)]0.95} = 1/7$$

$$\therefore Prob_2^2(D) = 0.684.$$

$$\therefore Prob_2^2(A) = 0.316.$$

Player 1 will, therefore, adopt a mixed strategy at node 3 if player 2 plays this mixed strategy at node 2.

2nd node ($j = 2$) At node 2 we can derive the following expected pay-offs for player 2.

$\Pi_2^2(D) = 0.8$ and

$$\Pi_2^2(A) = 3.2[r_1^2 + (1 - r_1^2)Prob_3^1(A)] + 0.4(1 - r_3^1)Prob_3^1(D)$$
$$= 3.2 - 2.8Prob_3^1(D) + 2.8r_2^1Prob_3^1(D).$$

Again if either of these expected pay-offs is greater than the other, then player 2 will adopt a pure strategy. If these expected pay-offs are equal, then player 2 (if rational) can adopt a mixed strategy at this node. This will occur when $Prob_3^1(D) = 6/7(1 - r_2^1)$. Given that r_2^1 is sufficiently small, player 2 will use a mixed strategy at node 2 if player 1 is anticipated to play the appropriate mixed strategy at node 3. This is similar to the prediction derived for node 3. The mixed strategies at nodes 2 and 3 are self-supporting in equilibrium.

If we assume that player 1 always plays across at node 1 (this assumption is validated below), then from Bayes' Theorem $r_2^1 = 0.05$. From the previous equation, therefore, player 2 will play a mixed strategy at node 2 if $Prob_3^1(D) = 0.902$ and $Prob_3^1(A) = 0.098$.

1st node ($j = 1$) In order to justify the use of mixed strategies derived above for nodes 2 and 3 all that is needed now is to demonstrate that, given these predictions, player 1 will play across at this first decision node. Again the expected pay-offs for player 1 at this node are given as $\pi_1^1(D) = 0.4$ and

$$\Pi_1^1(A) = 0.2(1 - r_1^2)Prob_2^2(D) + 1.6[r_1^2 + (1 - r_1^2)Prob_2^2(A)]Prob_3^1(D)$$
$$+ 0.8[r_1^2 + (1 - r_1^2)Prob_2^2(A)]Prob_3^1(A)(1 - r_1^2)$$
$$+ 6.4[r_1^2 + (1 - r_1^2)Prob_2^2(A)]Prob_3^1(A).$$

Given the previous mixed-strategy predictions we can calculate that $\prod_1^1 (A) = 1.036$. For player 1 playing across dominates playing down at this node, and so player 1 will always play across irrespective of their type. This pure-strategy prediction implies that $Prob_1^1 (A) = 1$ and $Prob_1^1 (D) = 0$ for a rational player.

This demonstrates that the use of mixed strategies at nodes 2 and 3 can form part of a sequential equilibrium. In fact it can be shown that this is the only sequential equilibrium for this game. This unique equilibrium is illustrated in Fig. 3.14.

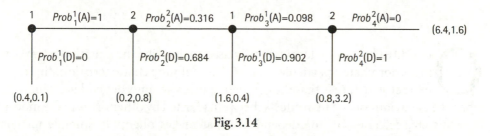

Fig. 3.14

These predictions conform to the typical pattern observed with sequential equilibrium. Initially there is a pure-strategy phase, where players co-operate. Players then adopt mixed strategies, where a player's reputation for being co-operative may be enhanced. Finally players adopt the pure strategy associated with non-cooperation.

Further Reading

Aumann, R., and S. Hart (1992), *Handbook of Game Theory with Economic Applications*, New York: North-Holland.

Bierman, H. S., and L. Fernandez (1993), *Game Theory with Economic Applications*, Reading, Mass.: Addison Wesley.

Dixit, A., and B. J. Nalebuff (1991), *Thinking Strategically: The Competitive Edge in Business, Politics, and Everyday Life*, New York: Norton.

Eatwell, J., M. Milgate, and P. Newman (1989), *The New Palgrave: Game Theory*, New York: W. W. Norton.

Gibbons, R. (1992), *Game Theory for Applied Economists*, Princeton: Princeton University Press.

Kreps, D. (1990), *A Course in Microeconomic Theory*, New York: Harvester Wheatsheaf.

Kreps, D. (1990), *Game Theory and Economic Modelling*, Oxford: Clarendon Press.

Rasmusen, E. (1993), *Games and Information*, Oxford: Blackwell.

Varian, H. (1992), *Microeconomic Analysis*, New York: Norton.

4
Oligopoly

OLIGOPOLY is the term typically used to describe the situation where a few firms dominate a particular market. The defining characteristic of this type of market structure is that the competing firms are interdependent. This occurs when the behaviour of one firm affects the profits earned by other firms in the industry. It is this characteristic of interdependence that makes oligopoly suitable for game theory analysis. Oligopoly can be contrasted with the two extremes of market structure. Under perfect competition all firms are price-takers, and so they are assumed to be independent of each other. In the case of monopoly, as there is only one firm in the market, there is again no interdependence.

Initially, in examining the behaviour of oligopolistic firms we consider one-off games where firms are assumed to interact with each other only once. In this context we present the now classic models of Cournot, Stackelberg, and Bertrand competition. Having discussed the outcome of these models, we then analyse how repeated interaction between firms can change their predicted behaviour. In particular we discuss the extent to which oligopolies can maintain a non-cooperative collusive outcome that maximizes joint profits. In discussing these issues many of the ideas presented in the previous two chapters are directly applied. One important contrast between the games previously discussed and those presented in this chapter is that now we represent the players making choices over a continuous, rather than a discrete, strategic variable. For example, we examine how ideas presented in the previous two chapters can be applied when firms must choose one particular output–price combination from a continuum of such choices as represented by the demand curve.

4.1 Three Models of Oligopoly

A number of different models have been developed that try to explain and predict the behaviour of oligopolistic firms. In this section we will examine three such models, each named after their originator. The distinguishing feature of these models of oligopoly is their underlying market structure. In *Cournot competition* firms simultaneously compete in terms of quantity supplied to the market. In *Stackelberg competition* one or more firms are able initially to precommit themselves to a particular output level. The remaining firms observe this level of output and then simultaneously determine their own optimal output levels. Finally, in *Bertrand competition* firms simultaneously compete in terms of the price they charge consumers. These differences fundamentally alter the underlying structure of the game between firms, and dramatically change the predicted behaviour of the firms involved. To illustrate these differences we initially focus our attention on the case of one-off competition between just two firms. More general models of oligopoly, where there are more than two interdependent firms, are examined in various exercises, while repeated interaction between firms is analysed in the next section.

4.1.1 Cournot competition

As stated above in Cournot competition firms simultaneously decide how much of the good they will supply to the market. Once aggregate supply is determined the price is set so that the market clears. To examine this type of competition we initially assume that two firms produce an identical product. As the output decisions are taken simultaneously each firm supplies the market without observing the other firm's level of supply. The market price, P, is determined so that aggregate supply, Q, is just demanded. We assume that total demand for the product is determined according to the inverse demand curve $P = a - Q$, where a is a positive constant. There are assumed to be constant marginal costs equal to c and no fixed costs. Each firm is assumed to maximize profits.

From this informal description we can identify the three basic requirements for a normal form game.

(1) The players
These are the two firms. We will call them firm A and firm B.

(2) The strategies available to each player
As this is a static game the available strategies are the same as the possible actions of the two players. The available strategies are therefore the possible quantities of the good each firm can supply to the market. We will assume that firms A and B can supply any positive level of output, and denote these as q_A and q_B respectively.

(3) The pay-offs
These are the profits each firm receives. These are denoted as Π_A and Π_B for firms A and B respectively.

Furthermore we also know how much *information* each player has when deciding upon their optimal strategy, and the *timing* of these events. We can therefore represent this competitive structure as an extensive form game. This is shown in Fig. 4.1.

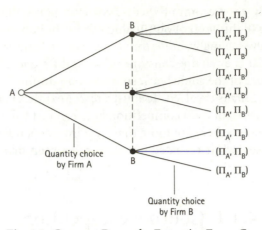

Fig. 4.1 Cournot Duopoly: Extensive Form Game

This extensive form game illustrates the essential elements of Cournot competition. In particular it shows that both firms make their supply decisions before knowing how much the other firm has supplied to the market. This is represented by having all of firm B's decision nodes in the same information set. This is also true for firm A as it is depicted as only having one decision node, the initial node. It should be noted, however, that Fig. 4.1 does simplify the game described above by assuming that each firm has only three possible levels of output. In contrast, we assumed above that the firms can supply any positive level of output. This means there are an infinite number of actions available to each firm. It is clearly impossible fully to represent all these possibilities diagrammatically, and so the extensive form game depicts only a representative sample of the available strategies. Once each firm has chosen its optimal level of supply, the market price is determined, and the firms receive the corresponding level of profit. As we are restricting ourselves to one-off competition between firms in this section, the game is assumed to end when firms have received these profit levels.

Having depicted Cournot competition as a game between interdependent firms, we can now apply the solution techniques discussed in Chapter 2 to predict the outcome of this market structure. An obvious solution technique to use in this static game is the concept of Nash equilibrium. This involves determining each firm's optimal strategy dependent on what it expects the other firm to do. Diagrammatically this involves drawing each firm's so-called reaction function. This shows a firm's optimal supply of output for every possible quantity chosen by the other firm. (The term 'reaction function' is a misnomer because strictly it is not possible for either firm to react to each other's output decision in this static game.)

To find each firm's reaction function we differentiate the firm's profit function with respect to its own output level and set this equal to zero. Rearranging this yields the first-order condition for finding a maximum. The second-order condition, that the second derivative is negative, is then checked to ensure that a maximum has indeed been found. These calculations are performed below for firm A and firm B, under the assumptions of the model being used.

Firm A

$$\Pi_A = Pq_A - cq_A$$
$$\therefore \ \Pi_A = (a - q_A - q_B)q_A - cq_A$$
$$\therefore \ \frac{d\Pi_A}{dq_A} = a - 2q_A - q_B - c = 0$$
$$\therefore \ q_A = \frac{a - q_B - c}{2}.$$
$$\frac{d^2\Pi_A}{dq_A{}^2} = -2 < 0 \ \therefore \ \text{max.}$$

Firm B

$$\Pi_B = Pq_B - cq_B$$
$$\therefore \ \Pi_B = (a - q_A - q_B)q_B - cq_B$$
$$\therefore \ \frac{d\Pi_B}{dq_B} = a - q_A - 2q_B - c = 0$$
$$\therefore \ q_B = \frac{a - q_A - c}{2}.$$
$$\frac{d^2\Pi_B}{dq_B{}^2} = -2 < 0 \ \therefore \ \text{max.}$$

The penultimate line of these calculations is the *reaction function* for each firm. These functions show that the optimal level of supply for each firm is negatively related to the expected level of supply of the other firm. As an expected increase in one firm's supply causes the other firm to cut back on its supply the output of the two firms are said to be *strategic substitutes* for each other. (Conversely if strategic variables are positively related there are said to be *strategic complements*.) Diagrammatically strategic substitutes are illustrated by downward-sloping *reaction curves*. The reaction functions for firm A and firm B are plotted in Fig. 4.2.

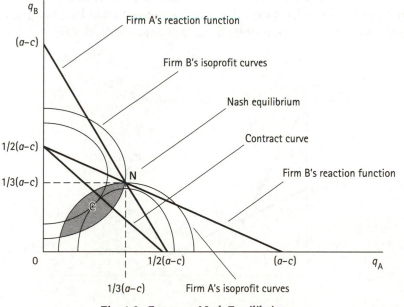

Fig. 4.2 Cournot–Nash Equilibrium

Ogliopoly

This diagram also shows the relationship between each firm's reaction curve and its isoprofit curves. In this diagram the isoprofit curve plots the different combinations of the two firms' output that yield the same level of profit for one of the firms. Profits are greatest when each firm is the sole supplier to the market. If one of the firms acts as a monopolist, it will supply $(a - c)/2$ units of the product to the market. This is equal to the intercept value of the reaction functions. The further away the firm is from this monopoly outcome the smaller its level of profit. This is indicated by moving on to isoprofit curves further away from the relevant intercept. As firm A is assumed to maximize profit given the expected level of supply by firm B, so its reaction function intersects its isoprofit curves where they are horizontal. Similarly, firm B's reaction function intersects its isoprofit curves where they are vertical. This represents maximum profit for firm B for each anticipated level of supply by firm A. In Nash equilibrium both firms must be maximizing profits simultaneously, given their beliefs about the other firm's level of supply. This means that both firms must be on their reaction curves simultaneously. In Fig.4.2 the reaction curves intersect only once, and so this corresponds to the unique Nash equilibrium for this model. From the diagram we can see that the Nash equilibrium is where each firm supplies an output equal to $(a - c)/3$. This can be confirmed algebraically by setting the two equations for the reaction functions equal to each other.

Although we have identified the output levels of $(a - c)/3$ as the unique solution to this model using the concept of Nash equilibrium, it should be noted that Cournot (1838) also claimed this output combination to be the equilibrium. Cournot, however, identified this as the equilibrium to the model by analysing how the firms would react when they were out of equilibrium. Cournot assumed that each firm believes that if it changed its own output level the other firm would not react by changing its output level. To show this yields the same equilibrium as before consider Fig. 4.3.

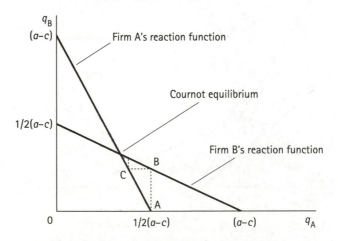

Fig. 4.3 Cournot Disequilibrium Dynamics

This diagram again plots the two firms' reaction functions. Assume initially that only firm A is producing in this market. As firm A is initially a monopoly it will produce the amount $(a - c)/2$ and be at point A. If now firm B enters the market, and assumes that firm A will maintain its initial level of supply, then it will produce at point B, which is on firm B's reaction curve vertically above point A. However, at point B firm A is off its reaction curve and so, if it assumes firm B will not change its level of supply, it will change its output to point C. It can be seen that this process will continue until we reach the Nash equilibrium. A similar argument could be advanced starting from any point in Fig. 4.3, with the two firms converging on the Nash equilibrium. As both methods yield the same equilibrium it is often called the Cournot–Nash equilibrium.

Although both the Cournot solution and the Nash equilibrium predict the same final output levels the concept of Nash equilibrium is theoretically much the stronger. Specifically, Cournot's methodology has two main weaknesses. *First*, it postulates that each firm is able to react to the other firm's output level. This is inconsistent with the initial structure of the game where it was assumed both firms set their output levels simultaneously. *Second*, although each firm assumes the other will not respond to output changes, this would in fact be falsified by actual behaviour if the firms did repeatedly interact, and were initially away from Nash equilibrium. This means that each firm's assumption about the behaviour of the other firm is not consistent with the model itself, and so is not a rational conjecture. Although Cournot's equilibrium is reasonable his analysis of what happens out of equilibrium must be regarded as unsatisfactory.

In contrast, the concept of Nash equilibrium does not introduce a dynamic process into an otherwise static model, nor does it introduce arbitrary behavioural assumptions. Instead each firm sets the equilibrium quantity based on rational beliefs about the behaviour of the other firm. It is via this rational decision-making process, where each firm explicitly takes into account its interdependence with other firms, that equilibrium is attained.

Before going on to discuss other models of oligopoly it is worth noting that the Cournot–Nash equilibrium is Pareto inefficient. If the two firms could co-ordinate their supply decisions, then they can potentially both earn greater profits. From Fig. 4.2 the Nash equilibrium is seen to be inefficient because at this point the two firm's isoprofit curves are not tangential. This implies there are other supply combinations where at least one firm is better off and the other firm no worse off. These combinations are shown as the shaded lens-shaped region in Fig. 4.2. The boundary of this shaded area is formed by the two isoprofit curves passing through the Nash equilibrium. Within this shaded area, therefore, both firms move on to isoprofit curves closer to their respective monopoly outcomes, and so both firms are better off. On the boundary itself, apart from where the isoprofit lines intersect, one firm is strictly better off while the other firm receives the same level of profit as in Nash equilibrium.

In order for an outcome to be Pareto efficient the isoprofit curves must be tangential. If this is the case, then one firm can only be made better off at the expense of the other firm's profit level. Also drawn in Fig. 4.2 is the *contract curve*. The contract curve shows the set of Pareto-efficient outcomes, where the firms' isoprofit lines are tangential. Exercise 4.2 demonstrates that along the contract curve joint supply is equal to $(a-c)/2$, which is the quantity a monopolist would supply to the market. Aggregate profits along the contract curve are therefore, in this model, equal to the monopoly profit level. Distribution of profits along this curve is, therefore, called a constant-sum game. If the two firms could fully co-ordinate their supply decisions, they would maximize joint profit by being on the contract curve. From this contract curve it can be seen, however, there are an infinite number of Pareto-efficient outcomes. This raises the question of which of these many output combinations firms might attempt to co-ordinate upon. In answer to this question, it seems reasonable to exclude points on the contract curve which are outside the shaded area. These outcomes can be rejected because one of the two firms strictly prefers the Nash equilibrium, and so will not maintain the collusive outcome. This leaves all the points on the contract curve within the shaded area. If the two firms are identical, one focal point for collusion is where both firms produce half the monopoly level of supply, and so each receives half the monopoly profit level. This focal point is labelled as point C in Fig. 4.2. Although this outcome might seem entirely reasonable, there is good reason to believe that in the game we are considering it is unsustainable. This is because point C is not a Nash equilibrium, and hence firms have the incentive unilaterally to deviate from it by changing their level of supply. The reason for this is that the cartel maximizes joint profits by acting like a monopolist, i.e. it restricts output and increases price. At this output level both firms, in general, will want to increase their own production, thereby increasing their own profits. Diagramatically at point C both firms are off their reaction curves. In Cournot equilibrium the total output is higher and the price is lower but at this point neither firm has an incentive to change its level of output. This is an example of a prisoners' dilemma game considered in Chapter 2. Each player has an incentive to deviate from the collusive outcome, with the result that the final equilibrium is Pareto inefficient.

This is the classic argument for why we might expect a cartel to be unstable. Each firm has a unilateral incentive to deviate from the collusive arrangement. We return to this issue of collusion, and specifically how a non-cooperative collusive outcome might be sustained, in section 4.2.

EXERCISE 4.1

Assume that there are $i = 1, \ldots, n$ identical firms in an industry, each with constant marginal costs of c and no fixed costs. If the market price, P, is determined by the equation $P = a - Q$, where Q is total industry output and a is a constant, determine the Cournot–Nash equilibrium output level for each firm. What happens as $n \to \infty$?

EXERCISE 4.2.

Find an equation for the contract curve for the model presented in Exercise 4.1 when $n = 2$. Show that along this contract curve aggregate supply of the good is equal to the quantity that a profit-maximizing monopolist would supply.

4.1.2 Stackelberg competition

With Cournot competition each firm chooses its desired level of supply simultaneously. In Stackelberg competition it is assumed that at least one of the firms in the market is able to precommit itself to a particular level of supply before other firms have fixed their level of supply. These other firms observe the leader's supply and then respond with their output decision. The firms able to initially precommit their level of output are called the market leaders and the other firms are the followers. Again to aid understanding, we examine the case of duopoly, where there is one leader and one follower. The extensive form game for this type of competition is shown in Fig. 4.4.

In Fig. 4.4 firm A is the leader and firm B the follower. The only difference between this diagram and the extensive form game drawn for Cournot duopoly, is that firm B's decision nodes are now in separate information sets rather than being in the same information set. This corresponds to the assumption that the follower now observes

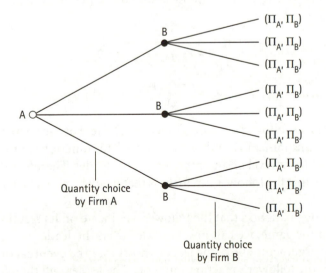

Fig. 4.4 Stackelberg Duopoly: Extensive Form Game

the leader's supply decision before choosing its own optimal response. This change in market structure significantly alters the predicted behaviour of the two firms.

In predicting the outcome of this extensive form game we need to realize that the game is no longer static but inherently dynamic. This raises the possibility of threats and promises being made and possibly acted upon. For example, firm B may threaten to produce such a large amount of the good that if believed the leader would set output equal to zero, thus leaving firm B the sole supplier. This represents one possible Nash equilibrium. There will, with a continuum of such threats and promises, be an infinite number of such Nash equilibria. The problem with this reasoning is that most of these equilibria involve the leader believing incredible threats or promises. They are incredible because they are not in the interest of the follower actually to carry them out if required to do so. In order to rule out such incredible threats and promises we require that the predicted outcome of the game be subgame perfect. To find the subgame perfect Nash equilibrium for this game we apply the principle of backward induction.

To see how the principle of backward induction may be applied in this situation we make the same assumptions previously used to analyse Cournot competition, except now we let firm A be the leader and firm B the follower. Using backward induction we start with the last period first, and initially determine the follower's output decision. Given that the follower is rational it will attempt to maximize its pay-off, here given in terms of its profit level, subject to the leader's known level of supply. The follower's profit function is given as

$$\Pi_B = Pq_B - cq_B$$

$$\therefore \Pi_B = (a - q_A - q_B)\, q_B - cq_B.$$

Differentiating this with respect to q_B and setting this equal to zero gives us the first-order condition for a maximum.

$$\therefore \frac{d\Pi_B}{dq_B} = a - q_A - 2q_B - c = 0$$

$$\therefore q_B = \frac{a - c - q_A}{2}.$$

This equation is the follower's reaction function. (Note that the term 'reaction function' is no longer a misnomer in this dynamic game.) This function shows the follower's optimal response for any level of supply chosen by the leader. Therefore the only credible threat/promise that the follower can make is that it will be on its own reaction function.

Having made the prediction that the follower will locate on its reaction function in the last period of the game, we can now consider what the leader will do in the first period. From the arguments above the leader knows that the eventual outcome of the game must be on the follower's reaction function. The leader will therefore maximize its own profits subject to this constraint. The first-order condition for a maximum is derived as follows, where we substitute firm B's reaction function in for its level of output.

$$\Pi_A = Pq_A - cq_A$$

$$\therefore \Pi_A = (a - q_A - q_B)q_A - cq_A$$

$$\therefore \Pi_A = aq_A - q_A^2 - \frac{a - c - q_A}{2}q_A - cq_A$$

$$\therefore \Pi_A = \frac{a - c}{2}q_A - \frac{1}{2}q_A^2$$

$$\therefore \frac{d\Pi_A}{dq_A} = \frac{a - c}{2} - q_A = 0$$

$$\therefore q_A = \frac{a - c}{2}.$$

This is the subgame perfect Nash equilibrium level of supply for the leader. Substituting this in to the follower's reaction function gives us that firm B's optimal response is to produce $q_B = (a - c)/4$. With one leader and one follower, the follower produces half the amount of the leader, and $Q = 3(a - c)/4$. These results are illustrated in Fig. 4.5.

The leader knows that if the follower is rational it will produce on its reaction function. Given this constraint the leader will maximize profits where its isoprofit curve is tangential to the follower's reaction curve. Firm A would ideally like to be the sole supplier in this market so that it could earn monopoly profits. This corresponds to point A in Fig. 4.5. However, the lowest isoprofit curve that it can reach, subject to the final output combination being on the follower's reaction function, is the one through point S. This is the Stackelberg–(subgame perfect) Nash equilibrium. Interestingly, with only

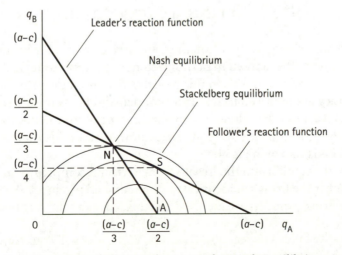

Fig. 4.5 Stackelberg-Subgame Perfect Nash Equilibrium

one leader and one follower, the leader produces the monopoly output level. (This result does not generalize to the case of more than one follower, as Exercise 4.3 demonstrates.) The leader, however, does not earn monopoly profits. This is because the follower's positive level of output drives down the market price that the leader receives. In the Stackelberg–Nash equilibrium the firms' isoprofit curves continue to intersect and so, as with the Cournot–Nash equilibrium, there are still potential gains to be had from collusion.

Fig. 4.5 also illustrates the Cournot–Nash equilibrium. Compared to this equilibrium the Stackelberg equilibrium entails higher profits for the leader and smaller profits for the follower. More information has actually made the follower worse off! In contrast, the ability of the leader to precommit itself to a particular level of supply has made that firm better off. In this model there is said to be a first-move advantage.

EXERCISE 4.3

Assume there are m identical Stackelberg leaders in an industry, indexed $j = 1, \ldots, m$, and n identical Stackelberg followers, indexed $k = 1, \ldots, n$. All firms have a constant marginal cost of c and no fixed costs. The market price, Q, is determined according to the equation $P = a - Q$, where Q is total industry output, and a is a constant. Find the subgame perfect Nash equilibrium supply for the leaders and the followers. Confirm the duopoly results for both Cournot competition and Stackelberg competition, and the generalized Cournot result for n firms derived in Exercise 4.1.

4.1.3 Bertrand competition

In Cournot and Stackelberg competition the firms' strategic variable is the quantity of the good they supply to the market. In Bertrand competition the strategic variable is the price firms charge their customers. In this model firms simultaneously announce the price at which they are prepared to sell their product, and then consumers determine the amount they will buy. The extensive form for this type of competition with just two firms is the same as for Cournot duopoly, except now firms decide on the price to sell their product. This is shown in Fig. 4.6.

The nature of the equilibrium that results from Bertrand competition depends critically upon whether the firms sell identical or differentiated products. We will initially assume that the firms' products are identical and then consider the case of product differentiation.

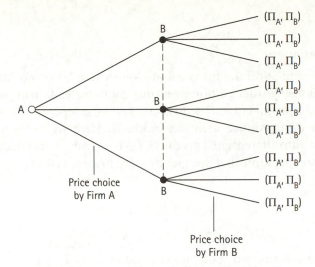

Price choice
by Firm A

Price choice
by Firm B

Fig. 4.6 Bertrand Duopoly: Extensive Form Game

Undifferentiated products

With undifferentiated products there is a unique Nash equilibrium, where the firms charge the same price, and just earn normal profits. To see that this is the case consider the following two-stage argument.

If the firms sell identical goods, then consumers will only buy from the firm offering the product at the lowest price. Therefore, if firms were to sell the product at different prices the firm with the lower price would capture the whole market. If in this situation this firm is making supernormal profits, then the other firm has an incentive to slightly undercut its competitor's price. Doing this it will capture the whole market and begin earning positive profits. If, on the other hand, the initial firm is earning less than normal profits, then that firm has an incentive to raise its price. This will be to where it either earns at least normal profits, or has zero sales and leaves the industry. From these scenarios it is clear that firms charging different prices cannot be a Nash equilibrium.

A similar argument can be made concerning firms charging the same price but earning more or less than normal profits. In this situation both firms will have an incentive either to slightly increase or decrease the price they charge. The unique Nash equilibrium is, therefore, all firms charging the same price and earning normal profits. This is identical to the perfectly competitive outcome. This result, that as few as two firms will yield the competitive outcome, is referred to as the *Bertrand paradox*. It is a paradox because it seems implausible to believe that so few firms would not find some way of colluding so as to move away from the competitive outcome in order to earn supernormal profits. One way of avoiding the Bertrand paradox is to allow firms to repeatedly interact. As argued in section 4.2, this allows the possibility of non-cooperative collusion, where firms can earn greater profits than those suggested by this one-off game. An alternative way of avoiding the paradox is to allow the firms to sell differentiated products. This situation is analysed below.

Ogliopoly

Product differentiation

With product differentiation the firms will no longer face all-or-nothing demand as experienced when they produce a homogeneous good. Instead, firms will now face a downward-sloping demand curve. The firms remain interdependent but this is not as extreme as when they produce identical products. Here we examine the case of Bertrand duopoly with differentiated products. Let two firms, A and B, set the prices p_A and p_B respectively. We assume that the quantity each firm sells is determined by the following equations

$$q_A = a - p_A + bp_B$$

$$q_B = a - p_B + bp_A.$$

where $b > 0$ reflects that the two goods are substitutes for each other. As with previous models we assume that the firms have constant marginal costs equal to c and no fixed costs. Assuming firms attempt to maximize profits, we can derive the Nash equilibrium as follows. First, we derive each firm's reaction function, which gives us their optimal price given the price the other firm sets.

Firm A	**Firm B**
$\Pi_A = p_A q_A - c q_A$	$\Pi_B = p_B q_B - c q_B$
$\therefore \Pi_A = p_A(a - p_A + bp_B) - c(a - p_A + bp_B)$	$\therefore \Pi_B = p_B(a - p_B + bp_A) - c(a - p_B + bp_A)$
$\therefore \dfrac{d\Pi_A}{dp_A} = a + bp_B - 2p_A + c = 0$	$\therefore \dfrac{d\Pi_B}{dp_B} = a + bp_A - 2p_B + c = 0$
$\therefore p_A = \dfrac{a + c + bp_B}{2}.$	$\therefore p_B = \dfrac{a + c + bp_A}{2}.$
$\dfrac{d^2\Pi_A}{dq_A} = -2 < 0 \therefore \text{ max.}$	$\dfrac{d^2\Pi_B}{dq_B} = -2 < 0 \therefore \text{ max.}$

These two reaction functions are plotted in Fig. 4.7.

The reaction curves for Bertrand competition are seen to be upward-sloping, and so the prices of the two firms are strategic complements. To find a Bertrand–Nash equilibrium both firms must be maximizing their profits simultaneously given the expected behaviour of the other firm. Again this means that both firms must be on their reaction curves. Setting the two reaction functions equal to each other we obtain the unique Nash equilibrium that each firm will set its price equal to $(a + c)/(2 - b)$. As with the Nash equilibrium associated with Cournot and Stackelberg competition, this outcome is Pareto inefficient. Both firms can be made better off if they set higher prices. These Pareto-dominant outcomes are shown as the lens-shaped area in Fig. 4.7. The problem with achieving one of these Pareto-dominant outcomes is that, again, at least one firm has an incentive to deviate from it. This justifies the Nash equilibrium as being the expected outcome for this particular model.

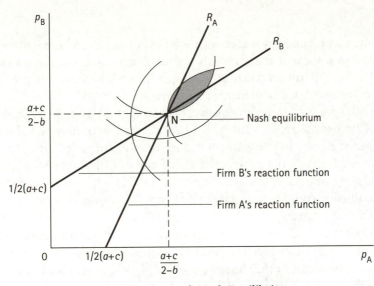

Fig. 4.7 Bertrand–Nash Equilibrium

4.2 Non–Cooperative Collusion

In the previous section we illustrated the three classic models of oligopoly as one-off games. The predicted outcome of each model was either a Nash equilibrium or a sub-game perfect Nash equilibrium. In all three models the equilibrium was shown to be Pareto inefficient. With effective collusion all firms could receive higher profits. The problem, however, is that without the use of legally enforceable contracts such collusion is not credible in these one-off games. This is because at least a subset of the firms involved in the collusion has an incentive to unilaterally deviate from it. This section extends our analysis of oligopoly by discussing the possibility of non-cooperative collusion when firms repeatedly interact. This is closer to reality for many oligopolies, and provides us with the opportunity to see how the issues of repeated games, as presented in Chapter 3, can be applied to oligopolistic competition. First, we examine the situation where firms experience infinite interaction with each other. We will then consider what happens when there are only a finite number of repetitions of the one-off game. In this latter context we discuss the role of multiple equilibria, uncertainty about the future, and uncertainty about one's competitors.

4.2.1 Infinite repetitions

With infinite interaction firms have the possibility of adopting punishment strategies that induce other firms to maintain the non-cooperative collusive outcome. This is because with repeated interaction there is the possibility of firms being punished if they break an explicit or tacit collusive agreement. For example, if one firm increases its output other firms may retaliate by increasing their output causing all firms to be worse off. If this effective punishment is sufficiently severe, firms will voluntarily maintain the collusive outcome. This involves firms forgoing an increase in short-run profits in order to avoid the costs associated with future punishment.

One particular form of punishment that firms might adopt is a *trigger strategy*. As discussed in Chapter 3 a trigger strategy is where a certain action by one player induces other players in the game to *permanently* change the way they act. With a trigger strategy, therefore, a firm faces the prospect of an infinite punishment period if it deviates from the collusive outcome. It was J. Friedman (1971) who first showed that non-cooperative collusion could be maintained if oligopolies continually interact and adopt an appropriate trigger strategy.

To see how adoption of a trigger strategy can lead to non-cooperative collusion we apply a specific trigger strategy to our model of Cournot duopoly. In section 4.1 it was shown that any point within the shaded region of Fig. 4.2 makes both firms better off compared to the Nash equilibrium. However, it was previously argued that given the symmetry of our model, and the assumption that firms will aim for a Pareto-efficient outcome, a focal point for attempted collusion is where each firm produces half the monopoly output level. This corresponds to point C in Fig. 4.2. If firms do seek to co-ordinate upon this output combination, then they may adopt the following trigger strategy

> Produce half the monopoly output level in the first period, and continue to do so if the other firm has always done so in the past. Otherwise produce the Cournot–Nash output level.

With this trigger strategy firms, in effect, promise to collude as long as they perceive that the other firm has always done so. The threat, however, is that if a firm deviates from the collusive outcome it will be punished by the other firm producing the Cournot–Nash equilibrium output level forever. For the collusive outcome to be a subgame perfect Nash equilibrium both the promise and the threat implied by this strategy must be credible.

The threatened punishment is clearly credible because if one firm is seen to have deviated from the collusive outcome, then it is always rational for the other firm to produce the output level associated with the Nash equilibrium. For the promise to be credible the present value of maintaining collusion must exceed the present value of deviating from it. This will be true provided that firms do not discount the future 'too much'. This is shown as follows. If both firms continue to collude, then they each earn half the monopoly level of profit, $\Pi_M/2$, in every time-period. Discounting this by the relevant discount factor $\delta = 1/(1 + r)$; $0 \leq \delta \leq 1$, we obtain the present value of always continuing to collude:

$$\frac{\Pi_M}{2} + \delta \frac{\Pi_M}{2} + \delta^2 \frac{\Pi_M}{2} + \delta^3 \frac{\Pi_M}{2} + \ldots = \frac{1}{1-\delta} \frac{\Pi_M}{2}.$$

If, alternatively, one firm deviates from the collusive outcome, then let the profit it earns in the first time-period be equal to Π_D (where the subscript D refers to deviation). In subsequent periods the most it can earn is equal to the Cournot–Nash equilibrium profit level Π_C. The present value of deviating is therefore:

$$\Pi_D + \delta \Pi_C + \delta^2 \Pi_C + \delta^3 \Pi_C + \ldots = \Pi_D + \frac{\delta}{1-\delta} \Pi_C.$$

Non-cooperative collusion will be maintained if

$$\frac{1}{1-\delta} \frac{\Pi_M}{2} \geq \Pi_D + \frac{\delta}{1-\delta} \Pi_C$$

$$\therefore \quad \delta \geq \frac{\Pi_D - \Pi_M/2}{\Pi_D - \Pi_C}.$$

As $\Pi_D > \Pi_M/2 > \Pi_C$, the right-hand side of the inequality will be between zero and one. This condition is therefore satisfied provided δ is sufficiently close to one. This confirms that non-cooperative collusion will be maintained provided that the rate of discount is not too small. When this condition is satisfied the resulting non-cooperative collusion is self-enforcing. Each firm, given the other firm has adopted the above trigger strategy, willingly maintains the collusive outcome.

One natural question that arises from the above analysis is what happens if the rate of discount is smaller than that necessary to maintain the collusive outcome? Here we discuss two possibilities.

One possibility is that the firms continue to adopt the previous trigger strategy where punishment is equivalent to the Cournot–Nash equilibrium being played forever. Although this punishment strategy cannot sustain joint output equal to the monopoly outcome, because firms are assumed to discount future profits too much, other less profitable collusive outcomes may be supported. As long as the rate of discount is not zero there always exist other sustainable collusive outcomes that yield greater present-value profits compared to the Cournot–Nash equilibrium. From these possible outcomes it seems reasonable to assume that firms will co-ordinate on the symmetric outcome which yields highest present-value profits given the firm's actual rate of time-preference. If the rate of discount is zero, i.e. firms are only interested in present profits, then we return, in effect, to the one-off game, and the only subgame perfect equilibrium is that the Cournot–Nash solution is played every period.

An alternative possibility in trying to maintain an otherwise unsustainable collusive outcome, is to make the threat of punishment more severe. Instead of seeking to collude on an alternative outcome that is sustainable with the proposed trigger strategy, the firms might try to adopt an alternative trigger strategy. In order for this alternative trigger strategy to sustain the desired collusive outcome it must credibly threaten a more severe punishment for deviation. The problem with this proposal is that in this model any *permanent* punishment which is more severe, implies that the adopted trigger strategy is not credible. This can be illustrated by the following argument.

The most severe trigger strategy possible is to punish a deviant with its so called *minimax punishment* forever. The minimax punishment is the worst outcome players can inflict upon another, given that the other player will be seeking to maximize his or her pay-off. In our Cournot duopoly model this corresponds to one firm seeking to minimize the other firm's profits given that that firm will always seek to be on its reaction function. This occurs when the punishing firm produces the perfectly competitive output $a - c$. If the other firm expects to observe this level of output, then from its reaction function it will voluntarily cease production and earn zero profit. This confirms that this is the minimax punishment. (Note that a firm cannot be forced to earn negative profits because it always has the option of leaving the market and just breaking even.) If a firm believes it will face this extreme punishment if it deviates, it clearly has a stronger incentive to maintain the collusive outcome. In this way the desired collusive outcome can be part of a Nash equilibrium. The problem with this punishment strategy, however, is that it is not credible, and so the collusive outcome supported by it cannot be subgame perfect. The reason the minimax threat in this model is not credible is because it is off the punishing firm's reaction function. If it believed the other firm were going to produce zero output, then its optimal output is the monopoly output level $(a - c)/2$, and not the competitive output level. For a trigger strategy to be credible the punishment to be inflicted must be on the punishing firm's reaction function. However, as the other firm will always seek to maximize its own profit level, it must also be on that firm's reaction function as well. The only credible punishment, given that the firms adopt a trigger strategy, must be a Nash equilibrium in the stage game. The only credible trigger strategy, within our duopoly model, is the one considered previously where punishment corresponds to the Cournot–Nash equilibrium.

The above argument seems to imply that a more severe punishment strategy will not be credible. This, however, is not the case. The above argument rules out more-severe *trigger* strategies, but not more severe *punishment* strategies in general. Indeed, Abreu (1986) has proposed a way in which firms can threaten more severe punishment for observed deviation, and yet for it to still remain credible. The way to make punishment more severe and remain credible is to move away from a trigger strategy and adopt a *carrot-and-stick approach*. Abreu's suggestion is that firms need not threaten an infinite punishment period, as suggested by the use of trigger strategies, but instead threaten only a temporary period of punishment. The reason a more severe punishment can now be credible is that firms are punished themselves if they do not punish other firms.

The strategy suggested by Abreu is as follows. If all firms adopt the punishment strategy within the punishment period, firms revert back to the collusive outcome. This is the carrot. If, however, firms deviate from the prescribed punishment, then punishment is continued. This is the stick. In this way firms are punished if they do not punish other deviant firms. This strategy, therefore, gives firms a greater incentive to punish other firms. As a result the punishment itself need no longer be the Cournot–Nash outcome. More severe punishment can become credible because all firms have an incentive to carry it out so as to avoid being punished themselves. With more severe punishment being credible the desired collusive outcome can be sustained for even smaller values of the discount factor. This possibility is demonstrated for our Cournot duopoly model in Exercise 4.4.

The above result is an application of the *Folk Theorem* as presented by Fudenberg and Maskin (1986). In this context the theorem states that all possible output combinations that Pareto-dominate the minimax outcome can form part of a subgame perfect Nash

---

EXERCISE 4.4*

In the text we derived that $\delta \geq (\Pi_D - (\Pi_M/2))/(\Pi_D - \Pi_C)$ is a necessary and sufficient condition for each firm in a Cournot competing duopoly to produce half the monopoly output level if it faces continual interaction and adopt the following trigger strategy: *Produce half the monopoly output level in the first period, and continue to do so if the other firm has always done so in the past. Otherwise produce the Cournot–Nash output level.*

(1) Determine the necessary and sufficient conditions for this collusive outcome to be maintained if the firms adopt the following alternative punishment strategies.

(a) Instead of a permanent switch to the Cournot–Nash equilibrium, deviation from the collusive outcome causes the other firm to produce the Cournot–Nash output level for only one period, and then reverts back to producing the collusive output level.

(b) Each firm produces the collusive output level initially, and if this outcome was maintained in the previous period. If, however, one firm deviates from the collusive output level, then it will be punished for one period by the other firm producing the amount q_p. If the non-deviant firm does indeed produce q_p in response to deviation by the other firm then both firms return to the collusive outcome in the following period. If, however, the punishing firm deviates from the punishment output level q_p, then it is, in turn, punished by the other firm producing q_p. This process continues indefinitely.

(2) Using the necessary and sufficient conditions just derived to maintain the collusive outcome for each of the above three punishment strategies, calculate the specific conditions for δ in the following model. Price is determined by the equation $P(\pounds) = 65 - Q$, where Q is the joint output of the two firms. Each firm has constant marginal costs equal to £5, and no fixed costs. For the carrot-and-stick punishment strategy given in (1)b calculate the necessary conditions when q_p is 25, 30, and 35. Identify which of these punishment strategies supports the collusive outcome with the lowest value of δ.

equilibrium provided firms do not discount the future 'too much', and that they adopt appropriate punishment strategies. The minimax outcome is where each player is trying to minimize other player's pay-offs. In Cournot duopoly this is when both firms receive zero profits. This theorem states, therefore, that all feasible profit allocations can be subgame perfect equilibria provided both firms earn at least zero profits and do not overly discount future profits. This is a strong result. Due to the resulting multiple equilibria implied by this theorem firms must somehow co-ordinate their output on one particular equilibrium. The selection process often used in the literature, and which has been applied above, is to suppose that the equilibrium will be symmetric and on the contract curve provided the discount factor is not too small.

To conclude our discussion on infinite competition between firms it should be noted that the above results strongly contrast with those derived when examining one-off competition between firms. There it was argued that non-cooperative collusion is not possible. By modelling infinite repetitions of these one-off games we have derived the opposite result. Provided firms are sufficiently interested in future profits non-cooperative collusion is now possible. In these infinitely repeated games collusion is sustained by the credible threat of future punishment. Given the stark contrast of these results it is important that we go on to explore the predicted outcome of competition between firms when the one-off game is only finitely repeated.

4.2.2 Finite repetitions

In Chapter 3 it was argued that there is a fundamental difference between infinitely repeated and finitely repeated games. This is demonstrated by the paradox of backward induction. The relevance of this paradox to finite interaction between oligopolies is that with a unique Nash equilibrium in the one-off game non-cooperative collusive outcomes are unsustainable. This can be applied to all three models analysed in section 4.1. Here we consider its application to Cournot competition.

Assume that a finite number of oligopolies Cournot compete with each other over a known finite number of time-periods. In applying the paradox of backward induction we consider the last period first. In this last period there can be no subsequent punishment for deviation from a collusive outcome. The only credible outcome in this period, therefore, is the Cournot–Nash equilibrium. We now consider the period before last. As both firms know that the Cournot–Nash solution will be played in the next time-period, there is again no effective punishment for deviation in this penultimate period. The Cournot–Nash equilibrium will, therefore, be played in this last but one period. This argument can be repeated for all successive time-periods until we reach the beginning of the game. The only subgame perfect Nash equilibrium for this finitely repeated game is that the Cournot–Nash equilibrium is played in every time-period. The paradox of backward induction rules out the possibility of non-cooperative collusion between oligopolies in finitely repeated games of complete information, where there is a unique

Nash equilibrium in the stage game. As many economists believe that oligopolies do collude so as to increase profit, a number of ways of avoiding the paradox have been applied to oligopolistic competition. Here we discuss three suggested ways oligopolies might succeed in colluding without assuming infinite interaction between firms.

Multiple Nash equilibria

In the one-off models we examined in section 4.1 there was shown to be a unique Nash equilibrium. This, however, need not always be the case. For example, with more complex demand and/or cost functions it is quite possible for there to be multiple Nash equilibria in these one-off games. Fig. 4.8 illustrates how non-linear reaction functions can generate multiple Nash equilibria when two firms Cournot compete. In this diagram there are three Nash equilibria at points A, B, and C. The existence of multiple Nash equilibria means that the outcome in the final period of play is no longer uniquely determined. This in turn means there is no unique subgame perfect equilibrium for the whole game. In particular, if the multiple Nash equilibria in the one-off game are associated with different levels of profit for the competing firms, a collusive outcome can be self-supporting in the early periods of the game.

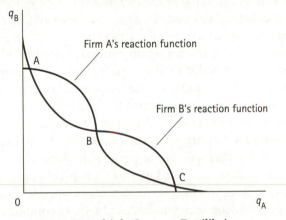

Fig. 4.8 Multiple Cournot Equilibria

Non-cooperative collusion is now possible because multiple Nash equilibria allow firms to be effectively punished if they deviate from the collusive outcome. If the punishment is sufficiently severe, then it will be in firms self-interest to maintain the collusive outcome. As the final period is approached the non-cooperative cartel will break down. This is demonstrated by the fact that the outcome in the final period must be a Nash equilibrium. Benoit and Krishna (1987) demonstrate that by combining multiple Nash equilibria in the stage game with a suitable carrot-and-stick punishment strategy the set of possible non-cooperative collusive outcomes is almost identical to that derived under infinite repetition, provided the game is repeated a sufficiently large number of times.

Uncertainty about the future

As discussed in Chapter 3 an alternative way of avoiding the paradox of backward induction is to introduce uncertainty about when the game might end. Without a known last period of interaction between competing firms the process of backward induction cannot be initiated. In this situation firms can credibly threaten future punishment if other firms deviate from the collusive outcome. Given that this future punishment may not be forthcoming, as interaction may have ceased before this is possible, this threat is not as severe as when made in an infinitely repeated game. However, similar results derived under infinite repetition can be reproduced when there is uncertainty about when finite interaction will end. Once again the non-cooperative collusive outcome can be sustained given that the firms do not overly discount future returns.

Uncertainty about competitors

A final way of avoiding the paradox of backward induction is by introducing incomplete information. In the context of oligopoly this involves competition between firms who are unsure about some aspect of their rivals' pay-off function. This may either be because firms are unsure about the *parameters* of their competitors' profit function, or the *objectives* of other firms. For example, firms may be uncertain about the demand or costs facing their competitors, which determine their rivals' profit function. Alternatively, it may not be clear whether other firms are interested in maximizing profits or have some other objective such as maximizing total revenue. Due to mutual interdependence firms will try and estimate the pay-off function of their competitors. This is necessary so that firms can attempt to predict the behaviour of other firms. Firms will then attempt to maximize their pay-offs based on these estimates. One important way firms seek to learn what their competitors are like, or the constraints they face, is by observing their current and past behaviour. Other firms realizing this may then seek to manipulate their own behaviour in order to influence the expectations of other firms. This, in turn, will be taken into account when firms interpret the actions of their rivals. Clearly solving such models can be quite complicated. As discussed in Chapter 3, a relevant equilibrium concept to use in models of incomplete information is that of Bayesian subgame perfect Nash equilibrium. With this type of equilibrium no incredible threats or promises are made or believed, and firms update their expectations rationally according to Bayes' Theorem. Typically the equilibrium need not involve firms playing the Nash equilibrium for the stage game in each and every period of the game. To illustrate the intuition behind this result consider a number of Bertrand-competing firms with incomplete information about each other's marginal costs of production.

As shown in section 4.1 Bertrand-competing firms can be made better off if they all set higher prices. Furthermore, as prices in the one-off game are strategic compliments, if a firm believes other firms are going to raise their price, it will also increase its price. Prices are, in turn, positively related to marginal costs of production. With uncertainty about other firms' marginal costs of production, each firm has an incentive to persuade its competitors that its marginal costs are high. In this way firms have an incentive to increase the price they set now so as to try and develop a reputation for having high marginal costs, and for setting high prices. In equilibrium it is possible for all firms to set high prices and a non-cooperative collusive outcome to be maintained in the initial periods of the repeated game.

The above argument illustrates how uncertainty can enhance the probability of non-cooperative collusion being sustained. This, however, need not always be the case. For example, most of the proposed ways in which collusion outcomes have been demonstrated to be self-supporting have relied upon firms being punished if and when they deviate from the collusive outcome. This mechanism presupposes that such deviation can be detected. If deviation from the collusive outcome can go undetected, then a firm may be able to cheat on a tacit agreement without fear of being punished. In this situation firms will have to find other ways in which to support the collusive outcome. This may involve the sharing of information on prices charged and quantities produced, or the development of punishment strategies conditional upon the observed market variables. Green and Porter (1984) and Porter (1983), for example, develop models where Cournot-competing oligopolies do not observe each other's output levels but only the derived market price. In these models the firms adopt a *trigger price strategy*, where each firm produces the collusive output level as long as the market price remains above the trigger price. If the market price falls below the trigger price, then a period of punishment where the Cournot–Nash equilibrium quantities are produced ensues. In this way collusion can be maintained as long as demand shocks do not cause the market price to fall below the trigger price. The typical equilibrium in models such as these involves alternating periods of collusive behaviour followed by price wars when demand for the good is sufficiently low.

4.3 Conclusions

This chapter has illustrated how game theory can be used to model the strategic interaction faced by oligopolistic firms. Initially one-off games were used to present the three classic models of Cournot, Bertrand, and Stackelberg competition. Each was shown to have a different underlying structure that greatly influences the way firms are predicted to behave. None the less each of the Nash equilibria associated with these models are Pareto inefficient. With different output combinations all firms could be made better off. This raises the question of whether firms are able to co-ordinate upon a more profitable outcome. If firms face a period of one-off competition, this seems unlikely. If, however, firms face continual interaction, non-cooperative collusion would seem possible. This derives from the possibility of firms being credibly threatened with future punishment if they deviate from the collusive outcome. In this way tacit collusion can be self-enforcing. The only exception to this is when the paradox of backward induction is applicable. However, as demonstrated in the text, this result depends on the extreme assumptions of a known end to competition, and common knowledge about all competing firms. In reality neither of these assumptions is likely to be satisfied.

Demonstrating the possibility of non-cooperative collusion is undoubtedly a major achievement of game-theoretical analysis. In one sense, however, such analysis is too successful, in that often there are a large number of feasible outcomes upon which firms may co-ordinate. In the text we argued that with such multiple equilibria it seems reasonable to assume that firms will co-ordinate on a focal point. This raises the question of what features of the underlying competition make one equilibrium more salient than another. Without greater attention being given to these factors we will be unable to confidently predict the outcome of oligopolistic competition in any specific market. These considerations are the subject of ongoing research, and some of the general issues involved are discussed in Chapter 12.

4.4 Solutions to Exercises

Exercise 4.1

The profit function for the i'th firm is equal to:

$$\Pi_i = Pq_i - cq_i$$

$$\therefore \Pi_i = (a - q_i - Q_{-i}) \cdot q_i - cq_i.$$

where the variable Q_{-i} refers to aggregate output of all firms excluding the i'th.

Differentiating with respect to q_i and setting this equal to zero gives us the first order condition for a maximum.

$$\frac{dq_i}{d\Pi_i} = a - 2q_i - Q_{-i} - c = 0$$

$$\therefore \quad q_i = \frac{a - Q_{-i} - c}{2}.$$

As all firms are identical, in Nash equilibrium they will all produce the same level of output, and so $Q_{-i} = (n-1)q_i$. Substituting this into the above equation gives us:

$$\therefore \quad q_i = \frac{a - c}{n + 1}.$$

This corresponds to the Nash equilibrium output level of each firm in the industry. With $n = 2$ we obtain the previous result that $q_i = (a-c)/3$. As $n \to \infty$ so industry output approaches the perfectly competitive outcome with price equal to marginal cost, and $Q = a - c$.

Exercise 4.2

There are two possible ways in which the equation for the contract curve can be found. The *first* method is to select a fixed level of profit for one of the firms and then maximize profit for the other firm. The *second* method is to maximize the weighted sum of profits of the two firms. Here we demonstrate the second method.

Define the weighted sum of the two firms profits as W so that

$$W = k\Pi_1 + (1-k)\Pi_2; 0 \le k \le 1$$

$$\therefore W = k(a-q_1-q_2-c)q_1 + (1-k)(a-q_1-q_2-c)q_2.$$

The first-order condition for a maximum is that the two partial derivatives $\partial W/\partial q_1$ and $\partial W/\partial q_2$ equal zero. From these two requirements the following quadratic equation can be obtained

$$(q_1+q_2)^2 - \frac{3(a-c)}{2}(q_1+q_2) + \frac{(a-c)^2}{2} = 0.$$

This equation has two solutions where joint supply, $Q = q_1 + q_2$, equals $(a-c)$ or $(a-c)/2$. The second solution corresponds to the output a monopolist would supply to the market, and so this is the solution that maximizes the sum of weighted profits. The equation for the contract curve is therefore written as

$$q_2 = \frac{a-c}{2} - q_1.$$

As stated in the text a Pareto-efficient outcome results when the two firms agree to divide the monopoly output level between them.

Exercise 4.3

To find the subgame perfect Nash equilibrium of this inherently dynamic game we use the principle of backward induction. We first find the reaction function of a typical follower. Throughout the following derivation we make use of the fact that in Nash equilibrium all leaders will have the same level of supply, as they are assumed to be identical. Similarly all followers will supply the same quantity. The profit function for any one follower is given as:

$$\Pi_k = Pq_k - cq_k$$

$$\therefore \Pi_k = [a - q_k - (n-1)Q_{-k} - mq_j]q_k - cq_k,$$

where the variable Q_{-k} refers to the aggregate output of all followers excluding the k'th firm. Differentiating this with respect to q_k and setting this equal to zero, gives us the first order condition for maximizing profits.

$$\frac{d\Pi_k}{dq_k} = a - 2q_k - Q_{-k} - mq_j - c = 0$$

$$\therefore q_k = \frac{a - c - Q_{-k} - mq_j}{2}.$$

As in Nash equilibrium all followers will have the same supply, we can rewrite this as:

$$q_k = \frac{a - c - mq_j}{n+1}.$$

In determining the optimal strategy for the leaders, we need to substitute this reaction function into their profit function. Again taking a representative leader j and letting the variable Q_{-j} represent the aggregate output of all leaders excluding this firm we have:

$$\Pi_j = Pq_j - cq_j$$

$$\therefore \Pi_j = [a - q_j - Q_{-j} - nq_k] q_j - cq_j$$

$$\therefore \Pi_j = aq_j - q_j^2 - Q_{-j}q_j - nq_kq_j - cq_j$$

$$\therefore \Pi_j = aq_j - q_j^2 - Q_{-j}q_j - n\left(\frac{a - c - mq_j}{n+1}\right)q_j - cq_j$$

$$\therefore \Pi_j = \left(1 - \frac{n}{n+1}\right)(a-c)q_j - \left(1 - \frac{nm}{n+1}\right)q_j^2 - Q_{-j}q_j.$$

Differentiating with respect to this firm's output, and setting this equal to zero yields the first-order condition for a maximum

$$\frac{d\Pi_j}{dq_j} = \frac{a-c}{1+n} - 2\left(\frac{n+1-mn}{n+1}\right)q_j - Q_{-j} = 0.$$

Once more in Nash equilibrium all leaders' supply will be equal to each other, and so:

$$q_j = \frac{a-c}{1+n+m-mn}.$$

This is the Nash equilibrium supply for any leader. Substituting this into the follower's reaction function gives us their equilibrium level of supply.

$$q_k = \frac{1}{1+n}\left(1 - \frac{m}{1+n+m-mn}\right)(a-c).$$

In Cournot duopoly we have either two 'leaders' and no 'followers', or no 'leaders' and two 'followers'. In each case we get the result that both firms supply $(a-c)/3$. For Stackelberg duopoly we get that the leader supplies $(a-c)/2$ and the follower supplies $(a-c)/4$. With n Cournot competitors, either all 'leaders' or all 'followers', each firm supplies $(a-c)/(n+1)$. These findings confirm previous results.

Exercise 4.4

(1a) Given the proposed punishment strategy, if a firm continually produces the collusive output level then its present value profits is:

$$\frac{\Pi_M}{2} + \delta\frac{\Pi_M}{2} + \delta^2\frac{\Pi_M}{2} + \delta^3\frac{\Pi_M}{2} + \ldots = \frac{(1+\delta)}{(1-\delta^2)}\frac{\Pi_M}{2}.$$

Alternatively if the firm deviates from the collusive outcome in the first period then it will rationally deviate in every alternate period, and so its present-value profit is, at most:

$$\Pi_D + \delta\Pi_C + \delta^2\Pi_D + \delta^3\Pi_C + \ldots = \frac{\Pi_D - \delta\Pi_C}{1 - \delta^2}.$$

The firms will maintain the collusive outcome if

$$\frac{(1+\delta)}{(1-\delta^2)}\frac{\Pi_M}{2} \geq \frac{\Pi_D - \delta\Pi_C}{1-\delta^2}$$

$$\therefore \; \delta \geq \frac{\Pi_D - \dfrac{\Pi_M}{2}}{\dfrac{\Pi_M}{2} - \Pi_C}.$$

Comparing this condition with that derived in the text when the punishment period is infinite, we can note that the set of discount values for which collusion on the monopoly outcome is possible is smaller. This is because the threatened punishment is less severe, and so firms are less likely to be deterred from deviating from the cartel.

(1b) In order for the collusive outcome to be maintained with this punishment strategy two conditions will need to be simultaneously satisfied. The *first* condition is that neither firm has an incentive to deviate from the collusive output level, given that the proposed future punishment is credible. The *second* condition is that neither firm has the incentive to deviate from producing the punishment level of output q_p, when required, given that the first condition is satisfied.

The first necessary condition is derived as follows. If a firm maintains the collusive outcome then present-value profits are:

$$\frac{\Pi_M}{2} + \delta\frac{\Pi_M}{2} + \delta^2\frac{\Pi_M}{2} + \delta^3\frac{\Pi_M}{2} \ldots = \frac{(1+\delta)}{(1-\delta^2)}\frac{\Pi_M}{2}.$$

If a firm deviates from the collusive output, then present value profits are at most:

$$\Pi_{\text{Dev.collusion}} + \delta\Pi_{\text{Punished}} + \delta^2\Pi_{\text{Dev.collusion}} + \delta^3\Pi_{\text{Punished}} + \ldots = \frac{\Pi_{\text{Dev.collusion}} - \delta\Pi_{\text{Punished}}}{1-\delta^2},$$

where $\Pi_{\text{Dev.collusion}}$ and Π_{Punished} are the period profits associated with deviating from the collusive outcome and being punished for so deviating respectively.

The firms will continue to produce the collusive outcome if the proposed punishment is credible and

$$\frac{(1+\delta)}{(1-\delta^2)}\frac{\Pi_M}{2} \geq \frac{\Pi_{\text{Dev.collusion}} - \delta\Pi_{\text{Punished}}}{1-\delta^2}$$

$$\therefore \; \delta \geq \frac{\Pi_{\text{Dev.collusion}} - \dfrac{\Pi_M}{2}}{\dfrac{\Pi_M}{2} - \Pi_{\text{Punished}}}.$$

Similarly the second necessary condition is derived as follows. If a firm produces q_p following deviation by the other firm then, if the first condition is satisfied, its present-value profits equal:

$$\Pi_{\text{Punishing}} + \delta\frac{\Pi_M}{2} + \delta^2\frac{\Pi_M}{2} + \delta^3\frac{\Pi_M}{2} + \ldots,$$

where $\Pi_{Punishing}$ is the expected level of profit when punishing the other firm. Alternatively, if it deviates from the proposed punishment level of output then present-value profits will be at most:

$$\Pi_{Dev.punishing} + \delta\Pi_{Punished} + \delta^2 \frac{\Pi_M}{2} + \delta^3 \frac{\Pi_M}{2} + \ldots,$$

where $\Pi_{Dev.punishing}$ is the expected profit level associated with deviating from the proposed level of punishment output. A firm will therefore maintain the proposed punishment strategy if the first condition is satisfied and

$$\Pi_{Punishing} + \delta\frac{\Pi_M}{2} \geq \Pi_{Dev.punishing} + \delta\Pi_{Punished}$$

$$\therefore \; \delta \geq \frac{\Pi_{Dev.punishing} - \Pi_{Punishing}}{\frac{\Pi_M}{2} - \Pi_{Punished}}.$$

(2) Under the trigger strategy where deviation from the collusive outcome causes firms permanently to switch to the Cournot–Nash equilibrium the collusive outcome is self-supporting if

$$\delta \geq \frac{\Pi_D - \Pi_M/2}{\Pi_D - \Pi_C} = \frac{506.25 - 450}{506.25 - 400} = 0.529.$$

With the punishment strategy given in (1a) the condition becomes

$$\delta \geq \frac{\Pi_D - \dfrac{\Pi_M}{2}}{\dfrac{\Pi_M}{2} - \Pi_C} = \frac{506.25 - 450}{450 - 400} = 1.125.$$

Finally, the results derived assuming the carrot-and-stick punishment strategy are shown in Table 4.1, where the binding constraint is underlined.

The results in the Table 4.1 indicate that as the punishment level of output q_p increases the minimum rate of discount needed to maintain the collusive outcome initially falls and then rises. This is confirmed in Fig. 4.9 where the two conditions over δ are plotted for values of q_p between 20 (the Cournot–Nash equilibrium output level) and 60 (the minimax output level). From these results the most effective punishment strategy in maintain-

Table 4.1

	$\delta \geq \dfrac{\Pi_{Dev.collusion} - \dfrac{\Pi_M}{2}}{\dfrac{\Pi_M}{2} - \Pi_{Punished}}$	$\delta \geq \dfrac{\Pi_{Dev.punishing} - \Pi_{Punishing}}{\dfrac{\Pi_M}{2} - \Pi_{Punished}}$
$q_P = 25$	$\delta \geq 0.391$	$\delta \geq 0.098$
$q_P = 30$	$\underline{\delta \geq 0.250}$	$\underline{\delta \geq 0.250}$
$q_P = 35$	$\delta \geq 0.191$	$\underline{\delta \geq 0.431}$

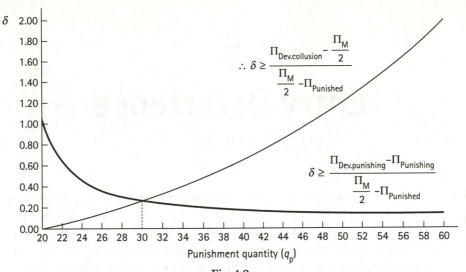

Fig. 4.9

ing collusion in this model is the carrot-and-stick punishment strategy when q_p is set equal to 30. With this punishment strategy collusion on the monopoly outcome can be sustained provided $\delta \geq 0.25$.

Further Reading

Friedman, J. (1977), *Oligopoly and the Theory of Games*, Amsterdam: North-Holland.

Gravelle, H., and R. Rees (1992), *Microeconomics*, London: Longman.

Jacquemin, A., and M. E. Slade (1989), 'Cartels, Collusion, and Horizontal Merger', in R. Schmalensee and R. D. Willig (eds.), *Handbook of Industrial Organization*, i, Elsevier Science Publishers.

Kreps, D. (1990), *A Course in Microeconomic Theory*, New York: Harvester Wheatsheaf.

Lyons, B., and Y. Varoufakis (1989), 'Game Theory, Oligopoly and Bargaining', in J. D. Hey (ed.), *Current Issues in Microeconomics*, London: Macmillan.

Martin, S. (1992), *Advanced Industrial Economics*, Oxford: Blackwell.

Phlips, L. (1995), *Competition Policy: A Game Theoretic Perspective*, Cambridge: Cambridge University Press.

Rees, R. (1993), 'Tacit Collusion,' *Oxford Review of Economic Policy*, 9: 27–40; repr. in T. Jenkinson (1996), *Readings in Microeconomics*, New York: Oxford University Press.

Shapiro, C. (1989), 'Theories of Oligopoly Behavior', in R. Schmalensee and R. D. Willig (eds.), *Handbook of Industrial Organization*, i, Elsevier Science Publishers.

Tirole, J.(1988), *The Theory of Industrial Organisation*, Cambridge Mass.: MIT Press.

Vickers, J. (1985), 'Strategic Competition among the Few—Some Recent Developments in the Economics of Industry', *Oxford Review of Economic Policy*, 1: 39–62, repr. in T. Jenkinson (1996), *Readings in Microeconomics*, New York: Oxford University Press.

5
Entry Deterrence

IN this chapter we continue to examine how game theory can be used to analyse the strategic interaction between firms. In the previous chapter this interaction occurred between firms currently competing against each other. In this chapter the interaction is between a firm already active in a specific market and a potential entrant or entrants into that market. In particular, we examine situations where a monopolist has the incentive to try and prevent other firms from entering its market and competing against it. If successful, the firm maintains its monopoly position. This issue is known as *entry deterrence*. Following standard practice the initial monopolist is called the *incumbent* and the potential competitor is called the *entrant* (even though it may subsequently decide not to enter the market). It is not necessary that the entrant produce an identical product as the incumbent, only that they are regarded as close substitutes. As a result of this assumption entry will have an adverse affect on the monopolist's profits.

In section 5.1 we critically analyse an early attempt to explain how a monopolist might attempt to deter future entry by increasing its current output. In doing this the monopolist hopes to convince the potential entrant that its level of sales will not be large enough to earn a positive rate of return. If the entrant believes this to be the case, it will stay out of the market. This argument is known as the Limit Price Theory. It is argued in this chapter, however, that this theory implies irrational behaviour by both the incumbent monopolist and the entrant. In section 5.2 we consider more recent game theory explanations of how an incumbent firm may credibly deter entry. Here we examine the role of predatory pricing, precommitment, and incomplete information.

5.1 Theory of Limit Pricing

In the basic textbook analysis of monopoly the possibility of future competition is ignored and the focus is on how a monopoly maximizes current profits. This is the static theory of monopoly. It shows that the monopoly, in order to maximize current profits, produces where the marginal cost curve cuts the marginal revenue curve from below. The firm then sets the highest price possible so as to just sell this level of output. This standard analysis is shown in Fig. 5.1.

In this diagram monopoly profits are maximized when marginal cost (MC) equals marginal revenue (MR). The firm produces Q_0 of the output per period of time with price set equal to P_0. Here the firm earns a return greater than is necessary to maintain it in this market, and so earns supernormal profits. This level of supernormal profit is equal to the shaded area in Fig. 5.1.

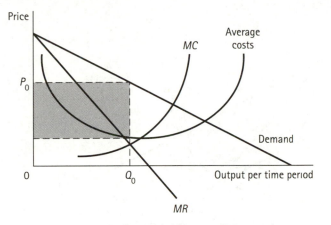

Fig. 5.1 The Static Theory of Monopoly

This analysis implicitly assumes that there are significant barriers to entry which prevent other firms from entering the market. These barriers, for example, might be due to government legislation, in which case we have a legal monopoly, or due to large economies of scale, where we then have a natural monopoly. With these barriers to entry the monopolist's position is assured and in this situation it can maximize current profits in every time-period. As other firms are unable to enter the industry the incumbent need not concern itself with the possibility of future competition. Bain (1956) noted that in the absence of these barriers to entry the presence of supernormal profits will attract other firms into the industry. This increased level of competition is likely to have an adverse effect on the incumbent firm's profits. If the monopoly is concerned with both current and future levels of profits, there is an incentive for it to try and deter entry provided such action is not too costly. Bain suggested that a monopoly could achieve this objective by increasing its output to an appropriate level and charging a correspondingly lower price. The appropriate level of output and price is determined so that the entrant believes its sales will be just insufficient to earn a normal rate of profit. Given this belief a rational entrant will not enter the market, and hence the monopolist's entry deterrence strategy is successful.

Bain's theory, which was later developed by Modigliani (1958) and Sylos-Labini (1962), starts with the critical assumption that potential entrants into a market believe that the incumbent firm will continue to produce the same level of output in the future.

Entry Deterrence

This is believed true irrespective of whether entry takes place or not. (This is similar to the behavioural assumption made by Cournot in his model of duopoly. There each firm believes the other firm will maintain its current level of output.) This assumption is also assumed to be common knowledge, i.e. the incumbent knows the entrant believes this, and the entrant knows that the incumbent knows this, and so on. This assumption gives rise to the concept of the *residual demand curve*. The residual demand curve shows how much demand is 'left-over' for the entrant once the incumbent has sold its level of output. This is illustrated in Fig. 5.2.

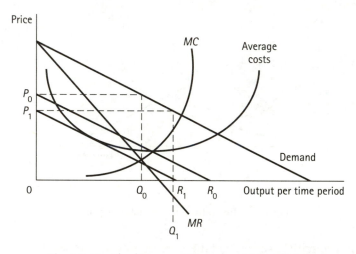

Fig. 5.2 Residual Demand Curves and Limit Pricing

In this diagram, if the monopoly is concerned with maximizing current profits, then, as we have seen, it produces output Q_0. With the incumbent producing this level of output the residual demand curve faced by the entrant is given by the curve P_0R_0. This is derived by shifting what remains of the incumbent's demand curve (all points to the right of Q_0) back to the vertical axis. If the entrant has the same cost curves as the incumbent, then the entrant can earn positive profits. This is because part of its residual demand curve lies above the average cost curve. With the prospect of earning supernormal profits the entrant will enter the market, and adversely affect the incumbent's future level of profits.

In order to avoid this prospect of reduced future profits the incumbent firm may set a different initial price and output combination that attempts to deter entry. Entry will be deterred if the entrant believes it will be unable to earn at least normal profits. This will arise when the residual demand curve is below the average cost curve at all levels of output. When the residual demand curve is tangent to the average cost curve the entrant is indifferent between entering and staying out of the market. We may assume that in this situation entry is just deterred. In Fig. 5.2 the residual demand curve tangent to the average cost curve is shown as P_1R_1. In order for the entrant to perceive this as its

---

EXERCISE 5.1

Find the output and price combination for the following incumbent monopolist that just deters entry, assuming the entrant believes that the monopolist will maintain its level of output in subsequent periods. The market demand curve is given by the equation:

$$P = 10 - 2Q,$$

where P is the market price and Q is total market output. Both the incumbent and the entrant are assumed to have the following identical total cost function

$$TC_i = 1/2 + 4q_i,$$

where $i = I$, E corresponds to the incumbent and the entrant respectively. TC_i are total costs for firm i and q_i is the level of output produced by firm i. Contrast this limit price strategy with the output and price combination when the incumbent firm maximizes current-period profits.

---

residual demand curve, and hence is just persuaded to stay out of the market, the incumbent needs to set a price of P_1 and sell the amount Q_1. This is the highest price at which entry is deterred and is called the *limit price*. The strategy of charging the limit price is called the *limit price strategy*. Under this strategy the monopolist sacrifices some of its current profits in an attempt to ensure higher profits in the future. It is argued that a rational monopolist will pursue this limit price strategy if the present value of profits in doing so exceeds the present value of maximizing current profits.

Bain's theory of limit pricing highlights that a monopoly facing the prospect of future competition, which adversely affect its future profits, may pursue strategic behaviour which is at variance with the aim of maximizing current profits. This model suggests that the traditional textbook analysis of monopoly is likely to give misleading predictions about monopoly behaviour, and the welfare implications of monopoly. For example, if we ignore the possibility of limit pricing, we are likely to overestimate the static, or dead-weight, welfare loss associated with monopoly. Clearly the Limit Price Theory has important policy implications concerning the regulation of monopolies. However, from a game theory point of view the theory of limit pricing seems far from satisfactory. This is because it seems to rely on both the incumbent firm and the potential entrant acting irrationally. The main criticism of Bain's theory relates to the entrant's belief that the incumbent will continue to produce the same level of output. This belief is maintained irrespective of whether the entrant intends to enter the market or not. There are situations where this assumption might be valid. For example, if the monopoly must publicly commit itself to a certain level of output, then the entrant's belief may be justified. None the less this assumption does not seem very realistic in many real-world situations. The normal expectation is that if the entrant enters the market it will force the monopolist to change its output–price combination. This is because the incumbent will realize it is now competing as a duopolist.

The incumbent may initially threaten to produce the same level of output, hoping to deter entry, but from the perspective of game theory this threat is not credible. Given that entry occurs, it is not in the incumbent's best interest to carry out this threat. From this perspective the limit price strategy, derived in Bain's model, is not a subgame perfect Nash equilibrium. For these reasons it seems necessary to reject Bain's theory of limit pricing as it is based on unreasonable behaviour by firms. It is irrational for the incumbent to issue such an incredible threat, and even more irrational for the entrant to believe it and act upon it.

One way of further understanding this criticism of Bain's model is to draw the extensive form for this model. It is assumed there are only two periods, and that the incumbent firm is free to change its level of output between them. This is done in Exercise 5.2.

EXERCISE 5.2

Draw the two-period extensive form game of entry deterrence under the following assumptions:

(1) At the beginning of the first period the incumbent chooses its output level which the (potential) entrant observes.

(2) At the end of the first period the entrant decides whether or not to enter the market, which is observed by the incumbent.

(3) In the second period we have the following situation: If the entrant has not entered the market, then the incumbent sets its output level so as to maximize monopoly profits. If the entrant has entered the market, we have the Cournot model of duopoly, i.e. both the incumbent and entrant choose their output levels simultaneously.

From the extensive form game drawn in answer to Exercise 5.2, it can be observed that beginning from the second period of play to the end of the game we have a series of separate subgames. To avoid the proposed equilibrium to the whole game involving incredible threats, we require that the solution must be a Nash equilibrium in all of these subgames. This is consistent with the equilibrium being subgame perfect. Bain's theory of limit pricing violates this requirement and so is not a subgame perfect Nash equilibrium .

To find the subgame perfect Nash equilibrium for the game given in Exercise 5.2 we use the principle of backward induction. This states that we must predict the outcome of the second period before we solve for the first period. If the entrant enters the market at the end of the first period, then the second period involves both firms Cournot competing. In this situation each firm sets the Nash equilibrium output associated with this type of competition, as explained in Chapter 4. If the entrant has not entered the market, then the incumbent is free to maximize current profits as predicted by the traditional theory of monopoly. Based on these predictions for the second period, firms will derive their optimal first-period actions. For the entrant it will only enter the market if it can make positive profits under Cournot competition. If not, it will stay out of the market. Significantly this entry decision is made irrespective of what the incumbent does in the first period of the game. In particular, the entrant ignores any limit price strategy pursued by the incumbent firm. The incumbent in turn realizes that nothing it does in the first period affects the entrant's entry decision. It is rational, therefore, for the incumbent to maximize current period profits in the first period.

In conclusion, there are only two subgame perfect equilibria for this game. The first equilibrium is where the incumbent firm remains a monopolist in both periods and maximizes current profits in each period. In this case the incumbent firm enjoys a natural monopoly. The second equilibrium is where the incumbent monopolist maximizes current profits in the first period, but faces duopolistic competition in the second period. Which of these equlibria occurs depends on the underlying parameters of the game. In neither equilibrium is there a role for entry deterrence or limit pricing.

The above argument has demonstrated that for the game described in Exercise 5.2, entry deterrence based on limit pricing implies irrational behaviour by both the incumbent and the entrant. It should be realized, however, that this model makes a number of simplifying assumptions. In particular, it assumes that there is limited interaction between the incumbent and the entrant, that there is no possibility of precommitment by the incumbent, and finally there is complete information. Recent game theory models have relaxed each of these assumptions to see if entry deterrence can be made credible. These extensions to the basic model are discussed in the next section.

5.2 Credible Entry Deterrence

5.2.1 Predatory pricing

The previous section analysed the situation where an incumbent firm modifies its current behaviour so as to deter future entry into its market. An alternative argument that has been put forward is that an incumbent can deter entry by engaging in a price war if and when any firm actually enters the market. Here the incumbent does not set a limit price but instead engages in predatory pricing when entry occurs. Limit pricing is where an incumbent sets a low price *before* entry occurs. Predatory pricing, in contrast, is where the incumbent sets a low price *after* entry has occurred. Typically, predatory pricing makes both the entrant and the incumbent worse off compared to accommodating entry. If this is true, the incumbent would always accommodate entry in a one-off game, and so the entrant is sure to enter if it can make positive profits. In this context, predatory pricing is irrational and entry is not deterred. However, Milgrom and Roberts (1982*b*) have shown that if the incumbent faces an infinite number of possible entrants, in different markets, then predatory pricing can be rational behaviour, and in equilibrium it deters entry. Consider the following so-called chain-store game.

A monopoly incumbent operates in an infinite number of separate but identical markets, and faces a potential entrant in each one. The entrants make their decision to enter each market sequentially. If entry occurs on any one market, then the incumbent has two options. It can either engage in predatory pricing and both firms make a loss, or it can accommodate entry and both firms earn positive profits, though this is less than the incumbent would have earned if it had remained the sole supplier. If an entrant does not enter, it is assumed to make zero profits, and the incumbent earns monopoly profits. These pay-offs are shown in Fig. 5.3 where the first pay-off refers to the incumbent (I) and the second pay-off to the entrant (E).

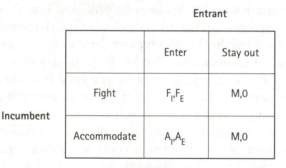

Fig. 5.3 Pay-offs for the Chain-Store Game

It is assumed that $M > A_I > 0 > F_I$ and $A_E > 0 > F_E$. With these assumptions the incumbent prefers its monopoly position to accommodating entry, which it prefers to fighting entry. An entrant will only enter a market if it expects to be accommodated. All previous outcomes are assumed to be observed by all players in the game.

Consider the first market and the first entrant. If the incumbent accommodates entry here, the other potential entrants will observe this and so rationally anticipate accommodation if they enter their respective markets. This is because in infinite supergames the nature of the game does not change between periods. This implies that if a decision is optimal in one period it must be optimal in all periods. With the expectation of accommodation, entry will occur in every market. If it was rational for the incumbent to accommodate the first entrant, it will accommodate all others. The incumbent's expected present value of profits from accommodating the first entrant is therefore

$$A_I + \delta A_I + \delta^2 A_I + \ldots = \frac{A_I}{1-\delta},$$

where δ is the appropriate discount factor.

On the other hand if the incumbent fights the first entrant, then successive entrants will expect the same behaviour, and so they will stay out of their respective markets. In this way the incumbent maintains its monopoly position in all succeeding markets. The expected present value of profits from fighting the first entrant is therefore

$$F_I + \delta M + \delta^2 M + \ldots = F_I + \frac{\delta M}{1-\delta}.$$

From these pay-offs the incumbent will fight the first entrant if

$$F_I + \frac{\delta M}{1-\delta} > \frac{A_I}{1-\delta}.$$

Rearranging this condition the incumbent will fight entry if $\delta > (A_I - F_I)/(M - F_I)$. As $M > A_I$ this condition is satisfied provided δ is sufficiently close to one, i.e. the incumbent does not discount the future too much. When this condition is met, entrants know that the incumbent firm will fight the first entrant, and so entry into every market is deterred. This result illustrates that, with the prospect of repeated entry, it may be credible for an incumbent to threaten predatory pricing, and in this way successfully deter entry. It should be noted that in this model the incumbent is free to maximize its current profits in every period. This is because entry is deterred not by what the incumbent does in pre-entry periods, but instead, because entrants know that the incumbent always has the incentive to fight such entry. This entry-deterrent result only holds true, however, if the number of markets where entry is possible is infinite. If the number of such markets is finite, then fighting entry is not credible and entry occurs in every market. This result is known as the chain-store paradox, and is an application of the paradox of backward induction. To understand this result consider the following argument.

Given the pay-offs in Fig. 5.3, the incumbent will definitely accommodate entry in the last market. This is because there are no future gains from doing otherwise, and so the firm maximizes current profits. The entrant into this market predicts this outcome, and so entry is followed by accommodation. In the penultimate market we get the same result. As the outcome of the final period has already been determined, there are again no future benefits of fighting entry, and so the incumbent will again accommodate. Once more the entrant knows this and so enters this market. This argument can be applied to all preceding markets until we reach the beginning of the game. The only subgame perfect equilibrium for this finite game is that entry occurs in every market and the incumbent always accommodates. Once more there is no possibility of entry deterrence.

5.2.2 Precommitment

The failure of the Limit Price Theory to explain entry deterrence, and the chain-store paradox, occur because the incumbent firm is unable to credibly precommit its future behaviour. Without such precommitment entry deterrence is not possible in these finite and complete-information models. For entry to be deterred the incumbent needs to find some way of credibly committing itself to a strategy which induces the entrant to perceive that if it enters the market, it will make a loss. The only way the incumbent can do this is by undertaking some action in the current period that affects the nature of competition in subsequent periods. In order for the current action to have the desired entry-deterrent effect it must, to some extent, be irreversible. If the incumbent's strategic action is easily reversible, then it will have no credible effect on the perceived nature of future competition, and so will not influence the entrant's decision of whether or not to enter the market. This highlights the importance of *sunk costs*, i.e. costs that cannot be recovered once they have been incurred. The role of sunk costs in determining the nature of competition within markets has been emphasized in the literature on contestable markets, as developed by Baumol, Panzar, and Willig (1982). Initially we examine a model developed by Dixit (1981). In this model, investment in capital in the current period affects that firm's future marginal costs. Due to this intertemporal link an incumbent can credibly deter entry into its market. We then discuss other ways in which an incumbent may successfully deter entry via precommitment.

Investment in capital

Dixit (1981) makes use of a two-period model. In the first period the incumbent is the sole supplier, whilst in the second period an entrant enters the market if it thinks it will earn positive profits by doing so. If entry does occur, then the two firms are assumed to Cournot compete. The possibility of precommitment by the incumbent is introduced by allowing it to invest in capital in the first period, which lowers its marginal costs in the second period. This investment can be in either physical or human capital, but it is assumed to be irreversible, and so in the second period such expenditure is regarded as a sunk cost. This investment is observed by the potential entrant. Via this intertemporal link the incumbent is able to affect the nature of competition in the second period, and so influence the entrant's entry decision. This can be shown using the reaction functions of the two firms as shown in Fig. 5.4.

In Fig. 5.4 the Nash equilibrium in the second period, if the entrant enters the market and the incumbent undertakes no strategic investment in the first period, is at point A. This is where the two initial reaction functions cross. As indicated by the isoprofit line through point A the entrant will earn a positive rate of return with this outcome, and so enters the market. However, the incumbent firm can alter this decision through strategic investment in capital in the first period. As increased investment reduces the

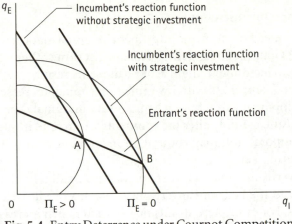

Fig. 5.4 Entry Deterrence under Cournot Competition

incumbent's future marginal costs, this investment in capital shifts the incumbent's reaction function to the right. With lower marginal costs the incumbent optimally produces more of its own product for each level of production by the entrant. This changes the nature of competition in the second period, and adversely affects the entrant's perceived rate of profit. With the appropriate level of investment the incumbent can reduce the entrant's expected rate of profit on entry to zero. This is achieved when the incumbent's reaction function cuts the entrant's reaction function at point B, which lies on the isoprofit line indicating zero profits for the entrant. The entrant's reaction function does not continue beyond point B as this would imply negative profits, which are avoided by staying out of the market. By optimally shifting its own reaction function to the right through increased investment in capital the incumbent credibly deters entry. Entry is deterred in this model because the entrant now perceives that if it enters the market the incumbent, based on its new reaction function, will act more aggressively and produce a higher level of output. With this expectation, the entrant perceives that it will make a loss on entry and so stays out of the market.

EXERCISE 5.3

Draw a diagram illustrating an incumbent's and an entrant's reaction functions when, if entry occurs, the two firms produce differentiated products and compete over price according to Bertrand competition. Explain and illustrate how, with this type of competition, strategic investment in capital by the incumbent can credibly deter entry.

Other forms of precommitment

So far we have examined how strategic investment in capital may commit an incumbent firm to future behaviour that deters entry. Here we list some other ways that have been suggested for how an incumbent might achieve the same result.

Research and development. As with investment in capital, increased expenditure on research and development can reduce a firm's future marginal costs. This can, if perceived to be successful, credibly alter the competitive outcome in subsequent periods. Again this intertemporal link may commit an incumbent firm to future action that deters entry into its market.

Advertising. Advertising can be a form of precommitment if its effects are durable. If its effects are durable, then current advertising expenditure will affect future competition between firms. For example, entrants may have to match increased advertising by the incumbent in order to compete effectively. This raises the entrants' costs and so may deter entry.

Switching costs. Switching costs are costs consumers incur when switching between different firms' products. This may, for example, be due to retraining costs or simply a dislike of change itself. In this case customers are likely to remain loyal to existing suppliers. Increasing current sales increases a firm's customer base and may put a future entrant at a competitive disadvantage, thus deterring entry. Long-term contracts with customers and network economies have a similar effect. Network economies arise when consumers derive greater benefits from a product, the greater the number of other people consuming the product. An obvious example is a telephone or computer network.

Learning by doing. This occurs when a firm's costs fall as the firm gains greater experience in producing its product. This cost benefit will accrue more quickly the greater the current rate of production. Once more an incumbent has the incentive to increase current production, so that future costs are lower. In this way the incumbent can ensure a competitive advantage in the future, which may once more deter entry.

5.2.3 Incomplete Information

A final way in which entry deterrence might be credible, even if the game is only finitely repeated, is if there is incomplete information about the type of incumbent the entrant is facing. For example, the entrant might not know the marginal costs of the incumbent, or whether the incumbent's managers obtain positive satisfaction from aggressively fighting entrants. In both these examples the entrant does not know for certain, at the beginning of the game, what pay-offs the incumbent will receive at the end of the game. To illustrate how incomplete information can lead to credible entry deterrence, we discuss two specific models. The first model was developed by Milgrom and Roberts (1982*a*), and shows how limit pricing can be seen as rational behaviour if there is uncertainty about an incumbent's costs. The second model developed by Kreps and Wilson (1982a), examines how the threat of predatory pricing can deter entry when there is uncertainty about the incumbent's incentives to engage in such aggressive behaviour.

Limit pricing

The model analysed here is based on a simplified version of the Milgrom and Roberts model, and is similar to the one presented by Fudenberg and Tirole (1986). Assume that there is only one incumbent and one potential entrant in an industry. The entrant observes the pricing policy of the incumbent in the first period, and then decides whether or not to enter the industry and compete against it in the second and final period of the game. The incumbent has one of two types of cost functions determined by nature. It has either low marginal costs equal to C_L with probability $Prob_L$, or high marginal costs equal to C_H with probability $Prob_H$. It is assumed that the entrant will only enter the market if it believes that the incumbent has high costs, or that the probability that it has high costs is sufficiently large. In this situation the incumbent has the incentive to signal that it is a low-cost firm and try to deter entry. However, the entrant will only believe that the incumbent has low costs if the signal is credible. For example, the entrant will not believe the incumbent if it merely announces that it has low costs. In order for the signal to be credible it must be costly. Milgrom and Roberts show that the limit price strategy can be rational, as it acts as a credible signal that a firm does indeed have low costs. It is credible because it is not in the interests of a high-cost firm to imitate it. To analyse this possibility in more detail, we will examine the equilibrium to this game, first under the assumption of complete information, and then introduce uncertainty about the incumbent's costs.

With complete information it is common knowledge what type of cost the incumbent has. If the incumbent has low marginal costs, then the entrant will definitely stay out of the market in the second period, and so the incumbent can set the monopoly price in both periods. This is equal to $(P_L^M | C_L)$ and the present value of profits for the incumbent is equal to $\Pi(P_L^M | C_L) + \delta \Pi(P_L^M | C_L)$, where δ is the discount factor. If the incumbent has high marginal costs the entrant will definitely enter the market in the second period. Here the incumbent sets the monopoly price in the first period, because with complete information it cannot hope to deter entry via limit pricing, and the Nash equilibrium duopoly price in the second period. These price levels are $(P_H^M | C_H)$ and $(P_H^D | C_H)$ respectively, and give the incumbent present-value profits equal to $\Pi(P_H^M | C_H) + \delta \Pi(P_H^D | C_H)$. With complete information the equilibrium to this entry game is very simple. By assumption the entrant enters when the incumbent has high marginal costs, with a probability of $Prob_H$, and stays out if the incumbent has low marginal costs, with a probability of $Prob_L$.

We now consider the effect of incomplete information on the equilibrium of this game. Assume now that only the incumbent knows for certain what type of cost function it has. In this situation the entrant will try and learn what type of costs the incumbent has from its behaviour in the first period. In signalling games such as this the

Entry Deterrence

Bayesian equilibrium can be one of two general types. It can either be a *pooling equilibrium* or a *separating equilibrium*. In a pooling equilibrium the players' types are not revealed by their actions because they do the same thing. In a separating equilibrium their type is revealed because their behaviour is different. Here we initially focus on the separating equilibrium and rule out the possibility of a pooling equilibrium. This is done by assuming that, based on its initial prior probabilities $Prob_L$ and $Prob_H$, the entrant expects to make a positive profit in the second period. This assumption implies that in a pooling equilibrium the entrant will definitely enter the market. With this prediction, however, the incumbent will have the incentive to set its monopoly price. As this price level differs between a high-cost and a low-cost incumbent there can be no pooling equilibrium. In the subsequent analysis we, therefore, assume that the prior probability that the incumbent has low costs is sufficiently large so that any equilibrium must be a separating equilibrium.

In a separating equilibrium the nature of the incumbent's costs are fully revealed. For this to be an equilibrium a high-cost firm must not imitate a low-cost firm, and a low-cost firm must not imitate a high-cost firm. These conditions require the equilibrium be *incentive compatible*. This requirement constrains the set of feasible actions available to each type of incumbent. We consider each of these types in turn.

The first condition, that a high-cost firm must not imitate a low-cost firm in the first period, will be satisfied if the following inequality holds:

$$\Pi(P_H^M \mid C_H) + \delta \, \Pi(P_H^D \mid C_H) > \Pi(P_L \mid C_H) + \delta \, \Pi(P_H^M \mid C_H). \tag{5.1}$$

The left-hand side of this inequality is the present value of profits for a high-cost firm given its cost function is revealed by its actions in the first period. If this is the case, it will charge its monopoly price in the first period and the Nash equilibrium duopoly price in the second. Total discounted profits will be the same as that derived under complete information. The right-hand side gives the present value of profits if the high-cost incumbent imitates a low-cost firm in the first period. P_L is the price charged by the low-cost firm in the first period, which in a separating equilibrium deters entry. As entry is deterred, the high-cost firm will set the monopoly price in the second period.

Similarly a low-cost firm will not imitate a high-cost firm in the first period if the following inequality holds:

$$\Pi(P_L \mid C_L) + \delta \, \Pi(P_L^M \mid C_L) > \Pi(P_H^M \mid C_L) + \delta \, \Pi(P_H^D \mid C_L). \tag{5.2}$$

The left-hand side is the present-value profits for the low-cost incumbent if it acts according to its type in both periods. As entry does not occur, the incumbent maximizes profits by setting its monopoly price in the second period. The right-hand side is the present value of profits if the low-cost incumbent initially imitates a high-cost firm. Here it sets the monopoly price associated with a high-cost firm in the first period. Entry is not deterred, but in the second period the entrant wrongly thinks it is competing against a high-cost incumbent. The incumbent will maximize its profits taking this false belief on the part of the entrant into account.

The above inequalities define the domain within which P_L must be set by the low-cost incumbent to guarantee a separating equilibrium. This will typically be less than the monopoly price a low-cost incumbent would set under conditions of complete information. (This is illustrated in Exercise 5.4.) In this situation the low-cost incumbent pursues a limit price strategy. As this is a separating equilibrium the entrant correctly perceives the cost function of the incumbent based on its pricing policy. This means that the entrant makes the same entry decisions as under certainty. It enters the market with a probability of $Prob_H$ and stays out of the market with a probability of $Prob_L$. If the limit price strategy does not affect the probability of entry it might be asked why the low-cost incumbent does not set its monopoly price in the first period. The answer is that if it did, the high-cost incumbent would have the incentive to imitate it. If this occurred, then the entrant perceiving the possibility of deception might enter the market, and so the low-cost incumbent would make smaller expected profits in the future. The limit pricing strategy, in this case, involves the low-cost incumbent reducing first-period profits so as to guarantee monopoly profits in the second period. The limit price strategy therefore deters entry from occurring when the entrant might otherwise have mistakenly perceived the incumbent to be a high-cost firm.

The above results are modified if the final equilibrium is a pooling equilibrium. As argued before if both types of incumbent set the same price in the first period, then the entrant learns nothing about its potential competitor. This means that in a pooling equilibrium the incumbent must perceive that it will make negative profits if it enters the market. Contrary to the separating equilibrium in a pooling equilibrium entry is always deterred. Again the first-period equilibrium price may be determined from the use of two necessary conditions. These relate to the fact that each type must prefer to charge the equilibrium price rather than set its monopoly price in the first period. In such an equilibrium it is typically the high-cost monopolist that now reduces its first-period price level and engages in limit pricing. By setting its price equal to what the low-cost monopolist would charge entry is effectively deterred and the incumbent is free to set the monopolist price in the second period.

EXERCISE 5.4*

Find the separating equilibrium behaviour of the low-cost incumbent in the following two-period model. The incumbent has marginal costs equal to either £4 or £2. Only the incumbent initially knows its exact costs. The entrant observes the incumbent's output decision in the first period and only enters the market in the second period if it believes that the incumbent has low marginal costs. If entry does occur, the two firms Cournot compete, and we assume that at this stage in the game the incumbent's true costs are revealed. Price, P, is determined by the following equation $P = 10 - Q$, where Q is the combined output of the two firms. Finally, it is assumed that the firms' discount factor is equal to 0.3.

Predatory pricing

In this second model of incomplete information it is assumed that potential entrants do not initially know for certain whether the incumbent has a preference for fighting entry, even if this involves reduced profits for that firm. Apart from this uncertainty the game is the same as the chain-store game with a finite number of markets. Clearly, if the probability that the incumbent is of this 'irrational' type is large, then entry is likely to be deterred. Kreps and Wilson (1982a) show, however, that entry can be deterred in the early stages of a repeated game even if this probability is very small. This involves a rational incumbent prepared to fight entry in early periods of the game. This is contrary to the chain-store paradox.

The reason entry is deterred is that now the rational incumbent has an incentive to act as if it were irrational in the early periods of the game. In this way the incumbent develops a reputation of being irrational, which deters future entry, and so raises the present value of expected future profits. The entrants know that the incumbent has this incentive to fight irrespective of its type in early periods, and so are deterred from entering. As we reach the end of the game the benefits of defending such a reputation diminish, as there is less time to reap future rewards. Towards the end of the game a rational incumbent will certainly accommodate entry. Before this stage in the game it is rational for the incumbent to play a mixed strategy. An entrant on the other hand will initially enter a market sometime during this mixed-strategy stage. If entry is accommodated, then it is known for sure that the incumbent is rational, and so entry occurs in all succeeding markets. If entry precipitates a price war, then the entrants will revise their probability that the incumbent is irrational, according to Bayes' Theorem. This increase in the entrants' perceived probability that the incumbent is irrational means that the incumbent now has a more valuable reputation to protect, and so it increases the probability that it will fight future entry. This in turn delays further entry. During the mixed-strategy stage the probability of fighting by the incumbent falls assuming there is no entry. Part of this Bayesian perfect equilibrium is illustrated in Fig. 5.5.

As in the infinite chain-store game entry is initially deterred, not from what the incumbent does pre-entry, but instead because potential entrants realize that the incumbent has the incentive to fight such entry. As a result the monopolist is free to maximize current profits in periods where entry does not occur. However, this is not

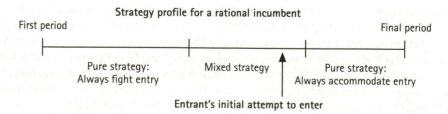

Fig. 5.5 Equilibrium for the Kreps–Wilson Model

the case when the incumbent engages in predatory pricing. In these situations the firm invests in a reputation for being irrational which deters future entry. This involves a reduction in current-period profits but has the benefit of increased future profits.

5.3 Conclusions

Static analysis predicts that a monopoly will attempt to maximize current profits by setting output where marginal cost equals marginal revenue. This implicitly assumes that there are significant barriers to entry that prevent other firms entering the market and competing away the monopolist's profits. If this assumption is relaxed, then the monopoly may have the incentive to strategically alter its behaviour in the current period, with the aim of deterring entry. One early attempt to model how a monopoly might accomplish this was provided by the Limit Price Theory. Here the monopoly increases its current output hoping that potential entrants believe that the remaining market is not large enough to support any more firms. A critical assumption in this theory is that the entrant believes the monopolist will continue to produce the same level of output even if entry occurs. This chapter has argued that this theory implies irrational behaviour by both the incumbent and potential entrants, and as a result should be rejected. Game theory has helped clarify the ways in which this theory is unsatisfactory. However, recent game theory models have suggested alternative ways in which an incumbent monopoly can strategically deter future entry. These models have been derived by relaxing certain assumptions made by the Limit Price Theory. In this way models incorporating the possibility of entry in an infinite number of separate markets, precommitment, and uncertainty have demonstrated that otherwise profitable entry may be deterred. These models represent significant advances in our understanding of how firms may strategically interact over time.

5.4 Solutions to Exercises

Exercise 5.1

From the market demand curve we can write the entrant's residual demand curve as

$$P_R = 10 - 2q_E - 2q_I.$$

The entrant's profit function is therefore given as

$$\Pi_E = (10 - 2q_E - 2q_I) q_E - 1/2 - 4q_E$$

$$\Pi_E = 10q_E - 2q_E^2 - 2q_I q_E - 1/2 - 4q_E$$

$$\Pi_E = 6q_E - 2q_E^2 - 2q_I q_E - 1/2.$$

Entry Deterrence

Differentiating this equation and setting it equal to zero gives us the entrant's first-order condition for maximizing its profits.

$$\frac{\partial \Pi_E}{\partial q_E} = 6 - 4q_E - 2q_I = 0$$

$$\therefore \ q_E^* = \frac{6 - 2q_I}{4}.$$

As expected the entrant's optimal level of output depends on the incumbent's level of output. Substituting this optimal level of output, q_E^*, back into the entrant's profit function we observe that its profit also depends on the incumbent's output level.

$$\Pi_E = 6\left(\frac{6 - 2q_I}{4}\right) - 2\left(\frac{6 - 2q_I}{4}\right)^2 - 2_{q_I}\left(\frac{6 - 2q_I}{4}\right) - 1/2.$$

According to the Limit Price Theory the incumbent, in order to deter entry, will set its output level so that Π_E equals zero. Setting the previous equation equal to zero gives us

$$36 - 12q_I - 1/2\,(36 - 24q_I + 4q_I^2) - 12q_I + 4q_I^2 - 2 = 0$$

$$\therefore \ q_I^2 - 6q_I + 8 = 0$$

$$\therefore \ (q_I - 4)\,(q_I - 2) = 0$$

$$\therefore \ q_I = 4 \text{ or } 2.$$

With the incumbent producing either of these outputs the entrant will make zero profits and so will not enter the market. Comparing these two output levels the incumbent makes a greater profit when $q_I = 2$, and sets $p = 6$. This is the limit price strategy.

If the incumbent firm were to maximize current-period profits, then it performs the following calculation.

$$\Pi_I = 10q_I - 2q_I^2 - 1/2 - 4q_I$$

$$\therefore \ \Pi_I = 6q_I - 2q_I^2 - 1/2$$

$$\therefore \ \frac{\partial \Pi_I}{\partial q_I} = 6 - 4q_I = 0$$

$$\therefore \ q_I = 1.5 \text{ and } p = 7.$$

As described in the text the limit price strategy involves the incumbent increasing its output and so reducing price.

Exercise 5.2

In the extensive form game drawn in Fig. 5.6 I refers to the incumbent firm and E to the entrant. The pay-offs are not shown but these are the present value of current and future profits for each firm. In order for the diagram to be manageable we have assumed that each firm has only three output levels that it can produce.

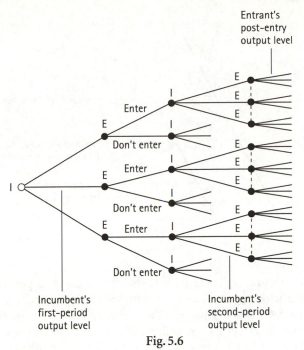

Entrant's
post-entry
output level

Enter

E

Don't enter

Enter

E

Don't enter

Enter

E

Don't enter

Incumbent's
first-period
output level

Incumbent's
second-period
output level

Fig. 5.6

Exercise 5.3

Fig. 5.7 illustrates the reaction functions for an incumbent and an entrant when they have differentiated products and price compete, according to Bertrand competition. As shown in Chapter 4 the reaction functions slope upwards. If one firm expects the other firm to raise its price, it will also raise its price. Profits for both firms are greater the farther out along their reaction curves they are. The initial equilibrium without strategic investment in capital is at point A. Here the entrant perceives it will make positive profits upon entry, and so enters the market. If, however, the incumbent invests in strategic capital, reducing its future marginal costs, its reaction function shifts to the left. With lower marginal costs the incumbent will optimally sell its product at a lower price for any given price set by the entrant. This reduces the profits of the entrant. With the appropriate level of strategic investment by the incumbent, the entrant will perceive that it will make a zero profit upon entry, and so it stays out of the market. This is shown in the above diagram by the new equilibrium at point B. The entrant's reaction function discontinues at point B, as at lower prices it perceives it will make a loss, and so does not enter the market.

Exercise 5.4

To find the separating equilibrium we adapt and apply the inequalities of (5.1) and (5.2) to this model. The equivalent inequalities for this model in terms of the firms setting output are:

$$\Pi(q_H^M \mid C_H) + \delta \Pi(q_H^D \mid C_H) > \Pi(q_L \mid C_H) + \delta \Pi(q_H^M \mid C_H)$$

$$\Pi(q_L \mid C_L) + \delta \Pi(q_L^M \mid C_L) > \Pi(q_H^M \mid C_L) + \delta \Pi(q_L^D \mid C_L).$$

Entry Deterrence

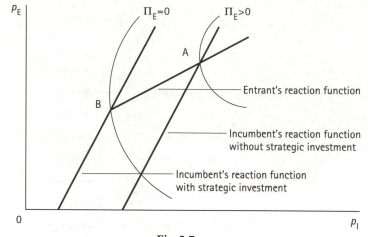

Fig. 5.7

where q^M and q^D are the incumbent's output levels when it acts as a monopolist and when it is in a duopoly respectively, each being conditional upon its costs. q_L is the equilibrium quantity that the low-cost incumbent sets in the first period. Given the details of the model we can find values for each of the above terms, except for the incumbent's profit level when setting q_L. Using the solution techniques discussed in Chapter 4, we obtain the following results.

$$\Pi(q_H^M \mid C_H) = 9,$$

$$\Pi(q_H^D \mid C_H) = 4,$$

$$\Pi(q_L^M \mid C_L) = 16,$$

$$\Pi(q_H^M \mid C_L) = 15,$$

$$\Pi(q_L^D \mid C_L) = 9.$$

Substituting these values into the above inequalities we get:

$\Pi(q_L \mid C_H) < 7.5$	$\Pi(q_L \mid C_L) > 12.9$
$\therefore (10 - q_L - 4)\, q_L < 7.5$	$\therefore (10 - q_L - 2)\, q_L > 12.9$
$\therefore q_L^2 - 6q_L + 7.5 > 0$	$\therefore q_L^2 - 8q_L + 12.9 < 0$
$\therefore q_L > 4.225$ or $q_L < 1.775$.	$\therefore 2.24 < q_L < 5.76$.

In order that the proposed solution be incentive-compatible for both the high- and low-cost incumbent firms, both these conditions must be satisfied simultaneously, and so we obtain the result that $4.225 < q_L < 5.76$. In contrast the monopoly output level for the low-cost firm is equal to 4. Therefore a low-cost incumbent needs to increase its output from the optimum quantity under complete certainty so as to clearly distinguish itself from a high-cost firm. This guarantees that entry does not occur, and the firm is assured of monopoly profits in the second period. The corresponding price in the first period for a low-cost firm is lower than it would have been with complete certainty, and so this strategy is equivalent to the limit price strategy.

Further Reading

Gilbert, R. J. (1989), 'Mobility Barriers and the Value of Incumbency', in R. Schmalensee and R. D. Willig (eds.), *Handbook of Industrial Organization*, i, Elsevier Science Publishers.

Gravelle, H., and R. Rees (1992), *Microeconomics*, London: Longman.

Martin, S. (1992), *Advanced Industrial Economics*, Oxford: Blackwell.

Ordover, J. A., and G. Saloner (1989), 'Predation, Monopolization, and Antitrust', in R. Schmalensee and R. D. Willig (eds.), *Handbook of Industrial Organization*, i, Elsevier Science Publishers.

Tirole, J.(1988), *The Theory of Industrial Organisation*, Cambridge Mass.: MIT Press.

Wilson, R. (1992), 'Strategic Models of Entry deterrence', in R. J. Aumann and S. Hart (eds.), *Handbook of Game Theory with Economic Applications*, New York: North-Holland.

6
New Classical Macroeconomics

IN the previous two chapters we have examined how game theory can be used to model the behaviour of individual firms. These were essentially microeconomic games. In this and the next chapter we present a number of macroeconomic games. In this chapter we analyse New Classical models based on the key assumptions of perfect competition and rational expectations. We give these models a game theory interpretation, and demonstrate how they modify the results of earlier models. It is argued that macroeconomic models concerned with optimal policy-making can be thought of as a game between the government and the private sector. From this perspective it is natural to expect each side to try and anticipate the actions of the other, and respond in an optimal way. Both New Classical and New Keynesian macroeconomics attempt to incorporate this insight by excluding irrational behaviour by both the government and the private sector. Relating this to the way agents formulate their expectations both these schools of thought have adopted the *Rational Expectations Hypothesis*.

The Rational Expectations Hypothesis, as originally defined by Muth (1961), states that 'expectations, since they are informed predictions of future events, are essentially the same as the predictions of the relevant economic theory.' In this strong version of the Rational Expectations Hypothesis agents' expectations of economic variables are the same as those derived from the relevant economic theory, conditional upon the information currently available to them. This version of the Rational Expectations Hypothesis assumes not only that individuals make the best use of all available information, but significantly, that the correct model of the economy is common knowledge. Agents then use this correct model of the economy to update their expectations. This does not necessarily mean that individuals' expectations are always proved correct. If there are random shocks hitting the economy, agents will inevitably make forecasting errors. Rather it implies that expectations must be correct *on average*. The Rational Expectations Hypothesis assumes that these errors will not be systematic. If agents do make systematic forecasting errors, then clearly they have an incentive to change the way they formulate their expectations. This process will continue until agents' expectations converge on the rational expectation. In effect the strong version of the Rational

Expectations Hypothesis assumes that this learning process has already been completed. A weaker version of the Rational Expectations Hypothesis assumes instead that agents only use currently available information in an optimal way. In this version agents may still need to learn the correct model of the economy. This may involve identifying either its structure or some particular parameter value. Despite the extreme nature of the strong version of the Rational Expectations Hypothesis it is this assumption that has typically been used in both New Classical and New Keynesian macroeconomics.

In adopting the Rational Expectations Hypothesis New Classical macroeconomics has highlighted the fact that results derived in earlier models were dependent upon agents having arbitrary expectations. In particular New Classical macroeconomics has significantly modified the predictions of earlier models related to government economic policy. To illustrate these advances we initially examine two specific examples. The *first* is the role of demand policy in stabilizing the economy. This is considered in section 6.1. Here we present the New Classical policy neutrality result, which states that a systematic demand management policy has no effect on real variables, such as output or employment. The *second* example is the nature of the political business cycle. This is considered in section 6.2. In this section we present the New Classical result that a government's long-run optimal monetary policy may be time-inconsistent, resulting in the economy suffering from inflationary bias. In section 6.3 we consider ways that time inconsistency may be avoided. This includes a discussion of the New Classical political business cycle, where, contrary to the policy neutrality result, systematic demand management can have short-run effects on real variables due to incomplete information.

6.1 Stabilization Policy

New Classical macroeconomics is characterized by two key assumptions. The *first* is that there is perfect competition in all markets. In particular all private sector agents are price-takers and markets clear instantaneously. As a result of this assumption private-sector agents are independent of each other. There is assumed to be interdependence, however, between the government and the private sector as a whole. The *second* key assumption is that agents formulate their expectations rationally. In early New Classical models, as developed by Lucas (1972), Sargent (1973), and Sargent and Wallace (1975), the main result derived was that a nominal demand shock will only effect real variables if it is *unanticipated*. If a demand shock is anticipated, than agents will instantaneously adjust wages and prices so that real variables remain unchanged. This result is illustrated in Fig. 6.1.

In Fig. 6.1 the aggregate price level (P) and real national income (Y) are determined where aggregate demand equals aggregate supply. The aggregate demand curve (AD) is assumed to be downward-sloping. This is due to the real balance effect. As the price level falls so the real money supply expands, and this increases aggregate demand for

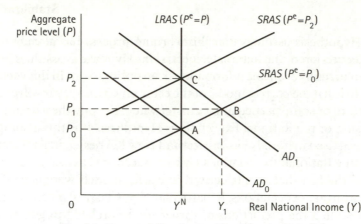

Fig. 6.1 Demand Shocks in a New Classical Model

goods and services. On the supply side the diagram distinguishes between the long-run and short-run aggregate supply curves. The economy is assumed to be in long-run equilibrium when agents' price expectations (P^e) are correct, and so $P^e = P$. In this situation all real variables are assumed to be at their natural rates. This implies that the long-run aggregate supply curve ($LRAS$) is vertical through the natural rate of output (Y^N). Real variables will only deviate from their natural values if price expectations are incorrect. This gives us the short-run aggregate supply curve ($SRAS$), which is assumed to be upward-sloping. If the price level is higher than expected firms increase their output, and real national income rises. This type of supply curve is known as a *Lucas supply curve*. Finally it is assumed that agents formulate their expectations according to the Rational Expectations Hypothesis. Fig. 6.1 illustrates the effects of a positive demand shock.

The economy is initially assumed to be in long-run equilibrium at point A, with the price level equal to P_0. Suppose now that aggregate demand increases, as shown by the upward shift in the aggregate demand curve from AD_0 to AD_1. This may be due, for example, to the government expanding fiscal or monetary policy, or some other exogenous shock. The effects on the economy depend on whether this shock is anticipated or unanticipated. If the shock is *anticipated*, then agents will adjust their expectations at the same time as aggregate demand increases. In this situation the new rational expectation for the price level is P_2, as this is the only price level consistent with long-run equilibrium. As the aggregate demand curve shifts up so the short-run aggregate supply curve shifts up by the same amount. The price level rises to P_2 and all real variables remain at their natural rates. The economy jumps from point A to point C. Anticipated demand shocks have no effects on real variables in either the short or the long run. If, on the other hand, the demand shock is *unanticipated*, then agents' expectations will not immediately adjust. With price-level expectations remaining equal to P_0, the economy will move up the original short-run supply curve to point B and output expands to Y_1. Only as agents discover that aggregate demand has increased will they adjust their expectations, and real variables return to their natural rates. In the absence of persistence effects which hinder the adjustment of real variables, the economy will jump to point C when agents learn that aggregate demand has increased to AD_1. In contrast to anticipated shocks, unanticipated demand shocks cause real variables to be temporarily away from their natural rates.

This key New Classical result that only unanticipated demand shocks can influence real variables has been used to challenge the Keynesian proposition that the government can use systematic demand policy to stabilize the economy. The reason such a policy must be ineffective in these New Classical models is that if such a policy where adopted, agents would anticipate policy-induced changes in demand, and so incorporate them into their expectations of the price level. With rational expectations any systematic demand policy will be fully anticipated and so have no affect on real variables. This is known as the *policy neutrality result*. Government stabilization policy will only be effective, in these models, if agents make systematic forecasting errors. This result can be illustrated using the following infinitely repeated policy game between the government and the private sector.

Assume that national income at time-period t (Y_t) is determined by the following Lucas supply curve

$$Y_t = (1 - \lambda)\, Y^N + \lambda\, Y_{t-1} + \beta(M_t - M_t^e) + \varepsilon_t;\ 0 \le \lambda \le 1 \text{ and } \beta > 0, \qquad (6.1)$$

where Y^N is the natural rate of output, M_t the money supply at time period t, M_t^e is the expected level of the money supply at time period t, and ε_t is a random demand shock to output. The random demand shocks are assumed to be serially uncorrelated with mean zero. The expected value of these shocks in any one period is therefore assumed to be zero. (6.1) is consistent with the New Classical proposition that only *unanticipated* demand shocks will influence real variables. In particular this equation states that if the money supply is greater than expected there will be a positive effect on output. It is further assumed that due to persistence effects output only gradually adjusts back towards its natural rate. The speed of adjustment is determined by the size of λ. If $\lambda = 0$, there are no persistence effects and output returns immediately to its natural rate when expectations are correct. If $\lambda = 1$, there is no such adjustment, and so output equals its previous-period level when expectations are proved correct.

The strategic variables for the government and the private sector are the money supply and its expected value respectively. Specifically, at the beginning of each period, before ε_t is observed, the government sets the value of the money supply, over which it has complete control. At the same time the private sector formulates its expectation of the money supply, which determines the level of wages and prices within the economy for that period. All variables determined in previous periods are assumed to be observed by the government and private sector.

Concerning each player's pay-offs, they are assumed to have the following utility functions The government's utility is given by the equation $V_t^G = -(Y^N - Y_t)^2$. With this utility function the government seeks to minimize output's deviation from the natural rate. The private-sector's utility function, on the other hand, is equal to

New Classical Macroeconomics

$V_t^P = -(M_t^e - M_t)^2$. The private sector, therefore, seeks to minimize its forecast error concerning the level of the money supply.

Although the government has the incentive to try and stabilize output around its natural rate, this is only possible, in this game, if agents act irrationally and make systematic forecasting errors. To see why this is true we initially assume that agents adopt non-rational expectations. Suppose, for example, that agents adopt naïve expectations, whereby the money supply expected this period is assumed to equal the previous period's value, i.e. $M_t^e = M_{t-1}$. With these naïve expectations (6.1) can be rewritten as

$$Y_t = (1 - \lambda) Y^N + Y_{t-1} + \beta (M_t - M_{t-1}) + \varepsilon_t. \tag{6.2}$$

In order to maximize its utility the government will set the value of the money supply so that the expected value of output is equal to its natural rate. From (6.2) the expected value of output is equal to

$$E(Y_t) = (1 - \lambda) Y^N + Y_{t-1} + \beta (M_t - M_{t-1}). \tag{6.3}$$

Setting this equal to Y^N, and rearranging gives us the following optimal money supply rule

$$M_t = \frac{\lambda(Y^N - Y_{t-1})}{\beta} + M_{t-1}. \tag{6.4}$$

Provided λ is greater than zero, the government will increase the money supply when output is below its natural rate, and reduce the money supply when it is above this rate. This equation corresponds to a policy of active demand management, where the money supply is determined by an optimal feedback rule dependent on last period's level of output. Substituting this equation back into (6.1) gives us the path output follows when the government pursues this optimal monetary policy. With these assumptions output is equal to

$$Y_t = Y^N + \varepsilon_t. \tag{6.5}$$

Equation (6.5) demonstrates that with naïve expectations the government is able to fully stabilize output around its natural rate, except for the occurrence of within-period shocks to the economy. This equation justifies the Keynesian claim that the government can use active demand management to fine-tune the economy. The New Classical insight, however, is that this result depends on agents making systematic, and hence predictable, forecasting errors. If, for example, the government, following Keynesian policy advice, set its monetary policy according to (6.4), then the private sector's forecasting error will be equal to

$$M_t^e - M_t = -\frac{\lambda(Y^N - Y_{t-1})}{\beta} = -\frac{\lambda\varepsilon_{t-1}}{\beta}. \tag{6.6}$$

As agents are assumed to be able to observe last period's random demand shock, ε_{t-1}, the expected value of this forecast error is, in general, not equal to zero. The private sector knowingly makes systematic forecasting errors. Adopting naïve expectations implies that the private sector is acting irrationally, in that it does not maximize its utility. Rationality dictates that agents recognize that the government will seek to manipulate the money supply in order to stabilize output, and this will influence their expectations accordingly. The only way the private sector can avoid making systematic forecasting errors is if they adopt rational expectations. As the name suggests this is the only mechanism for formulating expectations that is consistent with rationality in this game. Although the adoption of rational expectations is the optimal strategy for the private sector, the implication is that systematic monetary policy can no longer effect real variables. This is the New Classical policy ineffectiveness result. If there were an optimal policy rule, then the private sector would base their expectations upon it and so expectations would be proved correct. In this situation the path of output would be given by the equation

$$Y_t = (1 - \lambda) Y^N + \lambda Y_{t-1} + \varepsilon_t. \tag{6.7}$$

Comparing (6.7) with (6.1) it is clear that monetary policy now has no effect on output, and so stabilization policy is ineffective. Based on this policy neutrality result New Classical economists have proposed that the government's monetary policy should not target real economic variables, such as output or unemployment, but rather nominal variables, such as the rate of inflation. Furthermore, in order for the money supply to be as predictable as possible they argue that the government should follow a simple fixed policy rule. These arguments can, therefore, be used to justify Milton Friedman's (1968) proposal that the money supply should be allowed to grow at a constant rate of growth, and that the government should forgo attempts to stabilize the economy. This policy conclusion is further analysed in Exercise 6.1.

EXERCISE 6.1

(1) Draw a one-period extensive form game for the stabilization policy game described in the text.

(2) New Classical economists have argued that this model supports the view that the government should abandon stabilization policy and maintain a constant growth rate for the money supply. Explain why this policy conclusion is not, in general, a Nash equilibrium for this game.

(3) Explain how the policy recommendation in (2) of this exercise can be a Nash equilibrium if the government is able to precommit its monetary policy before agents determine their expectation of the money supply. How does this possibility alter the extensive form game drawn in answer to (1)?

New Classical Macroeconomics

As discussed above the New Classical policy neutrality result is contrary to Keynesian predictions about the effects of aggregate demand policy. In Keynesian models systematic demand policy is able to influence real variables. Based on this effectiveness, it is often proposed that the government use demand policy to stabilize the economy around full employment. Early Keynesian models justified these claims by assuming that agents had non-rational expectations. It should be noted, however, that assuming that agents respond optimally to the government's demand policy does not on its own guarantee that such a policy has no effect on real variables. Here we discuss a number of ways in which demand policy can be effective, whilst still assuming that all agents act rationally.

Information advantage

One way for systematic demand policy to influence real variables is to allow the government to have an information advantage. One example of an information advantage is where the government is able to observe events within the economy more quickly than the private sector. In this situation, without government intervention, the economy will remain away from its long-run equilibrium until agents correctly discern the shock and adjust wages and prices accordingly. With such an information advantage the government may be able to offset these exogenous shocks more quickly than the private sector. This will hasten the economy's return to long run-equilibrium, and stabilization policy is once more effective. A typical New Classical response to this observation is to ask why the government does not simply make known its information advantage to the private sector. In this way the government avoids having to implement a counter-cyclical demand policy, and adjustment back to long-run equilibrium is left to market forces. Howitt (1981), however, argues that it may be too costly for the private sector to be given all the relevant information. In this situation it may be more efficient for the government to collect the relevant economic data and respond by implementing the appropriate demand policy to stabilize the economy. This will only be true, however, if the government is able to respond quickly and accurately to any new information. If there is uncertainty about events within the economy, and lags associated with implementing policy, it is possible that the government's demand policy may be destabilizing.

Imperfect wage and price adjustment

The policy neutrality result obtained in the stabilization game was demonstrated by assuming a Lucas supply curve. With this type of supply curve only unanticipated changes in aggregate demand can effect real variables. This type of supply curve will be valid, however, only if there is perfect wage and price adjustment, with continuous market clearing. With imperfect wage and price adjustment nominal demand shocks can once again have real effects, even if expectations are formed rationally. This possibility has been denominated by Gray (1976), Fischer (1977), and Phelps and Taylor (1977). In these models either wages or prices are set one period in advance of when they will apply. Once wages and prices have been fixed aggregate demand policy can again have temporary effects on real variables, and may be used to offset demand shocks hitting the economy. The New Classical response to these models has been to question why there is imperfect wage and price adjustment. In Classical models such imperfections imply that agents are not fully optimizing, and so they are viewed as being inconsistent with the assumption of rationality. New Keynesian macroeconomics has attempted to meet this criticism by developing models where imperfect wage and price adjustment is consistent with rationality. Some of these models are examined in the next chapter.

Learning

The game used to illustrate the policy neutrality result also made use of the so-called strong version of the Rational Expectations Hypothesis. This assumes that agents know and use the correct model of the economy when formulating their expectations. This, however, ignores the question of how agents acquire this knowledge. The weak version of the Rational Expectations Hypothesis states that agents need only optimally use all the information currently available to them in formulating their expectations. This weak version does not assume that the correct model of the economy is common knowledge. If individuals have imperfect information about either the structure of the economy, or some particular parameter value, then a learning process is required. Given the endogeneity of agents' expectations this learning process need not always converge upon the true model of the economy. Even if convergence is guaranteed, prior to agents identifying the true nature of the economy, systematic demand policy can be effective in influencing real variables. Once again the policy neutrality result ceases to be valid, even though all agents are acting rationally.

One particular type of uncertainty that has been incorporated into macroeconomic policy games is incomplete information about the government's pay-off function. In these models the private sector is not certain about which type of government is in power. Once again such uncertainty may result in anticipated demand policy influencing real variables. This insight forms the basis of the New Classical business cycle, and is examined in section 6.3.

Multiple Equilibria

A final possible reason why the policy neutrality result may cease to be valid, even if agents are acting rationally, is if there are multiple rational expectations equilibria. With multiple equilibria a variety of expectations can be self-fulfilling and so fully rational. It may be the case that for some of these equilibria systematic demand policy can affect real variables. This possibility has been developed by a number of New Keynesian economists, and is examined in the next chapter.

6.2 The Political Business Cycle

In the stabilization policy game presented in the previous section the government's objective was to stabilize the economy around its long-run equilibrium. It has long been recognized, however, that governments may primarily be interested in political, rather than economic, objectives. From this perspective policy-makers will use economic instruments to try and secure political objectives. One approach which considers the government's strategic use of economic policy in achieving political objectives was developed by Nordhaus (1975). In this model the government uses monetary policy to influence the state of the economy. This in turn determines the popularity of the government. The prediction of Nordhaus's model is that the government will stimulate the economy just prior to a general election. By doing so the government hopes it will grow in popularity and obtain a majority of the votes at the forthcoming election. Subsequent to the election, the government will reverse this policy, and contract aggregate demand. It is this sequence of expansionary and contractionary demand policy over the life-time of a government that generates a political business cycle. Here we critically examine this model from a game theory perspective. The fundamental criticism is that the model's predictions are once more dependent on voters having non-rational expectations. If voters seek to avoid making systematic forecasting errors and adopt rational expectations, the model no longer generates a political business cycle. In section 6.3 an adapted version of this model shows that by introducing rational expectations the model now generates New Classical policy conclusions. Specifically, if the government has discretion over its monetary policy its optimal long-run monetary policy is time-inconsistent, and the economy experiences inflationary bias.

Nordhaus's model can be represented by the following infinitely repeated game between the government and voters. The government's objective is simply to stay in power by winning a majority of the votes at the next election. The proportion of votes it obtains is, in turn, determined by the state of the economy, as given by the current rate of inflation, $\overset{\circ}{p}_t$, and current rate of unemployment, U_t. We will assume that the proportion of votes cast for the present government is determined by the following equation

$$V_t = c - d(\overset{\circ}{p}_t)^2 - e(U_t - U^*)^2; \quad c, d, e \geq 0. \tag{6.8}$$

This equation is depicted in Fig. 6.2 as a series of indifference curves.

Along each indifference curve the proportion of votes cast for the government is constant. In the diagram each indifference curve is indexed by the percentage of total votes the government would receive if a general election were held in the current period. The government's popularity is maximized when inflation is zero and unemployment is at its optimal level, U^*. This is called the bliss point and is labelled point BP in Fig. 6.2. The further away the economy is from this bliss point the less popular the government, and the fewer votes it would receive in an election. These indifference curves represent the government's preferences.

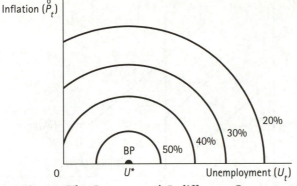

Fig. 6.2 The Government's Indifference Curves

Due to its control over money supply the government is assumed to be able to determine both the rate of inflation and the rate of unemployment, subject to the constraints imposed upon it. These constraints are given by the expectations-augmented Phillips curve and voters' current expectation of the inflation rate, $\overset{o}{p}_t^e$. The expectations-augmented Phillips curve is associated with Milton Friedman (1968) and is given by the following equation

$$\overset{o}{p}_t = a - bU_t + \overset{o}{p}_t^e; \quad a, b > 0. \tag{6.9}$$

This equation is consistent with the New Classical result that only unanticipated monetary policy will effect real variables. When expectations are correct the economy is in long-run equilibrium and unemployment is at its natural rate. Setting $\overset{o}{p}_t = \overset{o}{p}_t^e$ in equation (6.9) and rearranging we derive that the natural rate of unemployment, U^N, is equal to $a/b > 0$. Due to market imperfections it is assumed that this natural rate of unemployment is greater than the optimal rate of unemployment, i.e. $U^N > U^*$. If the government increases the money supply unexpectedly, inflation rises and unemployment falls. From (6.9) when inflation is greater than expected, unemployment is below the natural rate. Conversely, if the government unexpectedly reduces the money supply inflation falls and unemployment rises. Again from (6.9) when inflation is less than expected unemployment is above the natural rate. The expectations-augmented Phillips curve is depicted in Fig. 6.3.

The economy will be on the long-run Phillips curve (*LRPC*) when expectations are correct. When this occurs unemployment will be at its natural rate. The long-run Phillips curve is therefore vertical through this value. The short-run Phillips curves (*SRPC*) correspond to different values of inflationary expectations, and are downward-sloping for reasons explained above. The short-run curves cut the long-run curve when the expected rate of inflation equals the actual rate of inflation.

The second constraint upon the government is that of the voters' inflationary expectations. Nordhaus made the simplifying assumption that voters have naïve expectations so that the rate of inflation expected to prevail in the current period is equal to the rate of inflation in the previous period, i.e. $\overset{o}{p}_t^e = \overset{o}{p}_{t-1}$. Combining Figs. 6.2 and 6.3

New Classical Macroeconomics

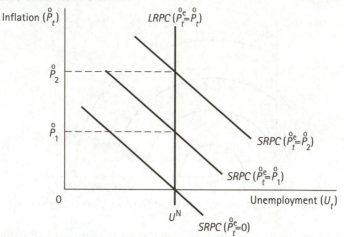

Fig. 6.3 The Expectations-Augmented Phillips Curve

together with this assumption of how voters formulate their expectations we are able to derive Nordhaus's political business cycle. This is shown in Fig. 6.4.

Assume that the economy is initially at point A and that the government is facing the run up to a general election. At point A the economy is in long-run equilibrium with zero inflation. From the indifference curve passing through this point we can see that currently 40 per cent of voters intend to vote for the government at the next election. If the government unexpectedly increases the money supply, however, it can increase its share of the vote. With expectations unchanged an increase in the money supply will cause the economy to move up the short-run Phillips curve passing through point A. The maximum share of votes the government can obtain given this short-run Phillips curve is 50 per cent. This occurs where the short-run Phillips curve is tangent to an

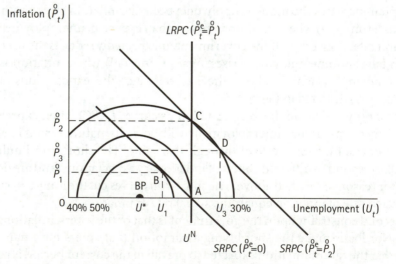

Fig. 6.4 The Political Business Cycle

indifference curve. The government, in order to increase its own popularity, will inflate the economy just prior to the election. The economy moves to point B with unemployment falling to U_1 and inflation rising to $\overset{\circ}{p}_1$. Point B, however, does not represent a long-run equilibrium as inflation is greater than expected. Subsequent to the election voters will observe the increase in inflation and so update their inflationary expectations. This adjustment causes the short-run Phillips curve to shift to the right. Inflation rises further and unemployment rises back towards its natural rate. This continues until the economy has returned to long-run equilibrium at point C. Unemployment is again equal to its natural rate and inflation equals $\overset{\circ}{p}_2$. With unemployment and inflation both higher the government is now less popular. At point C only 30 per cent of the electorate would vote for the present government. In order to increase its popularity, and secure victory at the next election, the government must reduce the rate of inflation. The government, therefore, reverses its previously expansionary monetary policy and reduces the money supply. Inflation falls and unemployment rises above the natural rate. The economy moves down the short-run Phillips curve to point D. Again this does not represent a long-run equilibrium, as inflation is now less than expected. As expectations are revised downwards so the short-run Phillips curve shifts to the left. Inflation falls further and unemployment returns to its natural rate. The economy returns to point A. The above process will be initiated once more as the next election approaches.

Over the lifetime of a single parliament we will observe the following sequence of events. The government initially pursues a contractionary monetary policy, which reduces inflation and causes unemployment to rise. The government then reverses this policy as a general election approaches, causing inflation to rise and unemployment to fall. These successive contractions and expansions of aggregate demand are the cause of the economy fluctuating around the natural rate. According to this model, therefore, it is the government manipulating economic policy for political objectives which causes the business cycle.

Although this model gives an interesting interpretation of the business cycle, and one that has a certain degree of intuitive appeal, from a game theory perspective it is critically flawed. The reason for this assessment is that it assumes that voters are far from rational. Prior to each election they are continually surprised that the government increases the money supply, even though the model predicts this outcome. Similarly, within the lifetime of each parliament the voters are continually surprised by the reduction in the money supply, even though, once more, the model predicts the government doing this. Voters' expectations are inconsistent with the predictions of the model itself. Furthermore, it is as if voters never learn from their previous experience. Instead of deriving voters' expectations from explicit maximization of their utility, which is consistent with rationality, this model merely assumes they have naïve expectations. As in the stabilization policy game this means that agents make systematic, and hence predictable, forecasting errors. If agents have an incentive to correctly forecast inflation, the assumption of naïve expectations implies irrational behaviour.

From a game theory perspective the assumption of naïve expectations cannot be part of a subgame perfect Nash equilibrium. In effect, Nordhaus assumes that voters accept the government's promise to maintain inflation at its current rate. This promise, however, is incredible. It is incredible because, if believed by the private sector, the government has an incentive to deviate from it. In order for the solution of the model to be subgame perfect voters must formulate their expectations in a way that predictable forecasting errors are avoided. This will occur if agents adopt rational expectations. This implies that with common knowledge of the correct model of the economy there is no political business cycle. This is demonstrated by the following argument. In equilibrium the government must have no incentive to change its monetary policy from the one expected by voters. If it had such an incentive, voters would perceive this and so modify their current inflationary expectations. This means the initial situation could not have been an equilibrium. In equilibrium, therefore, the government's monetary policy is completely anticipated and all real variables remain at their natural rates. Monetary policy now has no systematic effects on real variables, and there is no political business cycle. Nordhaus's model is unacceptable because it assumes voters do not act rationally, and the predictions of the model are not subgame perfect.

One way to reintroduce the possibility of a political business cycle is to assume agents have incomplete information. Economist's have recently developed this approach to generate New Classical political business cycle models. These models are discussed towards the end of the next section. Before that we discuss the important concept of time-inconsistency.

6.3 Time-Inconsistency

In New Classical macroeconomics the economy is defined as being in long-run equilibrium when expectations are correct. Only in the short run will agents' expectations remain incorrect. This distinction raises the possibility that a government's optimal *long-run* policy may differ from its optimal *short-run* policy. A government's optimal long-run policy is formulated under the constraint that agents' expectations are correct. In the short run, however, the government may have the incentive to produce an unanticipated policy shock. This will cause agents' expectations to be temporarily wrong. When the government has this incentive the optimal long run policy is said to be *time-inconsistent*. An optimal long-run policy is, therefore, time-inconsistent when the government has an incentive to deviate from it in the short run. If the private sector has complete information they will foresee this policy conflict. As a result they will rationally anticipate the government deviating from its optimal long-run policy. Only with a time-consistent policy does the government not have an incentive to deviate from it, and so expectations are justified. In an economy where agents' expectations are rational the equilibrium must involve the government pursuing a time-consistent policy. If the government's long-run optimal policy is time-inconsistent, this cannot be an equilibrium. This implies that in equilibrium the government is necessarily worse off. The government would receive a higher pay-off if it could persuade the private sector that it will maintain its optimal long-run policy. However, given the incentive to deviate, and with discretion over its own policy, this is not possible. The private sector would always anticipate deviation, and so the optimal long-run policy is no longer feasible. Once more we have an example of the prisoners' dilemma. Here the government is made worse off because it is unable to commit itself to its optimal long-run policy.

An alternative way of viewing time-inconsistency is to see it as a dynamic game played between the government and the private sector. Here the government tries to influence private-sector expectations. From this perspective Mankiw (1992) defines time-inconsistency as 'The tendency of policy-makers to announce policies in advance in order to influence the expectations of private decision-makers, and then to follow different policies after those expectations have been formed and acted on.' Using this definition we can illustrate the concept of time-inconsistency using the extensive form game shown in Fig. 6.5.

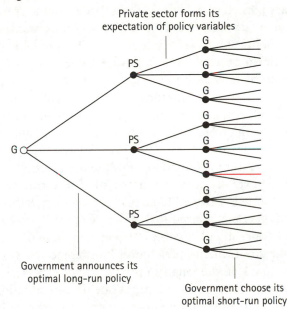

Fig. 6.5 Time-Inconsistency

In this game the government initially announces its optimal long-run policy in order to influence private-sector expectations. This optimal policy is formulated under the assumption that the private sector anticipates this policy and acts upon it. Having announced its policy intentions the private sector formulates its expectations. Clearly it has the choice of either believing the government's policy announcement, or not. Finally, having observed the private sectors' expectations, and consequent actions, the government enacts its optimal short-run policy to maximize its pay-off. This policy is determined on the basis of actual expectations held by the private sector. The long-run optimal policy is time-inconsistent if, were it to be believed, the government has an incentive to deviate from it. The long-run optimal policy is only time-consistent if it is the same as the short run optimal policy. If the private sector acts rationally, it will solve this dynamic game using the principle of backward induction. Using this principle it will anticipate the government's short-run optimal policy, and so recognize the government's incentive to renege on any preannounced policy that is time-inconsistent. With this reasoning the government has no influence over private-sector expectations, and so it may as well announce a policy that is time-consistent. The government no longer announces a policy it has an incentive to renege upon if believed. The time-consistent policy is, therefore, the policy associated with the subgame perfect Nash equilibrium for this dynamic game. Only credible threats and promises are made and believed. The promise to pursue a time-inconsistent policy is not credible and so not believed.

This concept of time-inconsistency has been used by New Classical economists to argue that discretionary monetary policy leads to a Pareto-inefficient outcome where the economy exhibits an *inflationary bias*. This result can be illustrated using a modified version of Nordhaus's political business-cycle model. This model is the same as the model presented in section 6.2 except for the following three changes. *First*, the government itself is assumed to be interested in economic, rather than political, outcomes. Specifically, equation (6.8) now represents the government's utility function. From this equation deviations of inflation and unemployment from their optimal rates reduce the government's level of utility. *Second*, the private sector are assumed to formulate their expectations according to the strong version of the Rational Expectations Hypothesis. Agents are, therefore, assumed to know the correct model of the economy and to rationally use all currently available information to formulate their expectations. *Third*, the policy game is assumed to be played only once rather than infinitely repeated. This assumption is later relaxed so that the effects of repeated monetary policy can be analysed. This one-off policy game is depicted in Fig. 6.6.

Fig. 6.6 illustrates the government's preferences indifference curves and the short- and long-run Phillips curves. In the long run private-sector expectations will be correct, and so unemployment must be at its natural rate. In this situation the long-run Phillips curve is the relevant constraint on government monetary policy. Facing this constraint the government maximizes its utility by setting the money supply consistent with zero inflation. The government's optimal long-run policy is, therefore, given by point A. In the short run, however, the private sector's expectation need not be correct. If the private sector believes that the government will pursue its long-run optimal monetary policy, it will anticipate zero inflation. The relevant constraint is now the short-run Phillips curve passing through point A. Given this constraint the government can increase its utility by unexpectedly inflating the economy. The government's utility is maximized when its indifference curve is tangent to this short-run Phillips curve. The government's optimal short-run monetary policy is to increase inflation to $\overset{o}{p}_1$ causing

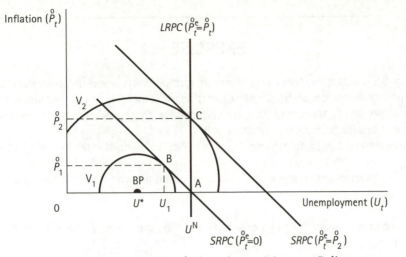

Fig. 6.6 Inflationary Bias of Discretionary Monetary Policy

unemployment to fall to U_1. This is given as point B in Fig. 6.6. Given this incentive to produce an inflationary surprise, it is clear that its optimal long-run monetary policy is time-inconsistent. As a result any statement that the government will pursue its long-run optimal monetary policy will not be believed by the private sector. Anticipating zero inflation cannot be a rational expectation. Instead the rational expectation for the private sector is to anticipate a policy that is consistent with the government maximizing its own pay-off function. In equilibrium the government will have no incentive to change its monetary policy, and expectations must be proved correct. This will occur when the government's indifference curve is tangent to the relevant short-run Phillips curve *and* on the long-run Phillips curve. This only occurs at point C. At this point the government has no incentive to change its monetary policy, and private-sector expectations are correct. This point corresponds to the Nash equilibrium of this one-off policy game. In equilibrium unemployment is at its natural rate and inflation is equal to $\overset{\circ}{p}_2$. Compared to the optimal long-run monetary policy at point A inflation is higher and there is no consequent reduction in unemployment. The economy is, therefore, said to experience an inflationary bias equal to $\overset{\circ}{p}_2$. This level of inflationary bias reduces the government's level of utility with no gain to the private sector. The final outcome is therefore Pareto inefficient.

From the previous analysis discretionary monetary policy is seen to lead to a Pareto-inefficient outcome and inflationary bias. A common New Classical policy conclusion from this result is that the government should renounce discretionary policy and pursue fixed policy rules instead. In this way it is hoped the government can commit itself to its optimal long-run policy and avoid the adverse consequences of time-inconsistency. This, however, is not the only way the government might seek to avoid the problems associated with time-inconsistency. This and other ways that have been proposed to avoid the problems associated with time-inconsistency are discussed below.

EXERCISE 6.2

In Fig. 6.5 it is assumed that the government formulates its monetary policy subsequent to the private sector formulating their expectations, and that this policy need not be the same as that previously announced. This exercise modifies these assumptions and examines the implications for government monetary policy.

How is the extensive form game depicted in Fig. 6.5 changed in the following situations?

(1) The government for some reason is unable to renege on its initial policy announcement.

(2) The private sector forms its expectations at the same time as the government enacts its policy.

Using Fig. 6.6 what will be the equilibrium level of inflation and unemployment in each of these alternative games?

EXERCISE 6.3

Using short-run and long-run Phillips curves identify the time-consistent monetary policy under each of the following assumptions:

(1) The government delegates its monetary policy to an independent central bank, which is required solely to target price stability.

(2) The natural rate of unemployment is the optimal rate of unemployment.

6.3.1 Precommitment

The first scenario in Exercise 6.2 corresponds to the situation where the government is able to effectively precommit itself to a particular monetary policy prior to the private sector formulating its expectations. If the government is able credibly to precommit itself to maintaining the economy at point A in Fig. 6.6, then agents will expect zero inflation and this would be the new long-run equilibrium. From this perspective the lack of precommitment is a basic cause of time-inconsistency. Various suggestions have been made as to how a government can precommit itself to an otherwise time-inconsistent optimal monetary policy.

Legislation

One extreme way for the government to precommit itself to a particular monetary policy is via legislation. Such legislation may be viewed as working in one of two ways. Either the government is explicitly prohibited from varying its monetary policy from previously published targets, or the process of such deviation is so time-consuming and expensive that it is not in the government's interest to pursue it. As a result of such legislation the government is no longer able to operate a discretionary monetary policy, and the problem of time-inconsistency is avoided.

One example of such legislation is for the government to delegate monetary policy to an independent central bank, which is instructed to maintain price stability. This possibility was considered in question (1) of Exercise 6.3. If the monetary authority is only concerned with achieving an inflation target, then it has no incentive to deviate from its optimal long-run policy of price stability. In this situation the optimal long-run monetary policy is time-consistent, and there is no inflationary bias.

Apart from the practical difficulties of implementing such legislation, and obtaining politicians consent to restrict their own powers, it is questionable whether such a severe restriction of the government's power is desirable. For example, if the monetary authority is constrained to follow a specific monetary policy rule, this will restrict its ability to enact desirable policy initiatives related to stabilization policy. Although the problem of inflationary bias may be overcome, this may be offset by other problems such as welfare-reducing fluctuations in unemployment.

Monetary targets

A second suggestion for how a government might be able to precommit itself to an otherwise time-inconsistent monetary policy is to announce monetary targets that the government intends to meet. Clearly, the announcement on its own does not make the targets credible. The idea instead is that having published the monetary targets it will be too embarrassing for the government to renege on them subsequently. From a game theory perspective the government receives a lower pay-off when it is observed to deviate from previously published monetary targets. In this way such announcements might become credible and so believed, and acted upon, by the private sector.

An example of the UK government using monetary targets in this way was in the early 1980s, when Mrs Thatcher's government published its Medium-Term Financial Strategy (MTFS). The MTFS set forth the government's targets for public spending and the growth rate of the money supply. It was hoped that these targets would be believed by the public, and hence the government's anti-inflation policy would not cause excessive unemployment. Unfortunately the economy entered a particularly severe recession with unemployment going above 3 million. From such evidence it would appear that politicians merely saying that they are going to undertake a particular policy does not make it more credible. One reason for this is that the government inevitably seeks to blame factors outside of its control as the cause of policy targets not being achieved. The government does this to try and reduce its own political embarrassment, but if agents perceive the government will do this then the initial credibility of policy targets is undermined.

Exchange rate targets

An extension to the idea of the government announcing monetary targets is that it announces an exchange rate target instead. Under a fixed exchange rate regime the government is unable to pursue an independent monetary policy. Instead interest rates are subordinated to the role of maintaining the target exchange rate. With no discretion over monetary policy it is argued that maintaining a fixed exchange rate policy overcomes the problems of time-inconsistency. However, the problem of credibility is merely switched from monetary targets to the exchange rate target. If the government had an incentive to deviate from monetary targets, it seems reasonable to suppose that it now has an incentive to allow the exchange rate to deviate from its preannounced target. If, however, reneging on an exchange rate target entails greater political embarrassment for the government, then such a policy may be more credible than the government announcing monetary targets.

This analysis can be related to the UK's recent experience within the European Exchange Rate Mechanism (ERM) in the early 1990s. Here the government attempted to maintain its exchange rate within a prespecified band with respect to other European currencies. It was hoped that maintaining a high exchange rate would again enhance the credibility of the government's anti-inflationary policy, and so reduce the costs associated with reducing inflation. Once more, however, the economy entered a severe recession. Despite successive government announcements that it was committed to maintaining the current exchange rate, and although the government spent billions of pounds trying to support sterling, it became increasingly less credible that the government could maintain such a high exchange rate. Eventually currency speculators, betting against the government maintaining its exchange rate target, forced the government to leave the ERM and allow sterling to depreciate. Again the government's policy was revealed to be time-inconsistent and so lacked credibility. It appears reasonable to conclude that precommitment, short of legislative changes, are unable to overcome the problems of time-inconsistency associated with monetary policy.

6.3.2 Supply-side policies

Part (2) of Exercise 6.3 illustrates that a government's optimal long-run monetary policy is only time-inconsistent if the optimal rate of unemployment differs from the natural rate of unemployment. If there is a divergence between these two rates, then there is an incentive for the government to renege on its commitment to price stability. The reason the natural rate is likely to be above the optimal rate of unemployment is due to labour market imperfections. These include the presence of proportional income tax and unemployment benefits that reduce the incentive to work.

One possible way of avoiding the problem of time-inconsistency in monetary policy is, therefore, to deal directly with these labour market imperfections. The benefit of doing so is not only reduced equilibrium unemployment, but also reduced inflationary bias. Even if such labour market imperfections cannot be totally eradicated, any reduction in the divergence between the optimal and natural rate of unemployment will reduce the extent of inflationary bias. Set against these benefits, however, are the possible costs associated with implementing these supply-side policies. The nature of these costs will typically be both economic and political.

6.3.3 Repeated monetary policy

So far we have only examined how the problems of time-inconsistency may be avoided in the context of a one-off game. In reality, of course, the government is involved in repeated interaction with the private sector. This changes the basic structure of the game being played. In particular, repeated interaction between the government and the private sector introduces the possibility that the private sector can credibly punish the government if it deviates from its optimal long-run policy of price stability. Given that this punishment is sufficiently severe the government is effectively deterred from temporarily inflating the economy. The government no longer has an incentive to produce unanticipated policy shocks, and so the problem of time-inconsistency is avoided. When this occurs the government's optimal long-run policy will be subgame perfect.

One model that demonstrates this result was developed by Barro and Gordon (1983). In this model the previous game is infinitely repeated, and the private sector is assumed to adopt a one-period punishment strategy. If the government maintains price stability, then the private sector continues to expect zero inflation. If, however, the government is observed to deviate from this policy, then, in the next period, the private sector will expect the rate of inflation associated with the time-consistent Nash equilibrium of the one-off game. If this expectation is fulfilled, then zero inflation is expected in the subsequent period, otherwise private sector expectations are unchanged. After the punishment period, therefore, bygones are bygones, and the government has the possibility of returning the economy to zero inflation at the natural rate of unemployment. Faced with the prospect of future punishment, it is not always in the government's interest to deviate from its long-run optimal policy. If this is true, then the problem of time-inconsistency is overcome. To demonstrate this result we need to compare the benefits of deviating with costs of future punishment.

If the government does not inflate the economy then it will receive utility equal to the social welfare function associated with point A in Fig. 6.6. Let this be equal to $V^G(A)$. The government will receive this in each and every time-period. Given that δ represents the appropriate rate of discount, then the present value for the government of not deviating (PV_{ND}) is equal to

$$PV_{ND} = V^G(A) + \delta V^G(A) + \delta^2 V^G(A) + \delta^3 V^G(A) + \ldots = \frac{V^G(A)}{1-\delta}.$$

In contrast if the government deviates from its long-run optimal policy it will receive, at most, $V^G(B)$ in the first period, followed by $V^G(C)$ in the second period. These are the levels of utility the government receives associated with points B and C respectively. If it was optimal for the government to deviate initially, then it will deviate at each subsequent opportunity. The present value of discounting is therefore equal to

$$PV_D = V^G(B) + \delta V^G(C) + \delta^2 V^G(B) + \delta^3 V^G(C) + \ldots = \frac{V^G(B) + \delta V^G(C)}{1-\delta^2}.$$

The problem of time-inconsistency will only be overcome if the government has no incentive to deviate from its long-run optimal policy. This will only occur if $PV_{ND} \geq PV_D$. This implies that

$$\frac{V^G(A)}{1-\delta} \geq \frac{V^G(B) + \delta V^G(C)}{1-\delta^2}$$

$$\therefore \quad \delta[V^G(A) - V^G(C)] \geq V^G(B) - V^G(A).$$

With the private sector adopting its one-period punishment strategy the government will maintain its optimal long-run policy provided that the discounted value of the next period's punishment, $\delta[V^G(A) - V^G(C)]$, is greater or equal to the current value of deviating, $V^G(B) - V^G(A)$. Whether this condition is satisfied can be related to three aspects of the government's preferences. *First*, this condition depends on the value of the government's discount factor, δ. The less the government discounts future utility the more likely its optimal long-run monetary policy will be time-consistent. With the government totally discounting future utility, i.e. $\delta = 0$, its current policy is unaffected by the threat of future punishment and so always deviates. This corresponds to the one-off policy game discussed previously. *Second*, the condition depends on the degree to which the government is concerned about inflation. Again this determines effectiveness of the punishment period. This is because the threatened punishment strategy is that inflation will be higher next period than it otherwise would have been. How effective this punishment is depends on how serious the government views higher inflation. This determines the value of $V^G(A) - V^G(C)$. If the government is relatively unconcerned with inflation, this threatened future punishment will not be effective in deterring deviation, and so the problem of time-inconsistency remains. If, for example, $V^G(A) - V^G(C) = 0$, then this means that the government is totally unconcerned about inflation and so, if it values higher employment at all, it will surely inflate the economy. *Third*, as just indicated, how highly the government values reductions in unemployment also determines whether the above condition is satisfied. This, together with the costs of increased inflation, determines the value of $V^G(B) - V^G(A)$. As discussed previously if the government is unconcerned with the level of unemployment then there is no time-inconsistency problem.

This result shows that provided the above condition is satisfied the problem of time-inconsistency is avoided. There are, however, two particular problems associated with this model. The first is the problem of *multiple equilibria*. This corresponds to the Folk Theorem of infinitely repeated games. The previous analysis has demonstrated that if the private sector adopts the assumed one-period punishment strategy, then the problem of time-inconsistency may be avoided. Given a positive discount factor, however, this is not the only credible punishment strategy that generates this result. For example, the private sector may either credibly threaten a longer period of punishment, or one where the punishment itself is more severe, or some combination of these. This aspect of multiple Nash equilibrium was discussed more fully in Chapter 4 in the context of oligopolies maintaining tacit collusion. In this context, however, indeterminacy due to multiple equilibria can be seen as greater criticism of the model. This is partly due to the increased difficulty of potentially millions of individuals co-ordinating their actions on one particular punishment strategy. There is also the problem of applying punishment strategies to the private sector which is that it is made up of numerous atomistic individuals. In this situation no one individual can influence the outcome of the game, and so there is little sense in talking about individual's choosing their optimal punishment strategy.

The second problem associated with the Barro and Gordon model is the assumption that the game is infinitely repeated. This seems to be especially unrealistic as the life of any one parliament is necessarily finite. If the policy game is not infinitely repeated, then the solution to the problem of time-inconsistency breaks down due to the paradox of *backward induction*. To see this suppose the game is played only a finite number of times. Using backward induction we start with the last period first. In this period there can be no future punishment, and so the government will certainly deviate from its optimal long-run policy by inflating the economy. The private sector will anticipate this and so the only possible solution in the last period is the Nash equilibrium of the stage game. Now consider the period before last. As the government knows that in the last period the Nash equilibrium will be played, there is again no effective punishment against deviation. The Nash equilibrium will be played in the last period whatever the government does in this penultimate period and so it might as well deviate now. Again, the private sector anticipates this and so the only outcome possible in this period is the Nash equilibrium. This logic can be applied to all succeeding periods until we reach the beginning of the game. The conclusion of backward induction is that the government will deviate in the first period, the private sector will anticipate this, and the economy will experience inflationary bias in every time-period.

As with previous applications this problem of backward induction can be avoided if we introduce uncertainty about when the game will actually end. This involves reinterpreting the rate of discount as follows

$$\delta = \frac{1 - Prob}{1 + r},$$

where *Prob* is the probability that the game ends in any one period, and *r* is the rate of time preference. With this type of uncertainty introduced into the model there is no definite last period from which to begin the logic of backward induction, and so once more Barro and Gordon's punishment strategy may be sufficient to avoid the time-inconsistency problem.

6.3.4 Incomplete information and reputation

As discussed in Chapter 3 one way in which the paradox of backward induction may be overcome is by allowing players in the game to have incomplete information. New Classical economists have used this assumption to show how the problem of time-inconsistency can, at least partially, be avoided. These models also provided a New Classical explanation of the political business cycle. A common method of incorporating incomplete information into a repeated policy game between the government and the private sector is to assume that the private sector does not know for certain which type of government is in power. Specifically, the private sector is unsure of the government's preferences as given by its utility function. This assumption has been adopted by Backus and Driffel (1985), and Barro (1986). Here we will examine one relatively simple example to illustrate the type of results that have been derived.

Suppose there are only two possible types of government. A '*strong government*' is only concerned with inflation, and so its indifference curves are horizontal straight lines. A '*weak government*' is concerned with both inflation and unemployment, and has indifference curves as shown in Fig. 6.2. Each type of government is assumed to maximize its own utility, while the private sector seeks to correctly anticipate future monetary policy, and hence the rate of inflation. This policy game is assumed to be played a finite number of periods. If there was *complete information* then from the principle of backward induction we would observe one of two possible outcomes in every period. These outcomes are illustrated in Fig. 6.7.

If a strong government is in power, then it never has an incentive to deviate from its optimal long-run monetary policy. In this situation we would always observe zero inflation and unemployment at its natural rate. This is shown as point S in Fig. 6.7. If, however, the government is weak, then it does have an incentive to deviate from its optimal long-run monetary policy. With complete information the private sector will anticipate this and the only possible equilibrium is the time-consistent monetary policy associated with inflationary bias. This is shown as point W in Fig. 6.7. This outcome will again be observed in every time-period.

With these two types of government only the weak government faces the problem of time-inconsistency. This implies that a weak government has the incentive to appear strong, and avoid inflationary bias. This type of deception will be possible, however,

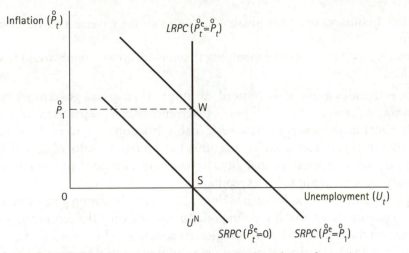

Fig. 6.7 Weak and Strong Government with Complete Information

only if there is incomplete information. With *incomplete information* the weak govern-ment may be able to develop a reputation for being strong by acting *as if* it were strong. This corresponds to a weak government renouncing the opportunity of inflating the economy and maintaining zero inflation. It forgoes the opportunity of increasing its utility in the short run so as to foster a reputation for being strong. In this context the term 'reputation' has the specific definition of the probability assessment of the private sector that the government is strong. In order to try and make accurate predictions of future monetary policy the private sector will try and discern which type of govern-ment is in power. It will do this by observing the government's policy actions. The equi-librium concept often used to solve dynamic games with incomplete information is that of sequential equilibrium associated with Kreps and Wilson (1982*b*). As discussed in Chapter 3 this equilibrium concept has two characteristics. *First*, the government's strategy is subgame perfect, i.e. no incredible threats or promises are made or believed. *Second*, the private sector update their beliefs in accordance with Bayes' Theorem. Specifically, adapting the equation derived in Appendix 3.1 the government's reputa-tion for being strong is determined by the following equation,

$$Prob(S \mid \overset{o}{P}_{t-1} = 0) = \frac{Prob(\overset{o}{P}_{t-1} = 0 \mid S) \cdot Prob(S)}{Prob(\overset{o}{P}_{t-1} = 0 \mid S) \cdot Prob(S) + Prob(\overset{o}{P}_{t-1} = 0 \mid W) \cdot Prob(W)},$$

where S corresponds to the government being strong, and W to it being weak. The prob-abilities in the equation, therefore, have the following interpretation:

Prob (S | $\overset{o}{P}_{t-1}$ = 0) = the probability that the government is strong, given that there has been no inflationary shock in the past.

Prob(S) = the prior probability that the government is strong.

Prob(W) = the prior probability that the government is weak.

Prob ($\overset{o}{P}_{t-1}$ = 0S) = the probability that a strong government would have set zero inflation. In our example this equals 1 because a strong government never inflates the economy.

Prob $(\overset{\circ}{p}_{t-1} = 0 \mid W)$ = the probability that a weak government would have set zero inflation.

One extreme example of this type of learning is when a weak government inflates the economy. As there are only two types of government, then the private sector will immediately infer that the government is weak. In this situation the government literally loses all credibility that it is strong. If on the other hand inflation is not observed, the private sector may well increase its probability assessment that the government is strong. In this case the government improves its reputation.

Typical results for a model such as this are as follows. A strong government will continue to pursue its optimal long-run policy of not inflating the economy. A weak government on the other hand will condition its action on which period of the game it is currently in. In early periods it never inflates, hoping to build a reputation for itself later in the game. In subsequent periods it will inflate with a positive probability, though less than one. In the final stages of the game it will definitely inflate so as to reduce unemployment below the natural rate. This description of a weak government's optimal strategy is illustrated in Fig. 6.8.

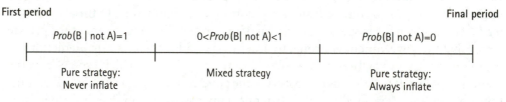

Fig. 6.8 Equilibrium Strategy for a Weak Government

During the first phase of this game neither a strong nor weak government inflates the economy, and so the government's reputation remains unchanged. This phase of the game is characterized as a pooling equilibrium. Here each type of government pursues the same optimal policy. In this situation the private sector receives no useful information to help it discern which type of government is in power. In the mixed-strategy phase the government's reputation for being strong will increase provided there is no inflationary demand shock. As the end of the game is approached the incentive for a weak government to inflate increases. At the end of this phase a weak government will certainly inflate the economy in order to reduce unemployment. If such a shock is observed, then the private sector knows for certain that the government is weak. Alternatively, if by the time the final phase is reached no inflationary shock has been observed, the private sector knows the government is strong. This final phase of the game is characterized as a separating equilibrium. Here the different types of government reveal their identity by pursuing diverse optimal strategies.

To complete the description of this game we can illustrate the effects of these equilibrium strategies for inflation and unemployment. This is shown in Fig. 6.9 using the expectation-augmented Phillips curve. Initially the private sector correctly forecasts that neither a weak nor a strong government will inflate the economy. Actual and expected inflation are, therefore, both equal to zero and unemployment is at its natural rate. In the pooling equilibrium phase of this game the economy remains at point S and the problem of time-inconsistency is avoided. In the mixed-strategy phase of the game there is a positive probability that the government will inflate the economy. The private sector's expected level of inflation will therefore be positive and the short-run Phillips curve shifts up. If there is no inflation, this causes unemployment to rise. In Fig. 6.9 we move to a position such as point A. With no inflationary shock the government's reputation for being strong increases. What happens next depends on which type of government is in power. If the government is weak, it will eventually inflate the economy. This is represented by the economy jumping from point A to point B where the government maximizes its utility subject to the appropriate short-run Phillips curve. Once the private sector discerns this demand shock they will know that the government is weak. The private sector now has complete information and the economy jumps to, and remains at, the time-consistent outcome for a weak government. This is point W. If the government is strong it will not induce a positive demand shock. When the separating equilibrium phase is reached the private sector will know that the government is strong. Once more the private sector has complete information and the economy returns to point S.

From this illustration it can be seen that the problem of time-inconsistency is initially avoided. Eventually, however, the economy experiences a temporary rise in unemployment above the natural rate. The path of inflation depends on which type of government is in power. For a weak government this predicted sequence of events is

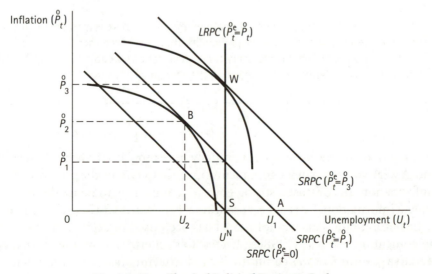

Fig. 6.9 New Classical Political Business Cycle

EXERCISE 6.4*

In the text we argued that a weak government can exploit the private sector's uncertainty about the government's preferences to partially avoid the inflationary bias associated with time-inconsistent monetary policy. In this exercise we provided a simple model that illustrates this result.

Assume that the government, via its monetary policy, can perfectly control inflation. Furthermore the government can be one of two types. Either it is strong or it is weak. A strong government is only concerned about the rate of inflation, and so never inflates the economy. A weak government, however, is concerned about both inflation and unemployment. Specifically, its welfare in time-period t is given by the following equation:

$$V_t^G = c - d(\mathring{p}_t)^2 - eU_t,$$

where $\mathring{p}_t$ and U_t are the rates of inflation and unemployment in time-period t respectively, and c, d, and e are all positive parameters. It is assumed the government does not discount future welfare, and so a weak government attempts to maximize the sum of its per-period welfare over all current and future periods. The constraint facing the government is given by the expectations-augmented Phillips curve. This is written as

$$\mathring{p}_t = a - bU_t + \mathring{p}_t^e,$$

where $\mathring{p}_t^e$ is the expected rate of inflation in period t determined at the beginning of that period, and again a and b are positive parameters. The private sector formulates its expectations rationally in accordance with Bayes' Theorem. Finally, it is assumed that this policy game lasts for only two periods.

(1) Determine the subgame perfect path of inflation if it is common knowledge the government is weak.

(2) Determine the sequential equilibrium path of inflation if there is incomplete information and the private sector's prior probability that the government is strong is 0.2. (Hint: initially determine the necessary condition for the weak government to be indifferent between inflating and not inflating the economy.)

strictly preferred to the government initially revealing itself through stimulating demand. A weak government is consequently made better off by the presence of incomplete information. In contrast a strong government is likely to be made worse off by incomplete information. This is because it now experiences a rise in unemployment above the natural rate. This type of model has been used to explain the sharp rise in unemployment in the early 1980s. Under this interpretation the newly elected Conservative government was committed to reducing inflation, even though it had yet to gain this anti-inflationary reputation. As a consequence expected inflation was higher than actual inflation, and unemployment rose above its natural rate. Only over time did the government's reputation improve, causing the private sectors' inflationary expectations and unemployment to fall. Even though agents formulate their expectations rationally, and wages and price are market-clearing we are still able to observe a political business cycle as the government attempts to develop a reputation for being anti-inflationary.

6.4 Conclusions

New Classical macroeconomics make two fundamental assumptions. These are that all agents formulate their expectations rationally, and that all markets are perfectly competitive. In early New Classical models it was assumed that the correct model of the economy is common knowledge. This is the strong version of the Rational Expectations Hypothesis. These models were used to challenge previous Keynesian results on the effectiveness of government demand policy. Two examples have been analysed in this chapter. The first refuted the effectiveness of government stabilization policy. The second denied the possibility of a political business cycle. In both instances Keynesian results were shown to depend on agents making systematic forecasting errors. This was argued to be inconsistent with full rationality, and that such results were not subgame perfect. As such they depended on the private sector believing and acting upon incredible policy statements by the government. To say the least, such an assumption is not a good foundation on which to base policy recommendations.

In the third section of this chapter we introduced the important concept of time-consistency. Using a one-off policy game it was demonstrated that if the government's optimal long-run monetary policy is time-inconsistent the economy will suffer from inflationary bias. In this situation the subgame perfect equilibrium will be Pareto inefficient. Various ways have been suggested how this inefficient outcome might be avoided. Here we discussed the role of precommitment, supply-side policies, and repeated monetary policy. In this final context we also considered recent New Classical models based on incomplete information. In these models it is no longer assumed that the correct model of the economy is common knowledge. Instead agents try to discern the correct model over time. This is the weak version of the Rational Expectations Hypothesis. These models tend to contradict earlier New Classical results. In particular with incomplete information systematic demand policy may well be able to influence real variables, and once more there may be the possibility of a political business cycle. Having initially refuted many Keynesian beliefs, recent New Classical models can be viewed as qualifying such results and rigorously identifying the underlying assumption upon which they depend. These advances have been made possible due to the incorporation of game-theoretic concepts in to mainstream macroeconomics. This process continues and it is hoped it will provided further insights in the future.

6.5 Solutions to Exercises

Exercise 6.1

(1) One possible extensive form representation for the one-period policy game between the government (G) and the private sector (PS) is shown in Fig. 6.10. Critically the government and private sector set their strategic variables simultaneously. This means that each of these two players' decision nodes are in the same information set. In order to incorporate random demand shocks to the economy, we introduce a third player called Nature (N). In this extensive form game each player is restricted to three possible actions. The pay-offs are given by the utility functions for the government and private sector, V_t^G and V_t^P respectively.

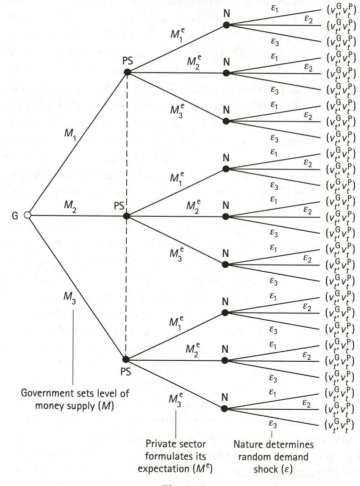

Government sets level of
money supply (*M*)

Private sector
formulates its
expectation (M^e)

Nature determines
random demand
shock (ε)

Fig. 6.10

(2) The policy of maintaining a constant growth rate of the money supply by the government is only a Nash equilibrium within this game if there are no random demand shocks to output. With no such shocks, and a fully anticipated monetary policy, output will remain at its natural rate. In this situation any systematic monetary policy will be a Nash equilibrium. If, however, demand shocks cause output to deviate from natural rate, then the government has an incentive to try and set the money supply above or below what is expected by the private sector. In this situation the government has an incentive to depart from any systematic monetary policy in order to try and stabilize the economy and increase its own utility. If there are no limits placed upon the value of the money supply, there is no systematic monetary policy that corresponds to a Nash equilibrium.

(3) One way of overcoming this unsatisfactory result that there is no Nash equilibrium for this infinite game with demand shocks is to allow the government to precommit its monetary policy. Now the private sector is able to observe the government's monetary policy before it formulates its expectations. In terms of the extensive form game depicted in Fig. 6.10, the private sector's decision nodes are no longer in the same information set, and so the dashed line disappears. As expectations are now always correct, the government is unable to effect the path of output. The government no longer has any influence over its own level of utility, and so any level of the money supply will be a Nash equilibrium. To justify the specific New Classical policy recommendation other considerations, such as the welfare costs of higher inflation, must be taken in to account.

Exercise 6.2

(1) With the government unable to renege upon its initial policy announcement, it acts as a Stackelberg leader. In this situation the policy announcement is identical to actual policy. The government no longer has two separate decisions to make concerning its policy announcement and actual policy. These two decisions reduce to the same thing. With the government moving first it only faces one decision node. The extensive form for this game is shown in Fig. 6.11. With the government committed to carrying out its preannounced policy, it will pursue its optimal long-run monetary policy. This is given as point A in Fig. 6.6. Inflation will be zero and unemployment at its natural rate. Once expectations are fixed the government would like to inflate the economy to increase its own utility, but is unable to do so.

(2) Given that the private sector formulates its expectation of monetary policy at the same time as the government enacts its policy, means that the government sets its monetary policy before observing expectations. The government, therefore, does not know for certain which decision node it is at following the private sectors' decision about expected inflation. The resulting extensive form game is shown in Fig. 6.12. Although the government is unable to observe the private sector's expectation, it can calculate what the rational expectation is. Assuming common knowledge of rationality implies that the solution must be a Nash equilibrium. As discussed in the text the only Nash equilibrium in this game is at point C in Fig. 6.6. Only at this point does neither player have an incentive to deviate. This equilibrium entails inflationary bias equal to $\overset{\circ}{p}_2$, and unemployment at its natural rate.

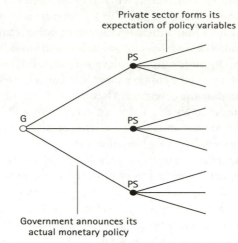

Private sector forms its
expectation of policy variables

Government announces its
actual monetary policy

Fig. 6.11

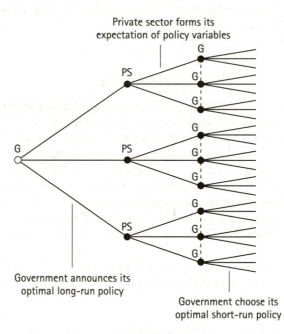

Private sector forms its
expectation of policy variables

Government announces its
optimal long-run policy

Government choose its
optimal short-run policy

Fig. 6.12

Exercise 6.3

(1) With the central bank only concerned with the rate of inflation, its indifference curves are represented as horizontal straight lines. This is illustrated in Fig. 6.13. In this situation the optimal long-run policy of maintaining price stability is time-consistent, and there is no inflationary bias. The monetary authority now has no incentive to induce the economy away from point A as this would reduce its welfare.

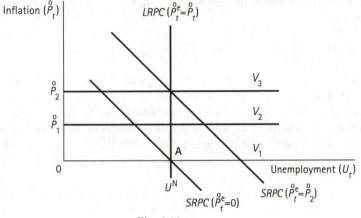

Fig. 6.13

(2) If the natural rate of unemployment is equal to the optimal rate of unemployment then the bliss point is on the long-run Phillips curve with zero inflation. This is given as point A in Fig. 6.14. The further away the economy is from this point the lower is the government's wel-

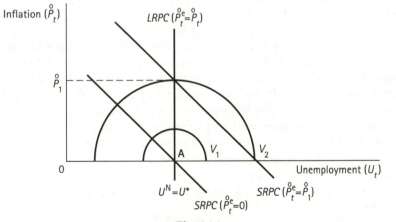

Fig. 6.14

fare. With the economy initially at point A, there is no incentive for the government to alter its monetary policy. If it were to do so, both inflation and unemployment would deviate from their optimal rates and the government's utility would be reduced. Once more the government's long-run optimal monetary policy is time-consistent and there is no inflationary bias.

Exercise 6.4

(1) To determine the subgame perfect path of inflation we start in the final period first and work backwards. In the second period a weak government sets monetary policy to maximize welfare in that period. From the model this equals

$$V_2^G = c - d(\overset{\circ}{p}_2)^2 - eU_2.$$

Rearranging the expectations-augmented Phillips curve and substituting for U_2, this can be rewritten as

$$V_2^G = c - d(\overset{\circ}{p}_2)^2 - \frac{e}{b}(a + \overset{\circ e}{p}_2 - \overset{\circ}{p}_2).$$

The government maximizes this function for a given value of $\overset{\circ e}{p}_2$. Setting the differential of this equation with respect to $\overset{\circ}{p}_2$ to zero and rearranging gives us the optimal inflation rate for period 2. This is equal to $e/2bd$. This corresponds to the unique Nash equilibrium in this period, and represents the level of inflationary bias due to time-inconsistency. Let this equilibrium value equal $\overset{\circ}{p}^*$. From the principle of backward induction we know that this unique Nash equilibrium must also be the outcome in the first period. In equilibrium, therefore, inflation is equal to $\overset{\circ}{p}^*$ in both periods.

(2) To determine the sequential equilibrium of this incomplete information game we again initially solve for the final period first and work backwards. In the final period the weak government will maximize welfare in that period by taking the private sector's inflationary expectations as given. This is identical to the problem solved in (1), and so in this period the government sets inflation equal to $\overset{\circ}{p}^* = e/2bd$. Solving for the first period is more complex. Now the government may have the incentive to try and deceive the private sector into thinking it is strong. The only way to do this is by playing a mixed strategy, with positive probabilities over zero and positive inflation. If, in this mixed strategy phase, the government adopts zero inflation, then its reputation for being strong increases. If, however, it induces positive inflation, the private sector will know it is weak. In this situation welfare in the second period is fully determined and so the government will seek to maximize welfare in the first period, again taking inflationary expectations as given. Therefore, if the government inflates the economy in the first period it will set it equal to $\overset{\circ}{p}^*$. The only possible equilibrium outcomes are either inflation equal to zero or $\overset{\circ}{p}^*$ in the first period, followed by $\overset{\circ}{p}^*$ in the second period. A necessary condition for this to be a sequential equilibrium is that the government is indifferent between the alternative pure strategies adopted in the mixed-strategy phase. To determine this condition we set the welfare levels associated with each pure strategy equal to each other.

If the government sets inflation to zero in the first period then its aggregate level of welfare is equal to

$$c - \frac{e}{b}(a + \overset{\circ e}{p}_1) + c - d(\overset{\circ}{p}^*)^2 - \frac{e}{b} - (a + \overset{\circ e}{p}_2 - \overset{\circ}{p}^*)$$

Alternatively, if the government sets inflation in both periods equal to $\overset{\circ}{p}^*$ then aggregate welfare equals

$$c - d(\overset{\circ}{p}^*)^2 - \frac{e}{b}(a + \overset{\circ e}{p}_1 - \overset{\circ}{p}^*) + c - d(\overset{\circ}{p}^*)^2 - \frac{ae}{b}.$$

It can be confirmed that these two expressions are only equal to each other if $\beta_2^e = \beta^*/2$. Finally, using this result we can solve for the probability distribution over pure strategies in the first period. This is done in the following way. We know that the expected rate of inflation in the second period equals the probability that the government is weak multiplied by β^*, i.e. $\beta_2^e = Prob$ (W | $\beta_1 = 0$). β^*. In equilibrium this must equal $\beta^*/2$. Using Bayes' Theorem this condition can be written as

$$\frac{Prob(\overset{o}{\beta}_1 = 0 \mid W).Prob(W)}{Prob(\overset{o}{\beta}_1 = 0 \mid W).Prob(W) + Prob(\overset{o}{\beta}_1 = 0 \mid S).Prob(S)} \cdot \overset{o}{\beta}^* = \frac{\overset{o}{\beta}^*}{2}$$

$$\therefore \frac{Prob(\overset{o}{\beta}_1 = 0 \mid W).0.8}{Prob(\overset{o}{\beta}_1 = 0 \mid W).0.8 + 0.2} = \frac{1}{2}.$$

From this condition we derive that in equilibrium $Prob$ ($\beta_1 = 0 \mid$ W) = 0.25. The unique sequential equilibrium is that the weak government plays a mixed strategy in the first period, with the probability of zero inflation equal to 0.25, and the probability of inflation set at β^* equal to 0.75. In the second period it adopts the pure strategy of setting inflation equal to β^*.

Further Reading

Blackburn, K. (1992), 'Credibility and Time Consistency in Monetary Policy', in K. Dowd and M. K. Lewis (eds.), *Current Issues in Financial and Monetary Economics*, London: Macmillan.

Hargreaves Heap, S. P. (1992), *The New Keynesian Macroeconomics: Time, Belief and Social Interdependence*, Aldershot: Edward Elgar.

Hoover, K. D. (1988), *The New Classical Macroeconomics*, Oxford: Blackwell.

Leslie, D. (1993), *Advanced Macroeconomics*, London: McGraw-Hill.

Levine. P. (1990), 'Monetary Policy and Credibility', in T. Bandyopadhyay and S. Clutah (eds.), *Current Issues in Monetary Economics*, London: Macmillan.

Peel, D. (1989), 'New Classical Macroeconomics', in D. Greenaway (ed.) *Current Issues in Macroeconomics*, London: Macmillan.

Phelps, E. S. (1992), 'Expectations in Macroeconomics and the Rational Expectations Debate', in A. Vercelli and N. Dimitri (eds.), *Macroeconomics: A Survey of Research Strategies*, Oxford: Oxford University Press.

Romer, D. (1996), *Advanced Macroeconomics*, New York: McGraw-Hill.

Schaling, E. (1995), *Institutions and Monetary Policy*, Aldershot: Edward Elgar.

Snowdon, B., H. Vane, and P. Wynarczyk (1994), *A Modern Guide to Macroeconomics: An Introduction to Competing Schools of Thought*, Aldershot: Edward Elgar.

7

New Keynesian Macroeconomics

IN his *General Theory of Employment, Interest and Money* (1936) Keynes set out to show that an economy could become stuck in an unemployment equilibrium due to insufficient aggregate demand. In such an equilibrium market forces on their own will not return the economy to full employment, and so government intervention, in the form of active demand management, is advocated. Following Hicks's (1937) interpretation of the *General Theory*, Keynesian results were initially derived under the assumption that wages and prices adjust slowly to clear markets. This allowed demand shocks to an economy to have real effects, and supports the need for government stabilization policy. In the 1970s this fundamental assumption of imperfect wage and price adjustment became increasingly criticized as being essentially *ad hoc*, and inconsistent with the rational maximizing behaviour of individuals. Furthermore, as discussed in the previous chapter, the way agents were assumed to formulate their expectations was also considered to be inconsistent with full rationality. So effective were these criticisms that New Classical economists, such as Lucas (1980), could even write about the death of Keynesian economics. Recently, however, Keynesian economics has experienced a significant revival, primarily due to the work of New Keynesian economists. The aim of New Keynesian Macroeconomics is to derive Keynesian results within models where agents fully optimize. Often New Keynesian models have sought to explain why agents might rationally avoid changing wages or prices, even though markets do not clear. In other New Keynesian models involuntary unemployment is possible even if wages and prices are completely flexible. A common feature on these New Keynesian models is that private-sector agents are interdependent of each other. This contrasts with New Classical models, where due to perfect competition, private-sector agents are assumed to be independent of one another. In this chapter we examine a number of New Keynesian models and give them a game theory interpretation.

In section 7.1 we examine efficiency wage models. In these models workers are more productive the higher the real wage rate. This provides firms with the incentive to increase the wage they pay their employees. With all firms seeking to pay a higher real wage there can be persistent involuntary unemployment. Efficiency wage models are therefore one reason why real wages may not fully adjust to their market-clearing level. These models support the Keynesian result that due to real wage rigidity an economy can experience an unemployment equilibrium. Section 7.2 goes on to critically discuss New Keynesian models where agents fail to adjust nominal wages and prices in response to demand shocks. Due to these nominal rigidities, demand shocks will cause real variables to deviate from their natural rates. These fluctuations can be used to justify the Keynesian proposition that government demand management is needed to stabilize the economy, and promote social welfare. In section 7.3 we analyse New Keynesian models which exhibit multiple equilibria, and specifically examine the issue of co-ordination failure. This occurs when agents within an economy co-ordinate upon a Pareto-dominated equilibrium. Once again the selected equilibrium may be characterized by involuntary unemployment, providing further justification for stabilization policy. We argue that co-ordination failure can occur even when wages and prices are completely flexible and agents have rational expectations.

7.1 Efficiency Wage Models

Involuntary unemployment occurs when there are workers prepared to work at the going wage rate but firms are unwilling to employ them. This situation is illustrated in Fig. 7.1.

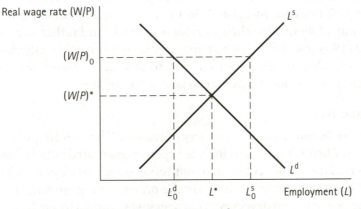

Fig. 7.1 Involuntary Unemployment

In this diagram the market-clearing real wage rate is $(W/P)^*$. With this real wage rate the demand for labour, L^d, equals the supply of labour, L^s, and the level of employment is L^*. Everyone who wants to work at the market-clearing real wage rate is able to find a firm willing to employ them. Anyone unemployed at this real wage rate must be voluntarily unemployed. If, however, the real wage rate is set above the market-clearing level, say at $(W/P)_0$, then there is excess supply of labour. With this real wage rate workers are willing to supply L_0^S amount of labour, but firms are only willing to employ L_0^d. Jobs will be rationed and involuntary unemployment is equal to the amount $L_0^S - L_0^d$. Involuntary unemployment will persist if real wage rigidity prevents the wage rate falling to its market-clearing level.

Two reasons often suggested why the real wage rate may fail to clear the labour market are the actions of unions, seeking to maintain their members' standard of living, and the government, via minimum wage legislation. Efficiency wage models identify another possible reason for why real wages may fail to fall in response to excess supply. In these models it is firms themselves who resist cuts in real wages. The reason for this is that a cut in the real wage rate reduces the efficiency of the workforce, leading to a reduction in profits. In these circumstances it can be rational for firms to pay an efficiency wage rate above the market-clearing real wage in order to maximize profits. The critical assumption behind all efficiency wage models is that worker productivity is positively related to the real wage rate. A number of reasons have been suggested for why this might be true.

Shirking

Many workers have some discretion over the level of effort they put into their job. Furthermore, their performance cannot always be directly observed by their employer. This might be because constant monitoring is too expensive or because productivity depends on the contribution of all the members in a team. In such circumstances it is not possible for employers to relate the wage paid to each worker to their individual productivity. If, however, increased effort reduces workers' utility, firms will need to find some way of motivating their workforce to work hard rather than shirk. Shapiro and Stiglitz (1984) show that firms paying an efficiency wage above the market-clearing wage rate can induce workers not to shirk, and this can increase firms' profits. A simplified version of this model is examined later in this section.

Labour turnover

Workers move between jobs for a variety of reasons. The resulting labour turnover is often costly for firms. These costs include expenses associated with hiring and training new workers. Firms will seek to economize on such costs by reducing the rate of turnover. One way to do this is to make the present job more attractive by paying a higher wage. Salop (1979) develops an efficiency wage model where firms increase their wage rate with the aim of economizing on labour turnover costs.

Adverse selection

Another reason why firms might have an incentive to pay an efficiency wage is to attract and maintain a high-quality workforce. Weiss (1980) presents a model where firms paying a high wage attract both more and a better quality of job applicants. Firms paying a low wage will experience adverse selection, where only poor-quality workers apply for vacancies. To economize on the costs associated with employing poor-quality workers, such as increased training costs or costs associated with firing unsuitable workers, a firm can increase its profits by paying a wage above the market-clearing level.

Sociological factors

A final reason why worker productivity might be positively related to real wages is due to sociological factors. A common theme in such explanations is that workers' morale is affected by, among other things, their rate of pay. With a higher rate of pay workers feel more valued by the firm and morale is boosted. Productivity is, in turn, assumed to be positively related to worker morale. This may be because teamwork is improved or because workers experience less stress-related illness and so take less sick leave.

For these various reasons increased wages are able to improve worker productivity, and so may actually increase firms' profits. To see the implications of this relationship we examine a simplified game theory version of the model developed by Shapiro and Stiglitz (1984). In this model it is assumed that there are a large number of identical firms and workers. These are the strategic players in the game. As all firms are assumed identical their equilibrium strategies must be the same. This is also true for all workers. Firms initially decide how many workers to employ and the real wage rate they are willing to pay. Having observed the firms' wage offer, workers then decide whether or not to accept it, and if so, how much effort to supply in return. These are the players' strategic variables. Firms and workers are mutually interdependent because both firms' profits, Π, and workers' utility, V, depend on the real wage rate, w, and the amount of effort supplied by workers, e. For simplicity we assume that workers have a discrete choice over the amount of effort to supply. Specifically they can either work hard all the time or none of the time. This is represented by setting e equal to either 1 or 0 respectively. If a worker shirks, then we assume there is a fixed probability, $Prob$, of being caught and fired. If a worker rejects a firm's wage offer, or is caught shirking and fired, then he expects to earn the outside or reservation wage, w_r. This is the income a worker expects to receive if he looks for work elsewhere.

Firms are assumed to maximize expected profits and workers' expected utility. We will assume the following specific pay-off functions for a representative firm and worker. The firm's profits are equal to:

$$\Pi = TR(N,e) - Nw, \tag{7.1}$$

where TR is the total revenue for the firm, and N is the number of workers employed by the firm. Total revenue is assumed to be positively related to both employment and effort over the relevant range of production. With either $N = 0$ or $e = 0$ for all workers we assume that total revenue is zero. Utility for a worker who works hard is equal to:

$$V_{(e=1)} = w - 1. \tag{7.2}$$

Utility for a worker who shirks depends on whether or not they are caught and fired. If they are not caught, then their utility equals:

$$V_{(e=0)} = w. \tag{7.3}$$

If they are caught shirking and fired, their utility equals the reservation wage and:

$$V_{(e=0)} = w_r. \tag{7.4}$$

Having defined the players, the strategic variables, the pay-off functions, as well as the timing of the decisions to be made and amount of information available to each player we can formulate this model as an extensive form game between a representative firm and worker. This is shown in Fig. 7.2.

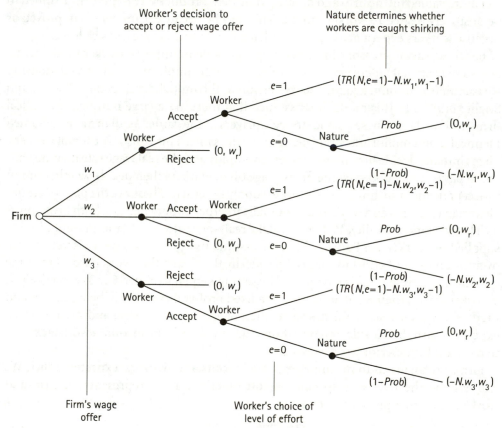

Fig. 7.2 Extensive Form Game for the Shirking Model

This extensive form game shows the representative firm first deciding upon its optimal wage offer. In Fig. 7.2 three possible wage offers are depicted, w_1, w_2, and w_3. Having observed the firm's wage offer the worker then decides whether or not to accept the job, and how much effort to supply. Finally, nature determines whether a worker who shirks is caught and fired, according to a given probability distribution. To find the subgame perfect Nash equilibrium for this game we apply the principle of backward induction. Working backwards the first strategic decision to be determined is the optimal level of effort workers will supply given that the real wage rate offered by the firm is acceptable. If the worker works hard, then utility is given by (7.2). Conversely from (7.3) and (7.4) the *expected* utility of shirking is given as

$$EV_{(e=0)} = (1 - Prob)w + Prob\, w_r. \tag{7.5}$$

The worker will therefore work hard if

$$w - 1 \geq (1 - Prob)w + Prob\, w_r. \tag{7.6}$$

Rearranging this inequality we get that the worker will work hard if

$$w \geq w_r + \frac{1}{Prob}. \tag{7.7}$$

In order for the employer to induce workers to work hard they must pay more than the reservation wage, w_r. The reservation wage, however, is determined in part by the wages set by other firms. We define the reservation wage as follows:

$$w_r = (1 - U)w + Ub, \tag{7.8}$$

where U is the unemployment rate and b the level of unemployment benefits. The reservation wage is equal to the probability of finding an alternative job offer multiplied by the real wage rate plus the probability of remaining unemployed multiplied by the level of unemployment benefit. This is equal to the expected level of alternative income. Substituting (7.8) into (7.7) and rearranging yields the condition that workers will only work hard if

$$w \geq b + \frac{1}{Prob\,U}. \tag{7.9}$$

If $Prob\,U = 1$, then the minimum wage the firms need pay to induce effort is equal to the level of unemployment benefit plus full compensation for the effort involved in working hard. However, $Prob\,U$ will only equal 1 if shirking is always detected, and as a result that individual remains unemployed. With $Prob < 1$ (i.e. there is imperfect monitoring) or $U < 1$ (i.e. there is some positive probability of finding alternative employment), then the real wage rate must be set above this minimum level in order to induce positive effort. In this case firms will have to pay workers a wage premium to induce them to work hard. If $Prob\,U = 0$, then the wage premium becomes infinite, and no finite wage induces workers to work hard. This is because there is either no chance of being caught shirking ($Prob = 0$), or because an alternative job, paying the same real wage rate, can always be found ($U = 0$). In order for equation (7.9) to be satisfied there must be some positive level of unemployment. This demonstrates that firms must pay an efficiency wage above the market-clearing wage rate if they are to induce effort from their workers. The reason for this is as follows.

If all firms pay the market-clearing wage rate, there is no incentive for workers to work hard. If workers are caught shirking and fired, then they can find another job paying the same real wage rate. With no effective punishment workers will definitely shirk.

Firms realizing this are willing to pay an efficiency wage above the market-clearing wage rate. This results in a positive level of involuntary unemployment. The effective punishment if a worker shirks and is caught, is that he faces a positive probability of being unemployed for a certain period of time. With all firms acting identically it is not wage differentials that induce workers to work hard, but rather the prospect that if caught shirking and fired workers could remain unemployed and only receive unemployment benefit. In this way unemployment acts as a worker discipline device.

So far we have only solved the worker's decision whether to work hard or not. To fully solve the model we must work back towards the firm's initial decision about its optimal wage offer. Before that we determine what characterizes an acceptable wage offer for the worker. It can first be noted that the worker will always accept a wage offer which satisfies (7.9). This is because any such wage rate, net of the disutility of work, must be greater than the reservation wage a worker earns if he rejects the job offer. Similarly, if the real wage rate does not satisfy (7.9), but is greater than the reservation wage, then the worker will again accept the job offer, but supply no effort. This implies that the worker will accept the job offer if the real wage rate is greater than b. If the wage offer is less than b, then the offer is rejected. This completes the description for the equilibrium strategies for the worker.

Given that the firm can also determine these optimal strategies for the worker its decision is straightforward. If it sets a wage below $b + 1/PrU$, then profits will always be less than or equal to zero. (Either its wage offer is rejected, in which case it earns zero profit, or accepted but the workers make no effort in which case the firm makes a loss.) The firm's optimal policy is to offer a real wage equal to $b + 1/ProbU$ if this generates positive profits, or zero otherwise. With a positive real wage rate the firm will hire workers until their marginal productivity equals the real wage rate. With a zero wage offer the firm sets employment equal to zero, and produces nothing. This completes the solution for this efficiency wage game.

7.2 Nominal Rigidities and the Business Cycle

As discussed in the previous section efficiency wage models provide one possible explanation for involuntary unemployment. However, such models are unable, on their own, to explain a further important Keynesian result. This is that nominal demand shocks can have real effects on the economy. In order for nominal demand shocks to influence real variables there needs to be some kind of nominal imperfection. New Classical macroeconomics attempts to explain fluctuations caused by nominal demand shocks by incorporating imperfect information about the aggregate price level into models of *perfect competition*. In contrast, one strand of New Keynesian macroeconomics analyses the effects of nominal wage and price rigidity in the presence of *imperfect competition*. With nominal rigidities wages and prices do not adjust instanta-

EXERCISE 7.1

The efficiency wage model presented in the text made two simplifying assumptions. *First*, workers only had a discrete choice over their level of effort, setting it equal to 0 or 1. *Second*, there was a fixed probability that a worker shirking would be caught and fired, equal to *Prob*. This Exercise relaxes both of these assumptions. Consider the model presented in the text when it is modified by the following alternative assumptions: (1) workers have a continuous choice over the level of effort supplied, provided e is between 0 and 1 inclusive and (2) the probability that a worker is caught shirking depends on the level of effort supplied according to the equation *Prob* = 1– *e*.

These modified assumptions also change the relevant definition of the utility associated with the reservation wage. In this current model a worker can be caught shirking and fired even if he is supplying a positive level of effort. The utility associated with alternative income must reflect this possible disutility of work. The reservation utility is therefore equal to

$$w_r = (1 - U)(w - e) + Ub.$$

Using this adapted model answer the following questions:

(1) What real wage rate will just induce the worker to accept the job?

(2) Determine an equation showing how a worker's optimal level of effort varies with the real wage rate. Plot this function.
(Hint: Find an equation for e that maximizes a worker's utility if he accepts a job offer.)

(3) What is the firm's optimal efficiency wage rate?
(Hint: To maximize profits firms will seek to minimize the wage rate per unit of effort, w/e.)

neously to offset shocks hitting the economy. These shocks therefore cause fluctuations in real variables. The main finding of this research has been that small nominal rigidities can, under imperfect competition, lead to large fluctuations in real variables. This in turn implies that there will be large changes in aggregate welfare. This result was developed independently by Akerlof and Yellen (1985), Mankiw (1985), and Parkin (1986), and has become known as the 'PAYM insight'.

Nominal rigidities are introduced into these New Keynesian models in one of two ways. Parkin and Mankiw assume there are small costs associated with changing nominal wages and prices. These so called '*menu costs*' include the physical costs of adjusting prices, such as printing new catalogues and price lists. They also cover the costs of having to calculate and renegotiate new prices. Alternatively Akerlof and Yellen introduce the concept of '*near rationality*'. This involves individuals suboptimizing, and so not behaving completely rationally, but only when the costs of doing so are small. The PAYM result is important because it is generally agreed that the costs of adjusting nominal wages and prices, and the costs associated with 'near rationality', cannot be very large. To illustrate this result we discuss the arguments presented in Mankiw (1985) and give them a game theory interpretation.

7.2.1 Small menu costs

In the argument that follows we assume that all firms are identical so that results derived for a representative firm apply to all firms in the economy. With imperfect competition firms face downward-sloping demand and marginal revenue curves. This is illustrated in Fig. 7.3.

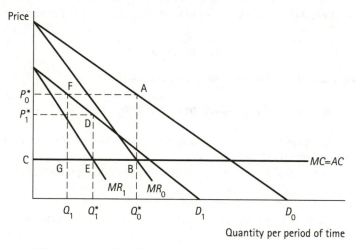

Fig. 7.3 Imperfect Competition and Small Menu Costs

The initial demand and marginal revenue curves for the representative firm are D_0 and MR_0 respectively. We assume that marginal cost, MC, is constant. The firm will maximize profits by setting output where marginal revenue is equal to marginal cost, and then setting the price just compatible with selling this level of output. Firms will initially set output equal to Q^*_0 and price equal to P^*_0. This gives them a level of super-normal profit equal to area P^*_0ABC.

Consider what happens if there is now a fall in nominal aggregate demand. This may, for example, be due to a contraction in the money supply. With prices unchanged this causes a fall in the real demand for goods and services. The demand and marginal revenue curves will shift to the left. The new demand and marginal revenue curves are shown as D_1 and MR_1 respectively. Price rigidity will be Nash equilibrium if the gain to a single firm from changing its price, given that all other firms maintain their current price, is less than the cost of changing the price. In such an equilibrium no one firm, acting in isolation, has the incentive to change its price. In this situation the general price level will remain unchanged. Price rigidity is therefore a Nash equilibrium if the costs to a firm of unilaterally changing its price outweigh the benefits. This will involve firms comparing their expected level of profit under the alternative strategies of changing or maintaining their current price.

If a firm maintains the price of P^*_0, then it will maximise its profit by producing the level of output Q_1. With this fixed price strategy the firm earns supernormal profits equal to the area $P^*_0\text{FGC}$. At this level of output, however, marginal revenue is greater than marginal cost, and so profits (excluding adjustment costs) will rise if the firm increases its level of output and reduces price. Profits are maximized if the firm produces Q^*_1, and cuts its price to P^*_1. The benefit of cutting its price is that the firm now earns a higher level of profit equal to the area $P^*_1\text{DEC}$. The cost of this strategy is the small menu cost of adjusting price. The firm will maintain its current price if this menu cost outweighs the increase in profit. Price rigidity will therefore be a Nash equilibrium if the menu cost is greater than $P^*_1\text{DEC} - P^*_0\text{FGC}$. When this necessary condition is satisfied the full effect of a nominal demand shock will fall on quantity adjustment. In this equilibrium all firms experience a fall in profit and consumer surplus is reduced. Social welfare is therefore significantly reduced following the fall in nominal aggregate demand. These are traditional Keynesian results.

It is important to realize that the above condition for price rigidity to be a Nash equilibrium will only be satisfied if there is imperfect competition. With imperfect competition the increase in profit from a firm reducing its price will only be of second-order magnitude (i.e. small). The increase in sales leads to greater profit, but this is partly offset by the fall in price. This is not true with perfect competition. This can be demonstrated by the following argument. Assume again that there is a fall in nominal aggregate demand. With perfect competition, and given the expectation that all other firms will maintain their initial prices, each firm believes it could capture the entire market with a slight price reduction. This would greatly increase the firm's profits, and certainly outweigh any possible menu costs. Each firm would therefore like unilaterally to reduce its price. This contradicts the assumption that other firms will maintain current prices. Under perfect competition complete price rigidity cannot be a Nash equilibrium. Instead the Nash equilibrium for perfect competition is immediate and complete price adjustment by all firms. For this reason small menu costs can only explain how nominal demand shocks have real effects on the economy if there is imperfect competition.

7.2.2 Aggregate demand externality

One interpretation of the PAYM result that allows us to see it more clearly as an application of game theory has been given by Blanchard and Kiyotaki (1987). They argue

---

EXERCISE 7.2

Determine the necessary condition, regarding the cost of adjusting prices, for complete price rigidity to be a Nash equilibrium in response to the following adverse demand shock. Assume there are n identical firms, indexed $i = 1, \ldots, n$, and that all firms are initially maximizing profits. The initial demand curve is given as p_i (£) = $250 - q_i$, where p_i and q_i are the price charged and quantity produced by firm i. After the demand shock this becomes p_i (£) = $230 - q_i$. Total costs for firm i, TC_i, are given by the equation TC_i (£) = $50.q_i$. Draw a diagram illustrating your results.

---

that the reason there can be large social costs associated with nominal price rigidity, even though it is not in any individual firm's interest to change its own price, is because there is a basic *aggregate demand externality*. This externality arises when there is imperfect competition.

The type of imperfect competition typically modelled in New Keynesian economics is *monopolistic competition*, which is associated with Chamberlain (1933). With this type of competition there are a large number of firms selling differentiated products. Product differentiation causes firms' products to be imperfect substitutes for each other, and so each firm has some degree of market power. The aggregate demand externality with this type of competition can be explained as follows. If only one firm adjusts its price in response to a fall in nominal demand, there is a small yet negligible effect on the aggregate price level. This implies that the fall in *nominal* aggregate demand translates into a fall in *real* aggregate demand. This will cause the economy to enter a recession. If, however, a significant number of firms reduce their prices, this will significantly reduce the aggregate price level, and so partially offset the fall in aggregate demand. In this situation the resulting recession is not so severe, and firms are less worse off. It is this interdependence under imperfect competition, via the level of aggregate demand, which constitutes the externality. Each firm in calculating its own optimal price strategy will ignore the effect it has on other firms, and so the resulting equilibrium will be Pareto inefficient. This result is illustrated in Fig. 7.4 for a reduction in the money supply.

In this diagram we assume there are a large number of identical firms engaged in imperfect competition. On the horizontal axis is the weighted price index for the economy as a whole, P, divided by the total amount of (nominal) money in the economy, M. This axis gives the inverse of the real money supply. On the vertical axis is the price of a representative firm, P_i, again relative to the nominal money supply. The diagram illustrates a number of firm i's isoprofit curves, indexed by the level of profit earned by that firm, Π. Moving farther to the right implies reduced demand for each firm's product, and correspondingly reduced profit. Each firm is assumed to be only interested in

150

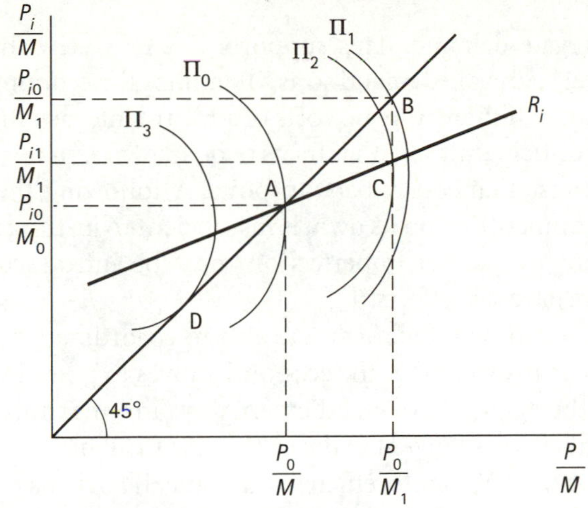

Fig. 7.4 Imperfect Competition and the Aggregate Demand Externality

maximizing its own level of profit, and ignores any effect its price has on real aggregate demand. This means that firms take the value of the real money supply as given and determine their own optimal price accordingly. To maximize profit firms set their price where the isoprofit line is vertical for each level of the real money supply. Joining these profit-maximizing positions together gives us firm i's reaction function, R_i. This curve shows how the firm's optimal price responds to changes in the inverse of the real money supply. In Fig. 7.4 it is assumed that this reaction function is upward-sloping. (It is possible for the reaction function to be downward-sloping, but this does not significantly alter the results of this section. As all firms are identical, the equilibrium involves firms setting the same price level. The resulting equilibrium is called a *symmetric Nash equilibrium*. This implies that the final equilibrium will be on the 45° line. With all firms initially setting their profit-maximizing price, the equilibrium will be at point A, where the reaction curve cuts the 45° line. In this Nash equilibrium all firms set a price of P_{i0} corresponding to the nominal money supply of M_0, and earn a level of profit equal to Π_0.

We now consider what happens if there is a contraction in the nominal money supply. If the amount of money in the economy contracts, to M_1, then with fixed prices the real money supply also falls. With fixed prices the economy moves to point B, and firms earn a smaller level of profits equal to Π_1. This point, however, is off each firm's reaction function, and so, ignoring menu costs, firms are suboptimizing. With each firm having a negligible impact on the aggregate price level, firms will maximize profit by cutting their price to P_{i1}, and moving vertically down to point C. This reduction in price increases profits to Π_2. Firms acting individually, however, will only reduce price if this increase in profit is greater than the menu cost of changing price. If the menu cost exceeds this second-order gain in profit, firms will maintain their initial price of P_{i0} and point B will be the new Nash equilibrium. In the absence of effective co-ordination no one firm has the incentive to change its price and the economy will enter a recession due to the fall in aggregate demand. This supports Keynes's view that the government should aim to target aggregate demand so as to stabilize the economy and avoid fluctuations in real variables. If there were no costs of adjustment, each firm would reduce its price immediately anticipating all other firms to do likewise. In this situation the economy would move instantaneously back to point A following the nominal demand shock. Imperfect competition, on its own, is insufficient to justify a Keynesian business cycle. Instead a further market imperfection must be introduced so that nominal demand shocks can have real effects.

It can finally be noted that if all firms are able to co-ordinate their prices, they can reduce prices to such an extent that the economy moves to point D. At this point firms have internalized the aggregate demand externality, and maximize joint profit. Here each firm's isoprofit curve is tangent to the 45° line, with all firms earning a profit equal to Π_3. This is the symmetric Pareto-efficient outcome. If all firms reduce their prices to the level associated with point D, real aggregate demand for goods is higher and all firms are made better off. However, as point D lies off each firm's reaction function, it does not correspond to a sustainable Nash equilibrium. Point D is not a Nash equilibrium because if firms believe other firms will set their prices consistent with this point, they have the incentive to set a higher price. Point A is the unique Nash equilibrium for the model depicted, and corresponds to an economy-wide prisoners' dilemma. Imperfect competition leads to prices being set too high and output too low, resulting in Pareto inefficiency. With sufficient nominal price rigidity expansionary monetary may be able to alleviate this problem and enhance social welfare. In this situation an increase in the money supply becomes equivalent to a co-ordinated reduction in prices by all firms. Real aggregate demand increases and all firms are made better off.

7.2.3 Combining real and nominal rigidities

The above analysis has illustrated that, given the presence of imperfect competition, small degrees of nominal rigidity can cause fluctuations in demand to have significant effects on real variables and welfare. One criticism made of these models, however, is that price rigidity will only be a Nash equilibrium under implausible parameter values. Most importantly, the supply of labour needs to be highly *elastic*. As most empirical evidence indicates that the supply of labour is highly *inelastic* this is a serious criticism. This criticism derives from incorporating the above partial equilibrium analysis, where we looked at the goods market in isolation, into a general equilibrium framework. The advantage of using a general equilibrium framework is that interactions between markets can be explicitly modelled. Consider, for example, the incorporation of the labour market into the above model. Given an adverse demand shock, and nominal price rigidity, firms will reduce their level of output. This in turn reduces their demand for labour. With inelastic labour supply this will cause the real wage rate to fall. This feeds back to affect the goods market by driving down marginal costs. With marginal costs falling firms have a greater incentive to cut prices. With plausible parameter values this increased incentive to reduce prices will dominate any small menu cost. With inelastic labour supply small menu costs, on their own, cease to be a plausible explanation of business cycle fluctuations.

To counter this criticism Ball and Romer (1990) have demonstrated that by *combining* both real and nominal rigidities Keynesian results can once more be re-established, without the need to assume unrealistic parameter values. Real rigidities are important because nominal price rigidity is only a Nash equilibrium if individual firms do not change prices in the belief that all other firms will maintain their prices. With this belief a firm perceives that changing its price represents a change in its *real* price in response to a *real* demand shock. If there is real price rigidity, this will reinforce the costs associated with nominal price adjustment. To illustrate this argument we will examine a number of real rigidities and indicate how they reduce the incentive of firms to cut prices following an adverse demand shock.

Efficiency wages

In the criticism outlined above the enhanced incentive for firms to reduce their prices resulted from declining real wages in the labour market. However, as we have seen in section 7.1, if firms pay efficiency wages above the market-clearing level, then labour is off its supply curve. In this situation a fall in demand for labour can reduce employment with little effect on the real wage rate. If this occurs, marginal costs will not fall greatly, and small menu costs may be sufficient to deter firms cutting prices. With efficiency wages price rigidity can be a Nash equilibrium for plausible parameter values.

This explanation suggests that interaction between the goods market and labour market strengthens the case for both wage and price rigidity. For example, firms might be prepared to reduce their prices following an adverse demand shock if they expect wages to fall. If, however, they anticipate wages to remain fixed, then given small menu costs they may decide to maintain current prices. Similarly, in the labour market, firms might be prepared to reduce wages if they expect prices to fall. If, however, if they expect prices to remain constant, then for efficiency wage considerations they will resist cuts to the nominal wage rate. In this way it is possible for the resulting Nash equilibrium to consist of complete wage and price rigidity, and for demand shocks to cause large fluctuations in output, employment, and welfare.

Thick market externality

Given the presence of trade frictions there are costs associated with undertaking mutually beneficial trade. This means buyers and sellers will only be brought together if they incur various search costs. For example, consumers will need to spend time searching the market for the best product to buy, while firms may need to incur advertising and promotional costs to attract new customers. Diamond (1982) has argued that these costs will be negatively related to the level of activity in the economy. When there are many potential trading partners, as in a boom, then search costs are likely to be lower than when there are few potential trading partners, as in a recession. As more people engage in economic activity, so search costs are reduced for other agents. This interdependence is called the 'thick market externality'. With search costs moving counter-cyclically due to this externality, firms are more likely to maintain prices following a nominal demand shock.

Customer markets

Closely related to the thick market externality, is the idea that customers will economize on search costs. Consumers can do this by having a low frequency of search relative to how often they buy a product. Following Okun (1975, 1981) markets with this characteristic are called customer markets. With this behaviour customers will only continue to buy a firm's product if they believe they are being charged an acceptable price. If customer's believe that a firm is charging a price significantly above what other firms are likely to be charging, they will stop buying from that firm and search elsewhere. This implies that the elasticity of demand is greater for a price rise than it is for a price fall. The demand curve is therefore kinked at the current price. If a firm *raises* its price, then its sales will fall due to some customers switching their demand to other firms, and the remaining customers buying less. If the firm *reduces* its price, it will sell more to current customers, but it will not immediately attract new customers from other firms, as they will not initially observe the price change. It is no longer sufficient that firms know that nominal demand has changed in order for it to change its price; consumers must also acquire the same information. This will tend to delay the change in price, and introduce a further degree of price rigidity into the economy.

Judging quality by price

Another possible outcome in markets where consumers have imperfect information is that they will judge a product's quality by its price. With this behaviour customers (or potential customers) infer that if a price increases this is due to an improvement in quality, while if the price falls this signals a deterioration in quality. Stiglitz (1987) has argued that in this situation firms will be reluctant to reduce prices following a negative demand shock for fear that consumers wrongly infer that quality has deteriorated.

Collusive oligopoly

Stiglitz (1984) has further argued that the gains derived from collusive oligopoly under imperfect information may prevent firms within a cartel from cutting their prices following a negative demand shock. This may happen if firms have imperfect information concerning the demand faced by other members of the cartel. In this situation one possible Nash equilibrium for maintaining a collusive outcome beneficial to all firms is to use price change as a trigger strategy. Each firm maintains the collusive price as long as other firms do so, otherwise each firm sets the Pareto-inefficient Nash equilibrium price. With this strategy firms may not reduce their prices following a fall in demand, due to the fear that this will be misinterpreted and cause other members of the cartel to revert to the non-collusive outcome. This would result in all firms being made worse off. Real price rigidity will be an equilibrium if the expected gains from maintaining prices outweigh the costs of not optimally adjusting to the demand shock.

Rotemberg and Woodford (1991) also appeal to collusive oligopoly to justify real price rigidity. They argue that the desired mark up of prices over costs falls in booms and increases in recessions. They suggest that this is because collusion is harder to maintain in booms due to increased competition. If this is true, then firms have less incentive to cut prices in a recession and so this again acts as a real price rigidity.

Staggered wage and price adjustment

A final argument for why prices might be sticky is that price adjustment across firms is not synchronized but staggered. With staggered price adjustment the length of time it takes for an economy to adjust to a nominal demand shock can be much greater than the length of time individual firms hold prices fixed. This is because with staggered price adjustment a change in price will correspond to a change in that firm's real price. If firms seek to avoid changes in relative price, they will wish to avoid large one-off price changes. For each successive price adjustment following a demand shock firms will only partially adjust towards the new long-run equilibrium. As all firms in the economy only partially adjust, the whole adjustment process is slowed down. The resulting price-level inertia implies that nominal demand shocks can have large and long-lasting real effects on the economy. This can be true even if individual firms change their prices frequently. Blanchard (1983) has further argued that if staggering occurs over firms at different stages in the chain of production, complete adjustment is further delayed.

Similar arguments can be made for wage adjustment. For example, workers might be prepared to take a cut in wages, following an adverse demand shock if all other workers accept a proportionate pay cut at the same time. However, with staggered wage contracts, adjustment will imply changes in relative wages. If workers are concerned about their wages relative to other workers, the adjustment process will be gradual, even if wages are changed frequently.

Each of the above real rigidities can reinforce the costs associated with nominal price adjustment. This increases the probability that firms will maintain prices and adjust quantities in response to demand fluctuations. It seems likely that the combination of empirically plausible menu costs, other real rigidities, and imperfect competition can cause nominal demand shocks to have real effects. This supports a basic Keynesian contention that the business cycle is demand driven and that there is a potential welfare-enhancing role for government stabilization policy via active demand management.

7.3 Co-ordination Failure

The previous section has argued that wage and price rigidity may form part of a Nash equilibrium in macroeconomic games characterized by imperfect competition. In this section we illustrate how interdependence can lead to the existence of multiple equilibria. Furthermore, we argue that these equilibria can be Pareto ranked. This means that from the perspective of social welfare some equilibria are better than others. This leads to the possibility of co-ordination failure. Co-ordination failure occurs when an economy co-ordinates on an equilibrium which is Pareto inferior compared to alternative equilibria.

The possibility of multiple equilibria and co-ordination failure has a number of significant implications. For example, it opens up a potentially important role for *government policy*. This involves the government attempting to induce the economy to co-ordinate upon a Pareto-dominant equilibrium. This may involve the government using active demand policy to prevent the economy becoming stuck in an unemployment equilibrium. Similarly, models with multiple equilibria can exhibit *hysteresis* effects, where shocks to the economy can have permanent effects. For example, Howitt and McAfee (1988) and Durlauf (1989) show that which of the many equilibria an economy co-ordinates upon depends on initial conditions.

An alternative implication is that the economy may switch between different equilibria due to changing *expectations*. This result would seem to support Keynes's proposition that 'animal spirits' can be an important influence on the level of economic activity and welfare. From this perspective these models are similar to 'sunspot equilibria' developed in overlapping-generation models. The idea here is that, because the economy does not process a unique equilibrium, agents will use a variable of no intrinsic importance, such as sunspots, to co-ordinate their beliefs upon one particular equilibrium. In this way an extraneous event can have real effects on the economy via its influence on agents' expectations. Given this possibility, the performance of different economies may be largely unrelated to underlying fundamentals. One method individuals might use to co-ordinate upon one particular equilibrium is to adopt common conventions. These conventions might in turn be related to certain institutions, such as the degree of centralization over wage-bargaining. Interestingly, the co-ordinating convention could also be the acceptance of a particular economic theory. Hargreaves Heap (1992) presents an overlapping-generation model where if agents formulate expectations according to Classical economic theory, an equilibrium consistent with these beliefs is selected. Alternatively, if agents formulate expectations according to Keynesian theory, the resulting equilibrium exhibits Keynesian features. Both methods of formulating expectations are self-fulfilling and so are rational. (A model with similar properties, based on monopolistic competition, is presented in Exercise 7.3.)

To examine some of these issues we initially state a general requirement for multiple equilibria to exist in macroeconomic games. This is based on the work of Cooper and

John (1988). We then discuss how this condition can be met in various economic contexts.

7.3.1 Multiple equilibria and strategic complementarity

Cooper and John (1988) demonstrate that a necessary condition for there to be multiple symmetric Nash equilibria is that the economy exhibits *strategic complementarity*. As discussed in Chapter 4, strategic complementarity refers to the situation where an increase in one player's strategic variable induces others to increase their strategic variable. Diagramatically this is represented by upward-sloping reaction curves. Conversely, strategic substitutability corresponds to downward-sloping reaction curves. To see that strategic complementarity is necessary for multiple symmetric Nash equilibria consider Fig. 7.5.

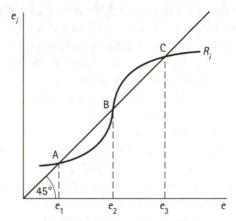

Fig. 7.5 Strategic Complementarity and Multiple Nash Equilibria

On the vertical axis is the value of a representative individual's strategic variable, e_i. The nature of this variable will depend on the economic model under consideration. On the horizontal axis is the aggregate value of this strategic variable, e. This is the weighted average of e_i over all individuals in the economy. It is assumed that due to the large number of individuals within the economy, each individual has a negligible effect on the value of e. A symmetric Nash equilibrium must lie on the 45° line. Fig. 7.5 illustrates individual i's reaction function, R_i. This reaction function shows how individual *i* optimally adjusts his or her strategic variable as e changes. (A specific application of this type of interdependence has been used in Fig. 7.4.) In Fig. 7.5 there are three symmetric Nash equilibria, at points A, B, and C. Given that the reaction function is continuous it should be clear that multiple intersections with the 45° line are only possible if the reaction curve is, at least in part, upward-sloping. Thus Cooper and John emphasize that a necessary condition for multiple equilibria is strategic complementarity. It should also be noted that strategic complementarity also provides a natural explanation of the *Keynesian multiplier* process. For example, if the strategic variable corresponds to firm's chosen level of output, then strategic complementarity implies that as some firms expand output this induces other firms to do likewise. In this way strategic complementarity is able to explain multiple expansions or contractions in national output. We now discuss how this general condition might be met, and how New Keynesian models can generate multiple Nash equilibria and co-ordination failure.

7.3.2 Possible causes of strategic complementarity

Aggregate demand externality

One way in which an economy can exhibit strategic complementarity is for there to be an aggregate demand externality. This has been demonstrated by Rotemberg and Saloner (1986, 1987), Blanchard and Kiyotaki (1987), Ball and Romer (1991), and Alvi (1993). In these models strategic complementarity arises because an increase in the general price level causes an individual firm, in the absence of menu costs, to increase its own optimal price. This can be explained as follows. The increase in the general price level has two effects on the individual firm's optimal price. *First*, for a given level of real aggregate demand the firm will want to maintain its price relative to other firms. This will induce the firm to increase its price level. *Second*, the increase in the general price level reduces the real money supply and real aggregate demand, and as a consequence of this, the firm will want to reduce its price. The net effect on the firm's optimal price is ambiguous. If the relative price effect outweighs the aggregate demand effect, there is strategic complementarity. If, however, the elasticity of aggregate demand to the real price level is greater than one, then the aggregate demand effect might outweigh the relative price effect. In this situation there is strategic substitutability. As discussed above, strategic complementarity is necessary for there to be multiple equilibria and co-ordination failure. The following argument illustrates how this can occur with an aggregate demand externality and small menu costs. In particular we argue that price rigidity itself is an example of co-ordination failure.

Suppose that the government reduces the nominal money supply. If other firms are expected to cut their prices, then with strategic complementarity, each firm will desire to cut its price. If, however, as a result of menu costs, other firms are expected not to cut their prices, then there is no relative price effect, and each firm has a smaller incentive to reduce its own price level. The implication is that the cost to an individual firm, in terms of reduced profit, of not adjusting its price, increases the greater the proportion of other firms changing their price. For certain values of menu costs there will be multiple equilibria. One possible equilibrium is where all firms expect other firms to adjust. With this expectation the cost of not adjusting is perceived to be large, and so each firm will adjust its price. Another equilibrium is where all firms expect others to maintain their current price. Here the perceived cost of non-adjustment is small, and can be smaller than the menu cost. If this condition is satisfied, none of the firms will adjust its price. In both equilibria, expectations are self-fulfilling and rational. In the second, equilibrium firms maintain their initial price and adjust quantities. Following a fall in the money supply this equilibrium will cause the economy to enter a recession and economic welfare is reduced. This argument illustrates that the combination of strategic complementarity, due to the aggregate demand externality, and small menu costs can lead to Pareto-ranked multiple Nash equilibria.

Before discussing alternative ways in which an economy might exhibit multiple equilibria it is useful to see that the above argument goes some way to meeting two related criticisms levelled against small menu costs being a justification of nominal price rigidity. The *first* criticism is that the small menu cost literature focuses on costs of price adjustment but ignores the costs of quantity adjustment. The argument here is that a firm will, contrary to the small menu cost literature, compare the cost of each type of adjustment following a nominal demand shock. If there are costs associated with quantity adjustment, it is no longer clear that firms prefer to maintain prices and allow quantities to adjust. The *second* criticism is that the standard presentation of how menu costs can lead to nominal price rigidity ignores dynamic considerations. The argument here is that the costs associated with a firm not adjusting its price will accumulate over time. Given that firms are concerned about future discounted profits this will increase their incentive to change price immediately following a nominal demand shock.

The reason the previous argument relating small menu costs to multiple Nash equilibria addresses these criticisms is that the type of shock a firm perceives it is facing depends on which equilibrium the economy co-ordinates upon. If firms expect other firms to adjust their prices, then they will perceive the shock as nominal. In this situation firms are indeed likely to adjust their prices. If, however, firms expect other firms to maintain their prices, then they perceive the shock to be real. In this situation firms are more likely to infer that quantity adjustments are necessary to re-establish long-run equilibrium. With this belief firms will resist price changes, and prefer quantities to adjust. This explanation of nominal price rigidity is no longer dependent on firms ignoring either quantity adjustment costs, nor the cumulative long-run effects of non-price adjustment.

Thick market externality

As discussed in section 7.2 thick market externalities occur when the cost of contacting potential trading partners is negatively related to the level of general economic activity. In a boom search costs are likely to be smaller than in a recession, and this provides a further inducement for firms to expand output. Once more we have strategic complementarity. As some firms expand their level of activity, this reduces the search costs of other firms. This provides the incentive for these other firms to increase their level of activity. This introduces the possibility of multiple Nash equilibria. If firms expect there to be a high level of economic activity, and consequently low search costs, then each firm will optimally produce a high level of output. If, however, firms expect a low level of economic activity, and consequently high search costs, they will produce a low level of output. Both of these scenarios generate self-fulfilling expectations and so represent possible Nash equilibria. As with the aggregate demand externality these equilibria are characterized by different levels of economic activity, and so will be Pareto ranked. Once more there is the potential for co-ordination failure.

Increasing returns

A final source of co-ordination failure is when production is characterised by increasing returns. With increasing returns production costs fall as output is expanded. In this situation production is more attractive when demand for the good is high. Again, if all firms expect a high level of aggregate demand, then they will expand their level of production. Alternatively, if they expect a low level of aggregate demand then they will cut back on production. Once more there is the possibility of Pareto-ranked multiple equilibria each characterized by self-fulfilling expectations. The implications of increasing returns have been developed by Kiyotaki (1988), Shleifer (1986), Shleifer and Vishny (1988), and Murphy, Shleifer, and Vishny (1989a, 1989b).

It should be noted that these final two mechanisms used to generate multiple equilibria in Keynesian models do not rely on imperfect wage and/or price adjustment. These models therefore demonstrate that co-ordination failure can result even if wage and prices are fully flexible. Indeed, models based on co-ordination failure and nominal rigidity are sometimes presented as alternative paradigms. However, models based on the aggregate demand externality show that these two approaches are closely related. As argued above, in certain models nominal price rigidity can itself represent a co-ordination failure.

EXERCISE 7.3.*

In the text we argued that price rigidity can itself be a co-ordination failure following a nominal demand shock. In this exercise we present a model where the resulting equilibrium depends on how agents expect others to react to a reduction in the nominal money supply. If agents have 'Classical' expectations, then the demand shock has no real effects. Conversely, if agents have 'Keynesian' expectations then there is co-ordination failure and the economy enters a recession. Consider the following economy of n firms, indexed $i = 1, \ldots, n$, that compete against each other according to monopolistic competition. Each firm faces the same demand function, given by the equation

$$d_i = \frac{1}{n}\left(\frac{p_i}{P}\right)^{-2}\left(\frac{M}{P}\right),$$

---

where d_i and p_i are respectively the demand and price of firm i's product, M is the nominal money supply, and P is the weighted average price level over all firms, defined as

$$P \equiv \sum_{i=1}^{n} p_i d_i \Big/ \sum_{i=1}^{n} d_i.$$

Each firm's total cost (TC_i) is given by the equation

$$TC_i = cPd_i^2$$

Firms attempt to maximize profits and ignore any effect their own price/output decisions have on the aggregate price level, P. Initially we assume that there are no menu costs associated with changing prices.

(1) Derive expressions for each firm's optimal output and price.

(2) Derive expressions for the Nash equilibrium of output and price for each firm.

(3) Derive expressions for each firm's price and output if firms maximize joint real profits and divide the optimal output level equally between themselves. Explain why the expressions derived here differ from those found in (2).

For all subsequent questions assume the following parameter values: $n = 20$, $c = 0.5$.

(4) If $M = 100$, what are the Nash equilibrium values for each firm's output and price?

(5) Assume now that the government reduces the money supply by 10 per cent. Calculate each firm's optimal price and output, and their resulting expected real profit level, under the following assumptions:
   (a) Each firm expects all other firms to reduce their prices by 10 per cent.
   (b) Each firm expects all other firms to maintain their initial prices.

(6) Calculate each firm's output and expected real profit level if instead of optimizing in (5), they maintain their initial price level. Again do this for each of the two assumptions about what other firms will do.

(7) From your results to (5) and (6), derive the range of values associated with the costs of changing prices for which both of the following situations are equilibria, dependent on expectations and a 10 per cent reduction in the money supply.
   (a) All firms reduce prices by 10 per cent.
   (b) All firms maintain their initial prices.

7.4 Conclusions

New Keynesian Macroeconomics attempts to derive traditional Keynesian results within models where all agents are assumed to act rationally. In part, this is a response to New Classical criticisms that earlier Keynesian results were dependent upon essentially *ad hoc* assumptions. In particular, as discussed in the previous chapter, many Keynesian results were initially derived in models where agents formulated their expectations in ways inconsistent with complete rationality. To meet this criticism New Keynesian economists have developed game theory models where agents determine their expectations according to the Rational Expectations Hypothesis. In this chapter we have analysed three separate, though related, strands of New Keynesian Macroeconomics. These were efficiency wage models, models based on nominal rigidities, and models where due to multiple equilibria there is the potential for co-ordination failure. In each case there is the possibility of sustained involuntary unemployment, and often a clear role for government stabilization policy. These results are no longer dependent on agents acting irrationally. Instead, the key assumption in all the models analysed is that private sector agents are interdependent. This contrasts with New Classical models where, due to the assumption of perfect competition, private-sector agents are independent. (In New Classical Macroeconomics there is none the less interdependence between the government and the private sector.) From this perspective which school of thought is viewed as offering the most relevant policy advice depends not so much on whether individuals act rationally or otherwise, but on the underlying structure of the economy being considered. In some economies New Classical models can be viewed as being the most relevant. In other economies New Keynesian prescriptions will be valid. With the widespread use of game theory models in both New Keynesian and New Classical macroeconomics there appears less reason to reject either school of thought on the grounds that they employ *ad hoc* assumptions concerning either the rationality of agents or wage and price adjustment. Instead we must now appraise the two schools of thought according to different criteria. In particular the empirical relevance of competing models is once more seen to be of paramount concern.

7.5 Solutions to Exercises

Exercise 7.1

(1) The expected utility for a worker accepting a job offer equals

$$V_A = (1 - Prob)(w - e) + Prob\, w_r.$$

Conversely the expected utility of rejecting a job offer is

$$V_R = w_r.$$

A worker will accept a job offer if

$$(1 - Prob)(w - e) + Prob\, w_r \geq w_r.$$

An offer will therefore be accepted if

$$w - e \geq w_r.$$

Substituting in the equation for w_r yields the following condition for an acceptable wage offer

$$w \geq b + e.$$

A worker will accept any job offer where the wage minus the disutility of work is greater than the level of unemployment benefit. As the worker can always set $e = 0$ the minimum acceptable real wage is b.

(2) Given that the wage offer is accepted a worker will determine his optimal level of effort by maximizing his utility, V_A. Substituting the equation $Prob = 1 - e$ into the expression for V_A gives

$$V_A = e(w - e) + (1 - e)[(1 - U)(w - e) + Ub].$$

Differentiating, setting this equal to zero and rearranging gives us the following equation for how workers determine their optimal level of effort:

$$e(w) = \frac{U(1 + w - b) - 1}{2U}.$$

This function is plotted in Fig. 7.6.

(3) Provided profits are positive firms will seek to minimize the wage rate per unit of worker effort, w/e. This corresponds to the maximum value of e/w. This value is represented by the slope of a line taken from the origin to the function $e(w)$. From the above diagram w/e is minimized when $e = 1$, and so firms set the real wage rate equal to $1/U + b + 1$. If $U = 0$, then firms always have an incentive to increase the wage rate. This cannot, therefore, represent an

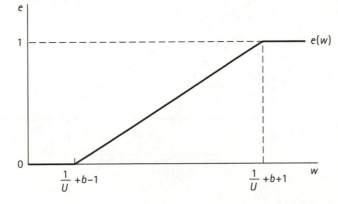

Fig. 7.6

equilibrium. As with the model in the text, the equilibrium must exhibit a positive rate of involuntary unemployment to induce workers optimally to supply effort.

Exercise 7.2

Multiplying the initial demand curve for firm i by that firm's level of output and differentiating gives us firm i's marginal revenue curve:

$$MR_i = 250 - 2q_i.$$

Setting this equal to marginal cost of £50 we can derive that the firm's initial profit-maximizing level of output is 100. The firm will just sell this amount when it sets its price equal to £150. Initial profits for each firm are therefore £10,000.

After the adverse demand shock the marginal revenue curve becomes

$$MR_i = 230 - 2q_i.$$

Setting this equal to marginal cost gives us the new profit-maximizing level of output of 90, and price equal to £140. With price adjustment each firm will earn profits equal to £8,100. From this level of profit, however, must be subtracted the cost of adjusting the price level, i.e. the small menu cost. Alternatively, if the firm maintains its initial price of £150, then the most it will be able to sell will be 80 units of the good. This yields a profit of £8,000.

The necessary condition for price rigidity to be a Nash equilibrium is therefore that the cost of adjusting prices for all firms is greater than £100. If this condition is satisfied, no firm has the incentive to change its price. Instead firms will reduce their supply of output by 20 per cent in response to the demand shock. These results are illustrated in Fig. 7.7.

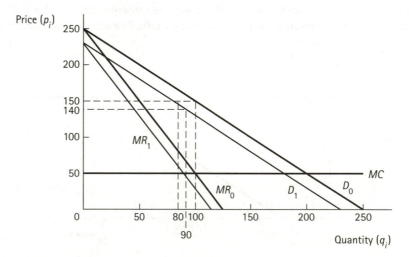

Fig. 7.7

Exercise 7.3

(1) Rearranging the demand function we can derive the inverse demand function for firm i

$$p_i = \left(\frac{MP}{nd_i} \right)^{\frac{1}{2}}.$$

From this expression we can formulate firm i's profit function

$$\Pi_i = d_i \left(\frac{MP}{nd_i} \right)^{\frac{1}{2}} - cPd_i^2.$$

By setting the differential of this equation, with respect to d_i, equal to zero, and rearranging, we can derive expressions for the firm's optimal output and price level.

$$d_i^* = \left(\frac{M}{16c^2 nP} \right)^{\frac{1}{3}}$$

$$p_i^* = \left(\frac{4c MP^2}{n} \right)^{\frac{1}{3}}.$$

(2) The Nash equilibrium for this model will exhibit two features:
   (a) All firms will be on their reaction functions, and so will set output and price according to the equations derived in (1).
   (b) All firms will set the same level of output and price, and so $p_i = P$, for all i. (As all firms face the same constraints, the equilibrium will be a symmetric Nash equilibrium.)
   From these two observations we can derive equations for p_i and d_i consistent with Nash equilibrium.

$$d_i = \frac{1}{4c}$$

$$p_i = \frac{4Mc}{n}.$$

(3) In this problem firms attempt to maximize joint profits, Π, given that all firm set the same price and produce the same output. We can therefore state that $P = p_i$ and $D = nd_i = M/P$. With these constraints joint nominal profit is equal to

$$\Pi = M - ncPd_i^2$$

and joint real profit is equal to

$$\frac{\Pi}{P} = \frac{M}{P} - ncd_i^2$$

$$\frac{\Pi}{P} = D - \frac{cD^2}{n}.$$

Setting the differential with respect to D equal to zero and rearranging gives us the following expressions

$$D = \frac{n}{2c}$$

$$\therefore d_i = \frac{1}{2c}$$

and

$$p_i = \frac{2cM}{n}.$$

Compared to the Nash equilibrium this joint profit-maximizing outcome involves firms doubling their output and halving their price. The reason for this is that by co-ordinating their price and output decisions they can internalize the aggregate demand externality. This involves firms recognizing that by reducing prices simultaneously their relative prices remain unchanged, but the real money supply expands. This increases the demand for all firms and makes them all better off.

(4) From the equations derived in (2) each firm's output is equal to 0.5, and prices are set equal to 10 in Nash equilibrium.

(5) and (6) The answers to these questions are given in Table 7.1, where P^e corresponds to the firm's expectation of the average price level, and Π_i/P^e is its expected real profit level.

(7) From examining the results derived in parts (5) and (6) we can state the following two results:

(a) If firm's expect all other firms to reduce prices by 10 per cent, then it is optimal for all firms to do so, provided the cost of changing prices (menu costs) are less than $0.375 - 0.368 = 0.007$.

(b) If firm's expect all other firms to maintain their initial prices, then it is optimal for all firms to do so, provided menu costs are larger than $0.350 - 0.349 = 0.001$.

Both of these scenarios will be Nash equilibria given that the following condition is satisfied:

$$0.001 < \text{menu costs} < 0.007.$$

Provided that this condition is satisfied, which equilibrium prevails depends upon firms' expectations. For example, if firms expect other firms to react according to Classical economic theory, and reduce prices in proportion to the fall in the nominal money supply, then the economy will co-ordinate on the first equilibrium. Alternatively, if firms expect other firms to react according to Keynesian economic theory, and keep prices constant, then the economy will co-ordinate upon the second equilibrium. In this sense economic theory itself can be a way for individuals to co-ordinate their expectations. Both types of expectation are

Table 7.1

	P^e	d_i	p_i	Π_i/P^e
Question (5a)	9.0	0.50	9.0	0.375
Question (5b)	10.0	0.48	9.7	0.350
Question (6a)	9.0	0.41	10.0	0.368
Question (6b)	10.0	0.45	10.0	0.349

rational as they are self-fulfilling, and generate either a 10 per cent reduction in price, or a 10 per cent reduction in the output.

Further Reading

Akerlof, G., and J. Yellen (1986), *Efficiency Wage Models of the Labour Market*, Cambridge: Cambridge University Press.

Hargreaves Heap, S. P. (1992), *The New Keynesian Macroeconomics: Time, Belief and Social Interdependence*, Aldershot: Edward Elgar.

Leslie, D. (1993), *Advanced Macroeconomics*, London: McGraw-Hill.

Mankiw, N. G., and D. Romer (1991), *New Keynesian Economics:* i and ii, Cambridge, Mass.: MIT Press.

Romer, D. (1996), *Advanced Macroeconomics*, New York: McGraw-Hill.

Snowdon, B., H. Vane, and P. Wynarczyk (1994), *A Modern Guide to Macroeconomics: An Introduction to Competing Schools of Thought*, Aldershot: Edward Elgar.

Weiss, A. (1991), *Efficiency Wages: Models of Unemployment, Layoffs and Wage Dispersion*, Oxford: Clarendon Press.

8

International Policy
Co-ordination

I N the previous two chapters we have discussed the role of macroeconomic policy from a purely domestic perspective. In particular we ignored the effects a country's economic policy might have on other countries. This is justified if the country under consideration is small. With this assumption it is legitimate to ignore any spillover effects that a country's macroeconomic policy might have on other countries because they are likely to be negligible. However, if we are interested in analysing large economies such effects may be significant, and need to be explicitly modelled. With spillover effects different countries are interdependent. This chapter illustrates that in the presence of spillover effects countries can benefit by co-ordinating their economic policies rather than setting them unilaterally. For this reason the prospect of policy co-ordination has especially appealed to the large G7 nations (USA, Germany, Japan, UK, France, Italy, and Canada), and in particular the G3 nations (USA, Germany, and Japan).

Policy co-ordination occurs when countries agree to pursue economic policies intended to promote the welfare of all nations involved in the agreement. This will involve countries explicitly taking into consideration the spillover effects their policies have on other countries. Spillover effects occur when one country's economic policy affects the economic performance of at least one other country. In the absence of policy co-ordination each country ignores these externalities and seeks to maximize its own individual welfare. With all countries acting independently the outcome will be a Nash equilibrium. With spillover effects this equilibrium is likely to be Pareto inefficient. This provides the incentive for countries to co-ordinate their policies. Policy co-ordination is, therefore, designed to avoid Pareto-inefficient outcomes.

Given that there is no supranational authority that can enforce agreements made between sovereign nations the appropriate tool for analysing economic policy co-ordination is non-cooperative game theory. From this perspective each country will only agree to policy co-ordination if it perceives this is in its own self-interest. As a result all agreements must be self-enforcing. To illustrate some of the issues involved in policy co-ordination we will focus on monetary policy. Specifically each section of this chapter addresses a separate question. In section 8.1 we ask the question: What are the main spillover effects of monetary policy? Here we discuss three ways in which aggregate demand policy in one country can spillover to effect the welfare of another country. These spillover effects are then illustrated using a modified version of the Mundell–Fleming model under the extreme assumptions of perfectly fixed and perfectly flexible exchange rates. In section 8.2 we ask the question: What are the consequences of these spillover effects? This section illustrates the potential gains from countries co-ordinating their monetary policies. This is done by using a two-country model and contrasting the possible outcomes under the alternative assumptions of no co-ordination and complete co-ordination. Although there are often potential gains from co-ordination, there are also problems for countries in realizing these gains. Some of these problems and how they might be overcome are discussed in section 8.3. This section therefore answers the question: What are the problems associated with monetary policy co-ordination? The final question we address in section 8.4 is: How large are the potential gains from policy co-ordination? To answer this question we review various studies that have attempted to estimate the possible gains from co-ordination.

8.1 Spillover Effects of Monetary Policy

As discussed in the introduction spillover effects occur when one country's economic policy affects the economic welfare of at least one other country. Here we discuss how such spillover effects can be associated with monetary policy. There are three broad ways in which any aggregate demand policy in one country can spillover to effect another country. These are the real income effect, the monetary effect, and the relative price effect. We discuss each of these effects in turn.

8.1.1 Real income effects

This linkage between countries takes place through the current account of the balance of payments. It occurs when a change in one country's national income increases its demand for imports from another country. This will stimulate aggregate demand in the overseas country, and alter its level of economic welfare. For example, if the UK increases the growth rate of its money supply this will stimulate domestic aggregate demand. This will cause aggregate demand in other countries also to expand as UK residents increase their demand for imports. Clearly the size of this spillover effect will depend crucially on the marginal propensity to import.

8.1.2 Monetary effects

In addition to real income effects there will also be monetary effects if nations seek to intervene in foreign exchange markets. The rationale for government's doing this is to influence the value of their exchange rate. This is done by either buying or selling foreign exchange. However, as foreign exchange constitutes part of a country's high-powered money supply this affects the quantity of money in the economy. With less than fully flexible exchange rates this provides another linkage between countries. Consider again the example of the UK expanding its domestic money supply which results in an increase in UK imports. This will improve the balance of payments of the UK's overseas trading partners. In the absence of exchange rate intervention the value of the foreign currency will appreciate against sterling. If this is viewed as undesirable the overseas government will sell its own currency and buy sterling on foreign exchange markets. The effect is that the foreign country accumulates sterling which leads to an expansion in its level of high-powered money. This in turn will lead to a multiple expansion in that country's own money supply. Once more domestic monetary policy affects aggregate demand and economic welfare in other countries. Only if exchange rates are completely flexible will there be no monetary effects.

8.1.3 Relative price effects

This final linkage occurs when the exchange rate between countries is allowed to appreciate or depreciate. This will cause a change in the relative price of goods and services between countries. This in turn affects the demand for imports and exports. With this linkage an expansion in the UK money supply will cause its trading partners to experience an exchange rate appreciation. This will make foreign goods and services less competitive, tending to reduce their exports and increase imports. This effect only works when there is less than completely fixed exchange rates.

As has been explained above, which of these effects operate, and which are dominant, depends on whether countries have fixed or flexible exchange rates. To see this we illustrate these spillover effects specifically for monetary policy in a modified version of the Mundell–Fleming model. This will be done under the alternative assumptions of fixed and flexible exchange rates. To illustrate the various spillover effects associated with monetary policy we make use of the so called IS/LM model. (This model is presented in most intermediate macroeconomic textbooks. If, however, the reader is unfamiliar with this model the rest of this section may be omitted.)

The basic two-country Mundell–Fleming model makes a number of simplifying assumptions. Significantly it assumes that both countries are small. It is this assumption that we modify and assume instead that both countries are large. Only with this modification can spillover effects be modelled, and the issue of policy co-ordination discussed. All other assumptions of the Mundell–Fleming model, however, are maintained. In particular, we assume that there is perfect capital mobility, and that increases in aggregate demand lead to an expansion in national income rather than wage and price inflation.

Figs. 8.1 and 8.2 illustrate the spillover effects following an expansionary monetary policy by one of two large countries. The first diagram corresponds to when both countries maintain a fixed exchange rate, and the second is when they allow the exchange rate to be completely flexible. Initially the effects of the monetary expansion are the same under each of these policy regimes. Prior to the change in monetary policy both countries are assumed to be in equilibrium at point A in both diagrams. Only at this point are the goods market and money market simultaneously in equilibrium. In country A the rate of interest (r) and national income (Y) are initially r_0 and Y_0 respectively. Similarly in country B they initially equal r^*_0 and Y^*_0. We now suppose that country A expands its domestic money supply. This is represented by the LM curve for that economy shifting to the right from LM_0 to LM_1. The increase in the money supply will cause the domestic rate of interest to fall, and this stimulates investment and aggregate demand. This leads to an increase in national income in country A, as shown by the economy moving to point B, where the new LM curve cuts IS_0. Output expands to Y_1 and the domestic rate of interest falls to r_1. As this economy is large the expansion in country A's domestic money supply will also lead to a significant increase in the world money supply. This will cause a fall in the world rate of interest. This reduction, however, will be less than the fall in the domestic rate of interest. We assume that the world rate of interest only falls to r_2. At point B, therefore, the domestic rate of interest is below the world rate of interest and so country A experiences an incipient balance-of-payments deficit. As national income in country A has increased, we assume that it also increases its demand for imports. In this two-country model this is equivalent to an increase in the demand for goods from country B. This real income effect is depicted by country B's IS curve shifting from IS_0^* to IS^*_1. This causes country B to adjust to point B with both a higher national income and interest rate. At this point the foreign rate of interest is above the world rate of interest. Country B will, therefore, experience an incipient balance-of-payments surplus. At point B neither country has balance-of-payments equilibrium. This disequilibrium will induce further adjustment and spillover effects, the nature of which depends on the exchange rate regime between the two countries.

Fixed exchange rates

With a fixed exchange rate, adjustment towards long-run equilibrium occurs via monetary effects. This effect is shown in Fig. 8.1. At point B country A is running a balance-of-payments deficit. In order to stop its exchange rate from depreciating the monetary authorities in that country must buy its domestic currency and sell foreign exchange. This will reduce the amount of high-power money in that economy and cause a multiple contraction in the domestic money supply. This is shown by a leftward shift of the

LM curve. In country B this process is reversed causing its domestic money supply to increase and its *LM* curve to shift to the right. These adjustments continue until both economies return to long-run equilibrium at point C. At this point both countries experience balance-of-payments equilibrium, and their domestic rates of interest equal the world rate of interest. With balance-of-payments equilibrium neither country need intervene any further in foreign exchange markets and so each country's domestic money supply remains unchanged.

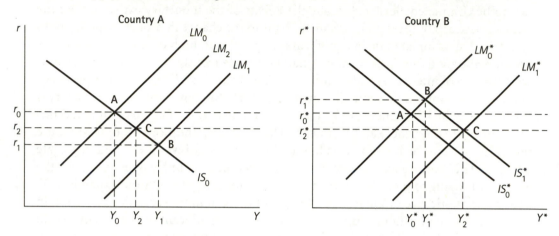

Fig. 8.1 Expansionary Monetary Policy with Fixed Exchange Rates

Flexible exchange rates

With a fully flexible exchange rate, adjustment towards the long-run equilibrium occurs via a change in relative prices. This effect is shown in Fig. 8.2. At point B country A is running an incipient balance-of-payments deficit. With flexible exchange rates country A's currency will depreciate. Similarly, country B's currency will appreciate. This change in the terms of trade makes country A's goods more competitive and country B's goods less competitive. With no adjustment lags this will cause the demand for country A's goods to increase, and its IS curve to shift to the right. In country B aggregate demand falls and its IS curve shifts to the left. These adjustments continue until both economies are in long-run equilibrium at point C.

The previous examples have illustrated the possible spillover effects associated with expansionary monetary policy. In particular, with fixed exchange rates expansionary monetary policy in country A leads to increased national income in both countries. Assuming this increases welfare in country B we can state there is a *positive spillover effect* from country A to country B. This contrasts with the result derived under flexible exchange rates where an expansionary monetary policy in country A, reduces national income in country B. This is a typical example of a beggar-my-neighbour policy. With welfare being reduced in country B, we have a *negative spillover effect* from country A. Although these example are useful in highlighting various possibilities it is important

172

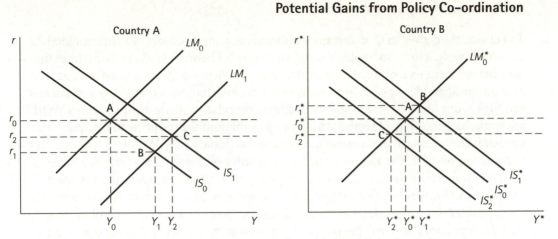

Fig. 8.2 Expansionary Monetary Policy with Flexible Exchange Rates

to realize that these results are model-specific. With a different set of assumptions these spillover effects may be negated or reversed.

8.2 Potential Gains from Policy Co-ordination

The previous section has illustrated how large countries typically face positive or negative spillover effects associated with aggregate demand policy. This causes economies to be mutually interdependent. In this context if each country sets its own monetary policy unilaterally, then there is the possibility that the final outcome will be Pareto inefficient. This will occur when government's have more policy objectives than policy instruments. If government's have at least as many independent instruments as

---

EXERCISE 8.1

In the text we illustrated the possible spillover effects associated with an expansionary monetary policy. This exercise shows how these spillover effects apply when a government adopts an expansionary fiscal policy.

(1) Using the modified Mundell–Fleming model presented in the text, illustrate the spillover effects when one country pursues an expansionary fiscal policy under fixed exchange rates.

(2) Repeat (1) under the assumption of flexible exchange rates.

---

objectives, then they can, if certain conditions are met, achieve all their objectives simultaneously. This is an application of Tinbergen's Theorem (1952) which states that for a government to achieve all of its independent policy objectives it must have at least as many independent policy instruments. In an international context government's can, in theory, offset adverse spillover effects originating from other nations. With fewer instruments than objectives this is not possible and the resulting inefficiency may be characterized by either expansionary or contractionary bias. Which of these occurs depends on whether the spillover effects are positive or negative, and the objectives of the government's involved. International policy co-ordination offers the prospect of increasing the welfare of all countries involved by taking the spillover effects explicitly into consideration when determining each country's optimal monetary policy. To discuss these possibilities we focus on a static two-country model and make use of the so called Hamada (1974, 1976, 1979) diagrams. Initially we examine an example where the final competitive outcome exhibits *recessionary bias*. We then consider an example of *expansionary bias*. Both examples assume that the exchange rate between the two countries is fixed.

8.2.1 Recessionary bias

To illustrate the possibility of recessionary bias we assume that both countries have two policy objectives but only one policy instrument. The policy objectives are assumed to relate to an optimal level of national income, and an optimal balance-of-payments surplus. This second objective assumes that for some reason both countries seek to accumulate foreign currency reserves, at least in the short run. The policy instrument is again assumed to be monetary policy, specifically related to the growth rate of the domestic money supply. Fig. 8.3 shows the Hamada diagram derived under these assumptions.

On the horizontal axis is the growth rate of the money supply in the domestic economy, $\overset{0}{M}{}^{s}$. On the vertical axis is the growth rate of the money supply in the foreign country, $\overset{0}{M}{}^{s*}$. With spillover effects a country's welfare will be determined by the policy stance within both countries. In particular the only way that either country can achieve a balance-of-payments surplus is for its money supply to expand slower than the other country's. Clearly, in this two-country model both countries cannot simultaneously run a balance-of-payments surplus. This represents a serious conflict of interest. This is illustrated by having separate bliss points for each country. A country's bliss point is the outcome of monetary growth rates that gives that country its highest possible level of welfare. The bliss point for the domestic country is at point B. This is above the 45° line, implying that ideally it desires the other country to have the faster rate of monetary expansion. This will secure the desired balance-of-payments surplus for the home nation. Similarly the bliss point for the foreign nation is at point B*. This is below the 45° line, again because it desires that the other country have the faster rate of monetary

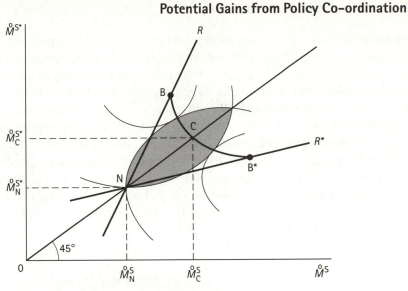

Fig. 8.3 Recessionary Bias

expansion. The further away each country is from its own bliss point the lower its economic welfare. Each country's set of indifference curves are therefore concentric around its bliss point. A number of these are shown in Fig. 8.3. With each nation ignoring the spillover effects associated with its own monetary policy we would expect this situation to lead to Pareto inefficiency. This can be confirmed from Fig. 8.3.

With no policy co-ordination each country will attempt to maximize its own welfare, taking the other country's monetary policy as given. This implies that each country seeks to be on its own reaction function. These are shown for the domestic and foreign countries as R and R^* respectively. For the domestic country its reaction function cuts its indifference curves where they are horizontal. This curve, therefore, shows where domestic welfare is maximized for variations in foreign monetary policy. For the foreign country its reaction function cuts its indifference curves where they are vertical. Both these reaction functions are upward-sloping. For a Nash equilibrium both countries must be simultaneously maximizing their own welfare, given the expected behaviour of the other nation. This only occurs at point N where the two reaction functions intersect. Here both countries set an identical growth rate for their money supply, and their balance of payments are in equilibrium.

Although neither country can improve on this Nash equilibrium acting independently, if they co-ordinate their monetary policies, both can be made better off. This is because the Nash equilibrium is Pareto inefficient. Diagramatically this is demonstrated by noting that at this equilibrium the two countries, indifference curves are not tangential. At any point within the shaded area of Fig. 8.3 both countries are better off compared to point N. For an outcome to be Pareto efficient the two countries' indifference curves must be tangential. The set of these outcomes is represented by the *contract curve* which joins the two bliss points. It may be supposed that policy co-ordination would seek to avoid Pareto inefficiency and so produce an outcome on this curve. With identical countries an obvious focal point for co-ordination is point C. At this point the two countries have identical monetary policies, and neither country has a balance-of-payments deficit or surplus. Compared to the Nash equilibrium this co-operative outcome involves the two countries increasing the growth rate of their money supply. From this perspective it can be seen that the Nash equilibrium exhibits a recessionary bias. This outcome is due to the competitive attempt by each country to run a balance-of-payments surplus. From point C each country has the incentive to reduce the growth rate of its money supply so as to try to improve its balance-of-payments position. However, with both countries ignoring the adverse effects its policy has on the other nation the resulting Nash equilibrium makes both countries worse off. Co-ordination is beneficial because it is able to avoid the adverse effects associated with such beggar-my-neighbour policies.

8.2.2 Expansionary bias

In order to illustrate the alternative possibility of expansionary bias we need only make a minor modification to the previous model. This is done by now assuming that both countries desire a balance-of-payments deficit rather than a surplus. All other assumptions remain unchanged. The Hamada diagram for this model is shown in Fig. 8.4.

With each country now desiring a balance-of-payments deficit, they will seek to have a greater monetary growth rate than the other country. The domestic country's bliss point (B) is now below the 45° line, and the foreign country's bliss point (B*) above the 45° line. With separate bliss points we again have a conflict of interest. The domestic country's reaction curve is shown as R, and the foreign country's reaction curve is R^*.

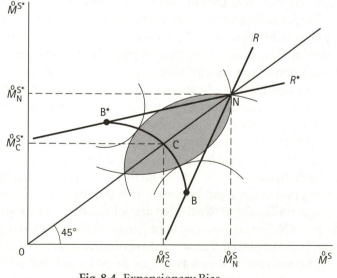

Fig. 8.4 Expansionary Bias

The Nash equilibrium is where these two curves intersect at point N. Once more this can be seen to be Pareto inefficient, with any point within the shaded region making both countries better off. Again the focal point for co-ordination is point C, which is the unique symmetrical Pareto-efficient outcome. Compared to this outcome the Nash equilibrium now involves both countries setting too fast a growth rate for their domestic money supply. This occurs as each country seeks to bid up the growth rate of its money supply, whilst again ignoring the adverse effects this has on the other country. In this situation such beggar-my-neighbour policy leads to an expansionary bias.

EXERCISE 8.2

Using the two-country Hamada diagrams presented in the text illustrate the following two scenarios. In each case state whether the Nash equilibrium is Pareto inefficient.

(1) There are no spillover effects between the two countries.

(2) There are spillover effects but the bliss points of the two countries coincide.

(3) There are spillover effects but each country has only one policy objective.

8.3 Problems of International Policy Co-ordination

The previous section presented examples where countries are motivated to overcome Pareto inefficiency by co-ordinating their economic policies rather than acting unilaterally. Despite the potential welfare gains of such co-ordination there are a number of problems that need to be overcome before these gains are realized. In this section we look at why these problems arise and how they might be overcome.

8.3.1 Sustainability

One of the major problems identified for international policy co-ordination is whether the agreed outcome is sustainable. As can be seen from the previous Hamada diagrams, all points on the contract curve, except at the bliss points, lie off both countries' reaction curves. Indeed, any agreement that co-ordinates monetary policy on a point other than the Nash equilibrium necessarily implies that at least one country has an incentive to renege upon the agreement. Once it is realized that countries have an incentive to renege upon the agreement no country will enter into policy co-ordination. In the static games considered in section 8.2 it appears that the only outcome can be the Nash equilibrium. This problem of sustainability is also relevant to dynamic games. In this context the problem is that of *time-inconsistency*. This issue was previously discussed in section 6.3 and arises when a government has the short-run incentive to deviate from its long-run optimal policy. In Figs. 8.3 and 8.4. the government's optimal long-run policy is associated with policy co-ordination at point C. However, as in the static model, government's may have a short-run incentive to deviate from this outcome. This problem is particularly severe when the game is known to be played only a finite number of times. In this situation backward induction predicts that all countries will pursue the Nash equilibrium every time-period, as this is the only subgame perfect Nash equilibrium for this game. This prediction appears to rule out the possibility of effective policy co-ordination. Fortunately a number of ways have been suggested for how government might overcome this problem of sustainability. Most of these proposals are closely related to those discussed when considering the time-inconsistency of domestic monetary policy. These include the importance of precommitment, an effective punishment strategy against countries that break international agreements (implemented either by other governments or the private sector), and countries being concerned with maintaining a favourable reputation for co-operation. In the context of international monetary policy one type of precommitment has received considerable attention. This is the situation where one country acts as the leader and then other countries follow its lead. This proposal is qualitatively the same as the Stackelberg model of duopoly presented in Chapter 4. Fig. 8.5 illustrates the outcome of this model for the example of recessionary bias discussed in the previous section. In this example both countries maintain a fixed exchange rate and desire a balance-of-payments surplus.

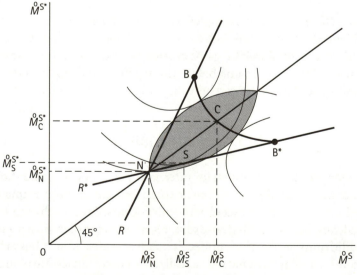

Fig. 8.5 Stackelberg Equilibrium

In this diagram the domestic country acts as the leader and the foreign country is the follower. As in the Stackelberg model of duopoly the leader sets its monetary policy at the point where its indifference curve is tangential to the other country's reaction curve. It, therefore, sets its monetary growth rate equal to $\overset{0}{\hat{M}}{}^S_S$. The follower then set its monetary policy consistent with this point. Its growth rate is therefore equal to $\overset{0}{\hat{M}}{}^{S*}_S$. As illustrated in Fig. 8.5 the leader will be made better off compared to the Nash equilibrium. The follower, however, may be made better or worse off depending on the structure of the model. Even if the follower is made better off the gains from such an arrangement are unlikely to be equally divided. As a result there will, in general, be some conflict over who should be the leader, which may cause this equilibrium to be unsustainable. Even if this equilibrium is maintained it is only a partial solution to the problem of time-inconsistency as it still yields a Pareto-inefficient outcome.

8.3.2 Inflationary bias

Another potential problem with the co-ordination of monetary policy is that it can worsen the inflationary bias within each country. If the costs associated with this increased domestic inflation outweigh the gains due to policy co-ordination, countries will prefer to act unilaterally. As discussed in Chapter 6 a country can experience inflationary bias if its optimal long-run monetary policy is time-inconsistent. Rogoff (1985) showed that policy co-ordination may increase the government's incentive to deviate from its optimal monetary policy. If this is perceived by the private sector, it will increase its inflationary expectations resulting in an increased level of equilibrium inflation. The reason the government has a greater incentive to deviate from its long-run optimal policy is because co-ordination can improve the trade-off facing the government over inflation and unemployment. Diagramatically the short-run Phillips curve becomes flatter under co-ordination as opposed to non-coordination. This can be explained as follows.

If one country expands its money supply in isolation, then its exchange rate will depreciate causing the cost of imports to rise, and this stimulates inflation. If, however, monetary policy is co-ordinated, and all countries expand their money supplies simultaneously, then the exchange rate effects are less severe and so inflation is tempered. The costs of expansionary monetary policy caused by higher inflation are less for a co-ordinated expansion of monetary policy than for an isolated expansion of monetary policy by one country. As the costs are lower, there is a greater incentive for the government to expand the money supply. Agents perceive this and so anticipate a faster growth rate of the money supply, and hence expect higher inflation. The optimal response for the government is then to produce this higher level of inflation. In equilibrium there is now a greater level of inflationary bias in the economy. This outcome is illustrated in Fig. 8.6. With no policy co-ordination the Nash equilibrium is at point A with

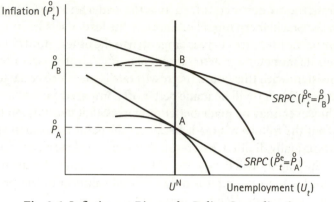

Fig. 8.6 Inflationary Bias under Policy Co-ordination

inflation equal to $\overset{o}{P}_A$. Under policy co-ordination the short-run Phillips curve is less steep and so the new Nash equilibrium is at point B with inflation equal to $\overset{o}{P}_B$.

8.3.3 Uncertainty

In our analysis so far we have assumed that all governments know the correct model of the economy. However, as governments typically base their forecasts on different models this assumption cannot be true. Furthermore, it is almost certainly true that no one knows the 'true' model of the economy. This basic uncertainty will clearly cause problems when governments attempt to co-ordinate their economic policies. With government's using different models they may be unable to agree on the most appropriate agreement, and negotiations may break down.

This issue of model uncertainty has been emphasized by Frenkel and Rockett (1988) who considered co-operation between the USA and other OECD countries. To represent model uncertainty they allowed each hypothetical policy-maker to choose one model from ten. Based on its chosen model the government then determines its optimal monetary policy. This gives a total combination of 100 policy formulations. Nature then chooses which of the ten models is actually true, giving a total of 1,000 possible combinations. Frenkel and Rockett then estimate whether there are potential gains from co-ordination in each of these possible scenarios. Their findings were that co-operation increased USA welfare in only 546 cases and improved welfare in the other industrialized countries in only 539 cases. In more than a third of the cases co-operation actually makes the countries worse off. These results, however, have been challenged by a number of authors. For example, Ghosh and Masson (1988) argue that these results depend on policy-makers acting irrationally. Instead of merely selecting one of the available models as true Ghosh and Masson argue that policy-makers will take uncertainty explicitly into account when formulating policies. This will involve two separate aspects. *First*, governments may view all the available models as being essentially plausible, and so base their policy proposals on some weighted average of their forecasts. *Second*, they may actively seek to learn which model, if any, is true. This will involve governments updating their beliefs about the true economic model using their observations of macroeconomic variables. Given these responses to model uncertainty the performance of economies with co-ordinated, rather than uncoordinated, policies improves substantially. Indeed, such arguments may actually reverse Frenkel and Rockett conclusions and suggest that the case of co-operation is strengthened given the presence of model uncertainty.

8.3.4 Reaction of other countries

A final problem associated with the policy co-ordination is that countries not involved in the policy agreement may react in such a way as to offset the gains from such an initiative. For example, if Europe and the USA jointly deflate their economies this will have an adverse effect on Japan's exports. As a consequence Japan may retaliate by using trade restrictions, with makes Europe and the USA worse off than if they had not agreed to deflate. The implication is that a set of countries cannot determine their optimal policies without determining how other countries will react. This complicates the process of deciding on which optimal policy combination to pursue, and may cause countries to act unilaterally.

8.4 Empirical Estimates of the Gains from Co-ordination

From the arguments outlined above it is clear that international policy co-ordination may enhance or reduce the economic welfare of the countries involved, and that ultimately this must be an empirical issue. The problem in this area is that direct comparison of the benefits of co-ordination against non-coordination is not possible. This is for the simple reason that a country cannot follow both policies simultaneously. In response to this problem empirical evidence of the gains from co-ordination have been estimated in one of two ways. The *first* approach uses simulation techniques based on *large-scale macroeconomic models*. These models are based on the econometric estimates of the main international spillover effects. In contrast the *second* method uses *small theoretical models* comprising only a few equations. In this approach parameter values are typically imposed on the model rather than econometrically estimated. With both approaches the economic welfare derived under the assumption of independent policy actions is contrasted with the co-operative outcome. Here we review a number of studies from each of these methodologies.

An early study that attempted to estimate the potential gains from policy co-ordination using an empirical macroeconomic model was undertaken by Oudiz and

International Policy Co-ordination

Sachs (1984). In this study Oudiz and Sachs estimate the potential welfare gains for the G3 nations (USA, Germany, and Japan) if they had co-ordinated their macroeconomic policies in the mid 1970s. This was done by initially computing each countries optimal policy consistent with the static Nash equilibrium and comparing this with the co-operative solution. In general the welfare gains were found to be small, with the estimated benefits for each country being approximately 0.5 per cent of gross national product (GNP) per year. Subsequent studies have tended to support these findings. For example, Hughes Hallet (1987) allowed for dynamic decision-making and estimated potential gains for USA, EEC, and Japanese co-ordination of between 0.5 and 1.5 of GNP. Other studies based on empirical models that report small gains from co-ordination include Canzoneri and Minford (1986), Currie, Levine and Vidalis (1987) and Minford and Canzoneri (1987).

Although employing a different methodology this result—that the gains from co-operation are generally small—has typically been confirmed by studies based on small theoretical models. One such study was undertaken by Currie and Levine (1985). Here the authors used a two-country model comprising eighteen equations. It was assumed that the spillover effects were constant and symmetric between the two countries. Once again the gains from co-operation are found to be small. Miller and Salmon (1985) use an even smaller theoretical model comprising only three equations per country. Interestingly in this model there is no long-run policy conflict between countries. This is because it was assumed that in the long run output returns to its natural rate and exchange rates are flexible. None the less policy co-ordination may result in net welfare gains by altering the adjustment path towards long-run equilibrium. Miller and Salmon report, however, that such gains are again only small. Other theoretical studies yielding similar results include Oudiz and Sachs (1985), Taylor (1985) and Levine and Currie (1987).

From these various studies it is reasonable to conclude that co-ordination can produce welfare gains, but that these gains are likely to be small. It needs to be stressed, however, that such results can only be indicative of the potential gains from co-ordination. In particular, these results should be viewed as tentative for two reasons. *First*, they are only as good as the models upon which they are based. This is particularly relevant here because one of the main international linkages is via the exchange rate, but this mechanism is generally poorly understood by economists. *Second*, these estimates typically assume that governments know the correct structure of the economy. As discussed previously, depending on how governments respond to model uncertainty, this may either enhance or detract from the gains from co-ordination.

8.5 Conclusions

The use of game theory to analyse policy co-ordination was initially undertaken in a series of seminal articles by Hamada (1974, 1976, 1979). Using simple symmetrical two-country models Hamada demonstrated that, given the presence of international spillover effects, the final outcome could be Pareto inefficient. This result implies that policy co-ordination may be used to overcome these inefficiencies. In recent years more complex models have been developed to test the robustness of this conclusion. In general these models have tended to qualify earlier results. For example, extending the model so that the policy game is not just between governments, but also against the respective private sectors, yields the result that policy co-ordination without government's having a strong reputation for being anti-inflationary, can worsen economic welfare. Similar results can be derived in models which incorporate model uncertainty, and the reaction of non-cooperating countries.

In addition to this theoretical research empirical estimates have been made to try and assess the importance of policy co-ordination. The finding of the majority of these models is that while gains from policy co-ordination do exist they are likely to be small. These estimates, however, are generally dependent on governments knowing the correct model of the global economy. Given the presence of model uncertainty, it is possible that the gains from policy co-ordination could be significantly enhanced. This is an important area of future research, which includes attempts to model how governments respond to model uncertainty, and seek to update their beliefs over time.

8.6 Solutions to Exercises

Exercise 8.1

(1) Fig. 8.7 depicts the situation when country A expands fiscal policy and maintains a fixed exchange rate with country B. Initially both countries are in long-run equilibrium at point A. When country A expands its fiscal policy its IS curve shifts from IS_0 to IS_1. This increases aggregate demand and both national income and the domestic rate of interest rise. With national income increasing the demand for imports from country B also rises. This stimulates aggregate demand in that country, and so its IS curve shifts from IS_0^* to IS_1^*. National income and interest rates correspondingly rise in country B. With national income rising in both countries world interest rates rise. This will be a weighted average of the two countries domestic interest rates, and we assume it is equal to r_2. From the diagram country A's interest rate is above the world rate of interest, and so that economy initially experiences a balance-of-payments surplus. The converse is true for country B, which experiences a balance-of-payments deficit at point B. Given this balance-of-payments disequilibrium the monetary authorities will need to intervene in the foreign exchange market in order to maintain the desired exchange rate. This will cause country A's money supply to expand and

country B's money supply to contract. Eventually, long-run equilibrium will be established at point C. In the diagram both countries' national income have risen following the expansionary fiscal policy in country A.

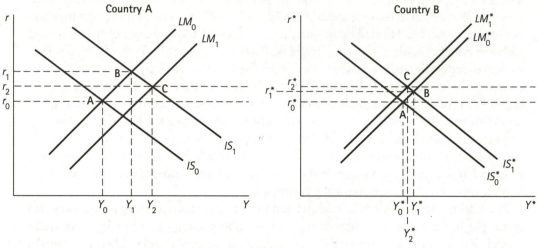

Fig. 8.7

(2) With flexible exchange rates the short-run analysis is identical to that discussed in (1). Initially both economies jump from point A to point B. This is replicated in Fig. 8.8. As with monetary policy the subsequent dynamics contrast with those experienced under fixed exchange rates. Now country A's currency appreciates, and country B's depreciates. This change in the terms of trade makes country A's goods less competitive and country B's more competitive. This causes country A's *IS* curve to shift to the left, and country B's *IS* curve to shift to the right. This continues until long-run equilibrium is established at point C. The diagram again depicts the situation where national income rises in both countries.

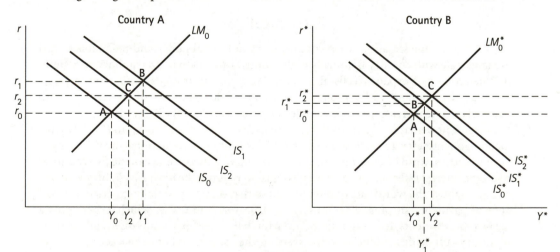

Fig. 8.8

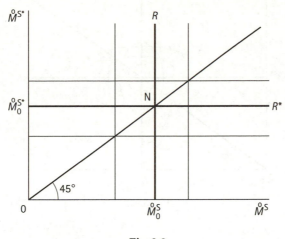

Fig. 8.9

Exercise 8.2

(1) With no spillover effects between countries each country's welfare is uniquely determined by its own monetary policy. In particular, changes in the other countries' money supply have no effect on domestic welfare. There is no longer a unique bliss point, but instead a bliss line. This is equivalent to that country's reaction function, and corresponds to that country's optimal monetary policy. In Fig. 8.9 the home country's optimal growth rate for its money supply is equal to $\overset{o}{M}{}^{S}_{0}$, and its reaction function is R. Similarly the foreign country's optimal growth rate is $\overset{o}{M}{}^{S*}_{0}$, and its reaction function is R^*. With no spillover effects the indifference curves are either horizontal or vertical. The Nash equilibrium (N) is where the two reaction functions intersect. At this equilibrium both countries obtain their greatest level of welfare by setting their optimal monetary policy. With no spillover effects there is no Pareto ineffi-ciency and no need for policy co-ordination.

(2) With spillover effects the indifference curves are no longer horizontal or vertical. However, with the countries' bliss points coinciding there is no inherent policy conflict. This is depicted in Fig. 8.10 as the point where the two countries' reaction functions intersect. (This diagram illustrates the special case where these curves are horizontal and vertical.) The indifference curves are concentric around this point. Again the Nash equilibrium is where the reaction functions intersect. As these must pass through the bliss points this is the Nash equilibrium. Once again the Nash equilibrium is Pareto efficient, and there is no need for policy co-ordination.

(3) With each country having the same number of independent policy instruments as targets they can, in these static models with complete information, achieve all their targets simul-taneously. Fig. 8.11 illustrates the case where each country has one target and one instru-ment. Even in the presence of spillover effects each country can achieve its policy objective by adjusting its own policy instrument. Thus the reaction curves depicted in Fig. 8.11 rep-resent the highest possible levels of welfare for each country. Where these two lines intersect

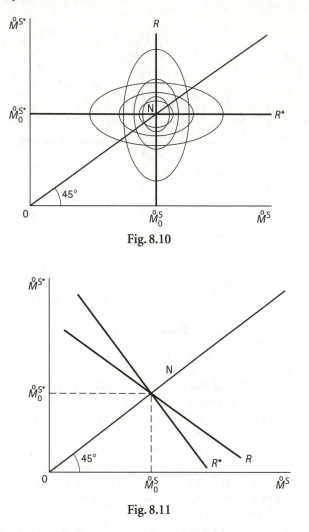

Fig. 8.10

Fig. 8.11

is the Nash equilibrium. With no policy conflict in equilibrium this equilibrium is again Pareto efficient.

Further Reading

Bladen-Hovell, R. C. (1992), 'International Monetary Policy', in K. Dowd and M. K. Lewis (eds.) *Current Issues in Financial and Monetary Economics*, London: Macmillan.

Buiter, W. H., and R. C. Marston (1985), *International Economic Policy Coordination*, Cambridge: Cambridge University Press.

Currie, D. A. (1990), 'International Policy Coordination', in D. T. Llewellyn and C. Milner (eds.), *Current Issues in International Monetary Economics*, London: Macmillan.

Currie, D. A., and P. Levine (1991), 'International Policy Coordination—A Survey', in C. J. Green and D. T. Llewellyn (eds.), *Surveys in Monetary Economics*, i, Oxford: Basil Blackwell; repr. in D. Currie and P. Levine (1993), *Rules, Reputation and Macroeconomic Policy*, Cambridge: Cambridge University Press.

Hallwood, C. P., and R. MacDonald (1994), *International Money and Finance*, Oxford: Blackwell.

Hughes Hallet, A. J. (1989), 'Macroeconomic Interdependence and the Coordination of Economic Policy', in D. Greenaway (ed.), *Current Issues in Macroeconomics*, London: Macmillan.

9
Strategic Trade Policy

T RADE policy is where the government of a country deliberately sets out to alter the pattern of international trade, so as to increase total domestic welfare, or the welfare of one particular sector in the economy. Strategic trade policy is when a government does this and explicitly takes into account the possible reactions of other agents that jointly determine the final outcome. This chapter analyses two broad ways in which governments can use strategic trade policy to enhance domestic welfare. The first is when international markets are perfectly competitive, and the second is when they are imperfect. As there are, as yet, no international organizations that can enforce agreements between nations, the analysis of strategic trade policy is best conducted using the tools of non-cooperative, rather than co-operative, game theory.

With perfect competition the case for government intervention in international trade is the well-known 'optimal tariff argument'. This argument is considered in section 9.1. Even if individual agents within an economy are all price-takers, the country itself, if large, can have significant market power. In this situation governments may exploit the country's market power via trade restrictions. This can improve the country's terms of trade and ultimately its economic welfare at the expense of other countries. When two or more countries engage in such beggar-my-neighbour policies, we have strategic interaction in the game theory sense. The first formal model of strategic tariff-setting was by Johnson (1954). He considered the situation of two countries simultaneously setting a one-off tariff, and showed the prisoners' dilemma result may apply with both countries being made worse off in the absence of co-operation. This analysis has been extended in a number of directions in recent years and presented using game theory analysis.

In section 9.2 we focus on more recent arguments for why governments might seek to influence international trade. These agruments derive from the observation that many international markets are imperfect and oligopolistic. In this context governments may be able to improve the competitive position of domestic firms by committing itself to a particular trade policy. For such trade policy to be strategic the government must consider the actions of either foreign firms, foreign governments, or both. This theory of strategic trade policy in the presence of oligopolistic competition was initially developed by Brander and Spencer (1983, 1984, 1985), and again has been extended in a number of directions.

9.1 Perfect Competition

9.1.1 The optimal tariff argument and retaliation

The optimal tariff argument is that a government a of large economy can improve domestic welfare by exploiting the country's market power in international trade. This is accomplished by imposing import tariffs which improve the country's terms of trade. This can be illustrated using the partial equilibrium diagram in Fig. 9.1.

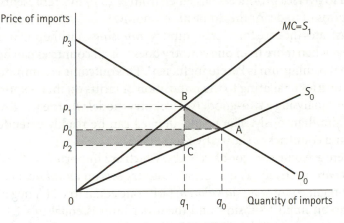

Fig. 9.1 The Optimal Tariff Argument

In this diagram the demand and supply curves for an imported good, before the imposition of a tariff, are D_0 and S_0 respectively. The supply curve is upward-sloping denoting that the country in question is large, and so collectively has a degree of market power. Under perfect competition, individuals acting in isolation ignore their influence on price and so continue to import the good until demand equals supply at point A. The government, however, by setting the optimal tariff can induce individuals to act as if they were a monopsonist and so raise total welfare. From the supply curve a monopsonist realizes that as it increases its purchase of imports, the price charged on all imports of that good rises. This means that the marginal cost curve, MC, lies above the supply curve, S_0. In this situation a monopsonist buys imports only up to the point where demand equals marginal cost at point B. The government can induce identical behaviour by imposing an *ad valorem* import tariff on the good. With an *ad valorem* tariff a proportion of the import price is now paid to the government. To offset this additional cost the exporter of the good will demand a higher proportionate price for each quantity it sells, and so the supply curve pivots upwards. With the optimal tariff being set the new supply curve S_1 will be identical to the monopsonist's marginal cost curve, MC.

Strategic Trade Policy

To measure the welfare implications for the domestic country we look at changes in consumer surplus and government revenue before and after the imposition of the tariff. For the domestic economy consumer surplus has been reduced from p_3Ap_0 to p_3Bp_1, but this is compensated by the increase in government revenue equal to p_1BCp_2. Domestic welfare increases as $(p_0 - p_2).q_1$ is greater than $1/2(p_1 - p_0)(q_0 - q_1)$. These are shown as the two shaded regions in Fig. 9.1. This increase in domestic welfare is at the expense of a fall in producer surplus accruing to foreign exporters. This is reduced from $0p_0A$ to $0p_2C$, and so foreign producer surplus falls by the amount p_0ACp_2. Global welfare is also reduced as measured by the dead-weight loss given by area ABC. Finally, as the price paid to oversea producers has fallen from p_0 to p_1 this represents an improvement in the terms of trade for the domestic economy.

Fig. 9.1 illustrates the case for a large country imposing a tariff upon its imports. The problem is that when more than one country does this all countries can be made worse off and the final equilibrium is Pareto inefficient. This outcome is commonly associated with other countries retaliating to the imposition of tariffs on their exports. We examine this issue by analysing a two-good, two-country model where each government sets its tariff rate simultaneously. The results derived can be readily extended to include many goods and countries as shown by Kuga (1973).

Assume there are only two goods, x and y, which are imported by the domestic and foreign country respectively. The domestic country sets an *ad valorem* tariff rate equal to *t* and the foreign country an *ad valorem* tariff rate equal to t^*. (A negative tariff rate corresponds to an import subsidy, and the lower limit is equal to –1.) The national prices of the two goods are related by the following equations

$$p_X = p_X^*(1 + t)$$
$$p_Y^* = p_Y(1 + t^*),$$

(9.1)

where p_X and p_Y are the domestic prices of goods x and y respectively, and p_X^* and p_Y^* are their prices in the foreign country. The relative price of the two goods on world markets is $p = p_x^*/p_Y$. An increase in p means that domestic imports are more expensive, and so the terms of trade have deteriorated. Each country's level of imports is determined by the terms of trade and its own tariff rate. Let $M(p, t)$ and $M^*(p, t^*)$ represent the domestic and foreign import functions. The balance of trade condition is

$$p.M(p, t) = M^*(p, t),$$

(9.2)

which determines p as a function of the two tariff rates. We assume that this function is continuous and differentiable. We also assume that an increase in either countries' tariff rate improves the terms of trade for that country, i.e. $dp/dt < 0$ and $dp/dt^* > 0$. This assumption is satisfied if the Marshall–Lerner condition is fulfilled, and all tariff revenue is redistributed to consumers. (The Marshall–Lerner condition is that the sum of import and export elasticities is greater than one.) The pay-offs to each country are given by the domestic and foreign social welfare functions $W = W(t, t^*)$ and $W^* = W^*(t, t^*)$. With these assumptions each country's welfare is reduced by an increase in the other country's tariff rate. We further assume that each country's welfare function has a unique maximum as its own tariff rate increases from zero, given the other country's tariff rate. The indifference curves corresponding to these social welfare functions are drawn in Fig. 9.2.

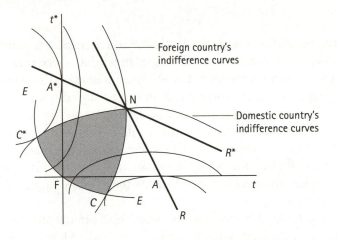

Fig. 9.2 Optimal Tariffs and Nash Equilibria

In this diagram the domestic country's welfare increases as we move downwards, and the foreign country's welfare increases as we move to the left. The diagram also shows each country's reaction curve, which gives us the country's optimal tariff corresponding to any tariff set in the other country. R is the domestic country's reaction curve, and R^* is the foreign country's reaction curve. We finally assume that these reaction curves are downward-sloping and cross only once.

As discussed above, the traditional optimal tariff argument assumes that only one country imposes an import tariff, so as to exploit its market power and maximize social welfare. If the foreign country abstains from setting a tariff, the optimal tariff for the domestic country is given at point A. In contrast, if the domestic country abstains from setting a tariff, the optimal tariff for the foreign country is given at point A^*. In the simultaneous game being played, neither of these outcomes is a Nash equilibrium, as the country setting zero tariffs is off its reaction curve. One Nash equilibrium is where the two reaction curves cross. Here both countries set positive tariff rates on imports. This equilibria is, however, Pareto inefficient, as at this point the two country's indifference curves cut each other rather than being tangential. Pareto efficiency requires that all mutually advantageous trade is undertaken, which implies that, through the process of arbitrage, relative prices in the two countries must be the same. That is

$$\frac{p_x}{p_y} = \frac{p_x^*}{p_y^*}.$$

Using equations (9.1), and the definition of the terms of trade, this can be rewritten as

$$\frac{p_x^*(1+t)}{p_y} = \frac{p_x^*}{P_y(1+t^*)}$$

$$\therefore \quad p(1+t) = \frac{p}{(1+t^*)}$$

$$\therefore \quad (1+t).(1+t^*) = 1.$$

This Pareto-efficient loci is shown by the contract curve *EE*. Along this contract curve the two countries indifference curves are tangential, which means that along this curve one country cannot be made better off without making the other country worse off. The shaded area in Fig. 9.2 corresponds to Pareto-superior outcomes as compared with point N. Co-operation, if it leads to tariffs being set within this shaded region, or on the contract curve itself between *C* and *C**, will make at least one country better off and the other country no worse off. One problem, however, is that there are an infinite number of Pareto-efficient outcomes, that make both countries at least as well off as at point N. This raises the problem of which of these many points countries should attempt to co-ordinate upon.

One suggestion is that the final outcome is derived from the process of countries systematically reducing tariff rates over a number of periods. Mayer (1981) considers formulae for reducing tariffs similar to those that have been used in previous GATT negotiations, such as the Kennedy and Tokyo Rounds. For example, one suggested formula is that starting from point N each country reduces its tariff rate by some equal proportion. This proportional cut is the largest possible, whilst leaving both countries better off. These new tariff rates then become the subject for the next round of negotiation. This process continues until no more Pareto improvements are possible. The appeal of this suggestion is that it is simplistic, and does seem to have been used in practice. One problem is that different proposed formulae have different effects on countries' welfare, and so bargaining is shifted from choosing a point in Fig. 9.2 to choosing an appropriate formula for reducing tariffs. A more fundamental problem is that, in general, all formulae are time-inconsistent. Once agreed upon at least one country will have an incentive to deviate from it. This is relevant here because as yet GATT does not have the authority to enforce such agreements.

An alternative method of predicting the outcome of co-operation is to note that an obvious focal point for co-ordination is that of free trade at point F. (Free trade need not always be Pareto superior to point N. This will only occur if the two countries are similar. Johnson (1954) shows that the country with the greatest import elasticity is more likely to prefer the Nash equilibrium at point N to free trade. Kennan and Riezman (1988) show that larger countries may also prefer this Nash equilibrium.) However, even if countries agree upon free trade as being the focal point for co-operation the problem still remains of how countries can be induced to observe it. Subsection 9.1.2 examines this issue, and in particular discusses how countries might pursue free trade, even though in the above static game both countries have an incentive to set positive tariffs.

EXERCISE 9.1

Redraw Fig. 9.2 assuming that only one of the two countries has any market power. What is the Nash equilibrium involving international trade for this static two-country/two-good model? Is this outcome Pareto efficient?

9.1.2 Free trade as a non-cooperative outcome

In the static tariff game analysed above free trade is not an equilibrium. However, as seen in previous chapters repeated interaction between players opens up the possibility of non-cooperative collusion, which in this context may result in countries pursuing free trade policies. We first consider the situation when such repetition is infinite or indefinite, and countries discount future returns by the factor δ. This discount factor either reflects countries' pure rate of time-preference, or includes the probability that interaction will cease at the end of the current period. From the Folk Theorem, as discussed in Chapter 4, we know that all rational and feasible outcomes can be sustained as a subgame perfect Nash equilibrium if the discount factor is not too small, and players adopt appropriate punishment strategies. If the discount factor is equal to one, i.e. countries do not discount future returns at all, then all the points in the shaded region of Fig. 9.2 can be sustained as a subgame perfect Nash equilibrium. Although there is clearly the problem of multiple equilibria this will not be too serious in this context if, as argued before, the free trade equilibrium acts as a focal point for all countries.

If the discount factor is not sufficiently large to maintain free trade as a subgame perfect Nash equilibrium, then an alternative punishment strategy must be sought that increases the costs of deviating from free trade. This will involve either increasing the length of the punishment period, or increasing the severity of the punishment within each period. The limit to the first option is to impose an infinite punishment period if deviation from free trade is observed. This is where the countries adopt a trigger strategy. This will reduce the required size of the countries' discount factor, and so increase the likelihood that free trade can be supported as an equilibrium. The problem with the second alternative is that the punishment itself must be credible. One such credible threat is to play the Nash equilibrium associated with point N. There is, though, an alternative punishment strategy that countries can credibly commit themselves to. This can be seen by noting that autarky is another Nash equilibrium to the static game analysed above. This was first noted by Dixit (1987). If one country sets its tariff so high that its imports are reduced to zero, then the outcome must be autarky, irrespective of the other country's tariff rate. Compared to the Nash equilibrium at point N autarky makes both countries worse off. As this is a Nash equilibrium it can form part of a credible punishment strategy. Using this as the punishment threat, a larger set of outcomes can be sustained as the equilibrium to the supergame compared with the alternative of using the Nash equilibrium at point N.

Although free trade might be sustainable if interaction between governments is infinite or indefinite, the paradox of backward induction again applies if the interaction is of definite finite length. In this situation an alternative mechanism must be found to support free trade. As in other applications of game theory, the main suggestions have been concerned with multiple equilibria, incomplete information, and bounded rationality.

As noted above the static tariff game has *multiple equilibria*, one associated with point N in Fig. 9.2 and another associated with autarky. Benoit and Krishna (1985) show that this general property of multiple equilibria in the stage game gives rise to the possibility of non-cooperative collusion. We know that in the last period of interaction the outcome must be a Nash equilibrium. However, with multiple equilibria this is indeterminant. Countries can use this indeterminacy to credibly induce other countries to pursue free trade in previous periods. For example, consider the static tariff game being played twice, and countries adopting the following punishment strategy:

> **Set a zero tariff initially. If free trade was observed in the first period then set tariffs associated with the Nash equilibrium at point N in Fig. 9.2 in the second period. Otherwise set the tariff rate so that imports are reduced to zero.**

The present value of national welfare of pursuing free trade in the first period with the expectation that other countries will follow the above punishment strategy is

$$V(F) + \delta V(N),$$

where $W(F)$ is the value of the social welfare under free trade, and $W(N)$ its value when the Nash equilibrium at point N occurs. In contrast the present value of welfare of not pursuing free trade in the first period is

$$V(D) + \delta V(A),$$

where $V(D)$ and $V(A)$ equal the value of the social welfare when that country deviates from free trade and autarky respectively. Countries will set zero tariffs in the first period if

$$V(F) + \delta V(N) \geq V(D) + \delta V(A)$$

$$\therefore \delta \geq \frac{V(D) - V(F)}{V(N) - V(A)}.$$

As $V(D) > V(F) > V(N) > V(A)$ this condition is satisfied provided countries do not discount the future too much. Extending the number of periods that countries interact, and assuming countries adopt appropriate punishment strategies, free trade can be sustained for a greater number of periods with a smaller discount factor.

An alternative approach in which free trade might be sustained in early periods of repeated interaction is by introducing *incomplete information* as shown by Kreps and Wilson (1982*a*). Suppose it is common knowledge there is a small probability that countries will always pursue free trade, perhaps due to ideological reasons. It is then rational for each country to encourage other countries initially to believe this about itself by setting zero tariffs in early periods of interaction. In this way free trade is sustained as part of a sequential equilibrium in all but the last few periods of interaction.

Finally, free trade might be sustained if countries are rational but only in a limited way, i.e. we introduce *bounded rationality*. As discussed in Chapter 3, Radner (1980) allows players to play suboptimal strategies as long as the pay-off per period is within ε of the optimal strategy. If the number of repetitions is large enough, then pursuing free trade can be an ε-equilibrium given that countries adopt appropriate punishment strategies.

9.1.3 Conjectural variations

Before leaving this topic of optimal tariff-setting, the conjectural variation approach taken by Thursby and Jensen (1983) deserves some discussion as it purports to show that tariffs will not be set at so high a rate as suggested by the previous static game analysis. This approach attempts to model the dynamics associated with tariff wars, where countries might reasonably expect other countries to react if they change their own tariff rates. For example, countries might expect retaliation if they increase their own tariffs. Conversely, they might expect other countries to follow them if they reduce their tariff rates. Thursby and Jensen model these beliefs by linking t^* with t and vice versa, via the conjectural variations $dt^*/dt > 0$ and $dt/dt^* > 0$. This implies that the reaction functions in Fig. 9.2 shift downwards as shown in Fig. 9.3.

The reason the reaction functions are downward-sloping is that they now cut the country's indifferent curves where they have the same slope as the value of the conjectural variation. (Figure 9.2 is the special case where the conjectural variations are set

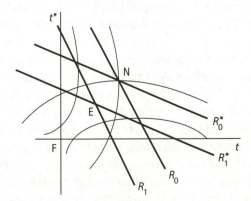

Fig. 9.3 A Conjectural Variation Equilibrium

equal to zero.) The equilibrium given these positive conjectural variations is where the new reaction curves intersect. This is at point E in Fig. 9.3. As drawn, tariffs are set lower than the Nash equilibrium at point N.

There are two serious problems that cause us to reject this approach in favour of the previous analysis. *First*, it is *ad hoc* to impose a positive value for the conjectural variations into the model. Instead, conjectures should be determined in a way that is consistent with the underlying structure of the model so that a rational conjectural variations equilibrium is determined. Bresnahan (1981) has shown, in the context of duopoly, that such rational conjectures will normally be negative, and so the resulting equilibrium for this model will involve higher, not lower, tariffs compared with point N. A *second* and more fundamental problem with this approach is that conjectural variations are inconsistent with the underlying nature of the static game. The reason for this is that it is impossible for any country to *react* in static games. This criticism is the same as that made against Cournot's disequilibrium analysis of oligopoly discussed in Chapter 4. In order to analyse countries' reactions in a consistent way the underlying game itself must be dynamic. This has already been examined in the above analysis of repeated interaction between countries.

9.2 Imperfect Competition

The previous section analysed the role of strategic trade policy when there is perfect competition in all markets in the sense that consumers and producers are all price-takers. In this situation firms earn normal profits and the only market power that exists is between countries. The optimal tariff argument is that governments can exploit this market power so as to increase national welfare. In this section we examine the possibility of welfare-enhancing trade policy when individual producers have market power, and industries are oligopolistic.

If an industry is characterized as oligopolistic, firms in that industry will typically be earning economic rent. This does not necessarily mean that firms are earning super-normal profits. Economic rent may be captured by the employees in the form of wages being above the minimum amount necessary to keep the workers in that firm, or by the government via increased taxation. As long as it is not distributed overseas increased economic rent earned by domestic firms increases domestic welfare. The insight of Brander and Spencer (1983,1984,1985), in a series of influential papers, was that the government, via strategic trade policy, might be able to improve the competitive position of domestic firms against foreign rivals. This raises the possibility of increasing the amount of economic rent domestic firms secure and, hence, national welfare. In effect economic rent is being transferred from other countries to the domestic economy and are therefore called *rent-shifting policies*. To analyse these policies we initially examine a simple model of Cournot duopoly, and then discuss various extensions.

9.2.1 Strategic trade policy with Cournot duopoly

The simplest example of a rent-shifting trade policy is in a two-period model. In the first period the government commits itself to a particular trade policy, such as an export subsidy or tax. In the second period domestic and foreign firms compete against each other. Let us assume that there is only one domestic and one foreign firm in a particular industry, and that they Cournot compete. In order to facilitate comparison with results derived in Chapter 4 we use the same specific demand and supply assumptions made in section 4.1. The two firms produce an identical product, and each firm produces its desired level of output without knowing the level of output the other firm has produced. The market price is determined so that the total quantity of the good produced, Q, is just demanded, according to the equation $P(Q) = a - Q$. There are assumed to be constant marginal production costs equal to c and no fixed costs. Each firm is assumed to maximize profits. We also assume that they sell all their output in a third country. This final assumption is made so that the effects on consumer surplus can be ignored.

From section 4.1 we know that in the absence of strategic trade policy each firm will produce an output equal to $(a - c)/3$ where the two firm's reaction functions intersect. This is illustrated in Fig. 9.4 where q and q^* represent the domestic and foreign firms' output, and R_0 and R_0^* their reaction curves in the absence of government trade policy. The equations for these reaction curve are: $q = (a - q^* - c)/2$ and $q^* = (a - q - c)/2$.

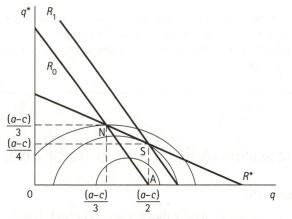

Fig. 9.4 Trade Policy with Cournot Competition

As shown by the isoprofit lines, if the domestic firm could commit itself to producing a higher level of output, then it could increase its level of economic rent by moving down the foreign firm's reaction function R^*. If such commitment were possible, profits would be maximized at point S, the Stackelberg equilibrium. The problem is that there is no credible way the domestic firm can commit itself to an output level off its own reaction curve. However, the government setting an appropriate trade policy in the first period can provide the needed precommitment. This can be seen by noting that the domestic firm's reaction function depends on its level of marginal costs. The government can in effect reduce these marginal costs by paying the firm an export subsidy for each unit of the good sold. This induces the domestic firm to increase production for each level of output produced by the foreign competitor. This is represented by the domestic firm's reaction function shifting to the right. With the optimal export subsidy the domestic firm's reaction function can be shifted so that it intersects the foreign firm's reaction function at point S. This then becomes the equilibrium for the second period, and domestic rent is maximized, at the expense of foreign rent.

This and similar models have been used to explain and justify governments targeting specific industries for export promotion via the use of trade policies. For example, it has often been argued that French and Japanese governments have targeted certain sectors of their economies with the aim of giving them a competitive advantage over foreign competitors. However, both the theoretical results and the issues involved in practical implementation have been subject to a number of criticisms. These criticisms are now discussed as we look at various extensions to the basic Cournot duopoly model, presented above.

EXERCISE 9.2

For the two-period model analysed in the text above, derive the optimal levels of output each firm will produce and the unit export subsidy the government pays the domestic firm. By how much will domestic welfare increase in monetary terms as a result of the government paying this subsidy?

9.2.2 Extensions to the basic Cournot duopoly model

Domestic consumption

In the basic duopoly model analysed above it was assumed that there was no domestic consumption of the good in question. This simplified the analysis as it meant there were no changes in consumer surplus as a result of introducing export subsidies. This is no longer the case if there is domestic consumption of the subsidized good. With an export subsidy the domestic firm will switch sales from the domestic to the overseas market. This will raise the price of the good in the domestic economy, and so there will be a corresponding fall in consumer surplus. This exacerbates the already inherent market failure due to imperfect competition. This loss needs to be set against any gains from the trade policy, but it is now possible for there to be a net welfare loss for the economy as a whole.

An alternative policy in this situation would be for the country to pay a production subsidy rather than an export subsidy. With a production subsidy the effects on international markets are the same as before, but now the domestic consumers will also benefit as the firm will increase sales to the domestic market thus lowering the price domestic consumers have to pay. Domestic welfare increases by more than previously indicated in the basic model with an export subsidy.

Nature of competition between firms

The Cournot model of duopoly assumes that the two firms compete in terms of quantity produced. However, as discussed in Chapter 4, this is not the only way in which firms might compete. One alternative is the Bertrand assumption that firms compete in terms of price. Unfortunately the implications for trade policy are highly sensitive to the nature of competition between firms. The reason for this is that in the Cournot duopoly model an export subsidy is only welfare-enhancing because it causes the foreign firm to cut back on its production. Without this reduction in foreign sales, increased domestic sales would reduce the price of the good to such an extent that domestic profits would fall. The welfare effects, therefore, depend crucially upon the reaction of the foreign firm to the imposition of a domestic subsidy. This, in turn, depends on the nature of competition between the two firms. This issue has been analysed by Eaton and Grossman (1986). For example, they showed that when the two firms produce differentiated products and compete in prices the optimal trade policy is not an export subsidy but an export tax. This is illustrated in Fig. 9.5.

In this diagram the domestic firm charges price p and the foreign firm charges p^*. The reaction curves are upward-sloping. If a firm expects its competitor to set a higher price, then it is optimal for that firm to also set a higher price. The domestic and foreign reaction curves without government intervention are R_0 and R^* respectively. The

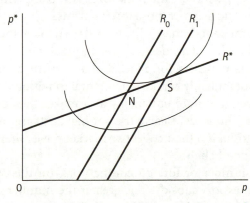

Fig. 9.5 Trade Policy with Bertrand Competition

isoprofit curves for the domestic firm are also shown. The higher the isoprofit line the greater the level of domestic profit. The Nash equilibrium in the absence of any trade policy is at point N. If the domestic firm could precommit itself to a higher price level, then its profits would be maximized at point S, the Stackelberg equilibrium. If, however, firms set prices simultaneously, then this optimal price level for the domestic firm is not credible, as it is off its own reaction function. Once again point S can only be achieved if the government commits itself to a trade policy that shifts the domestic firm's reaction function from R_0 to R_1. The appropriate policy here is an export tax as this will credibly commit the domestic firm to raise its price to cover this increased cost. The foreign firm perceives this commitment and so raises its price also. As the prices set by both firms have increased, the domestic firm does not suffer too large a fall in market share. The domestic firm's net profit falls but this is more than compensated by increased tax revenue the government now receives. This can be seen from Fig. 9.5 by noting that the firm has moved on to a higher isoprofit curve representing increased gross profits to the firm. Once more national welfare has increased as a result of strategic trade policy. If the government mistakenly paid an export subsidy, in the belief that the two firms competed in terms of quantity, then the domestic firm's reaction curve would shift to the left. The resulting Nash equilibrium would involve lower national welfare. Clearly, the government needs to be sure about the nature of competition between domestic and foreign firms in order to enact the appropriate optimal policy. This is not always an easy thing to discover.

Number of firms

One obvious way in which the Cournot duopoly model can be extended is to change the number of firms competing against each other. One trivial example is the possibility that there is only one firm in the industry. In this situation there is no case in favour of strategic trade policy. A monopolist, as it faces no strategic interdependence with other firms, is able to maximize its economic rent without the need for government intervention. Of more interest is when there are more than two competing firms. This can be due to either more domestic firms or more foreign firms.

An increase in the number of domestic firms tends to weaken the case for export subsidies. The greater the number of domestic firms the greater will be total domestic output, as individual firms compete for market share. With a sufficient number of domestic firms, an export subsidy can be detrimental to national welfare. In this situation an export tax is again welfare-enhancing as it makes the domestic firms behave more like a monopolist. This is identical to the optimal tariff argument, where individual firms are too small to exploit their collective market power themselves, but the government can do so on their behalf.

An increase in the number of foreign competitors, on the other hand, tends to increase the case for an export subsidy. The greater the number of foreign firms, the greater the fall in foreign production given an increase in domestic production. In response to a domestic subsidy each foreign firm may reduce its output by a smaller amount, but in aggregate foreign output falls further. This means that increased domestic production as a result of the export subsidy does not depress prices by so much. As a result the gain in domestic rent is greater the more foreign firms there are.

Retaliation

So far we have only examined strategic trade policy under imperfect competition on the assumption that only one government enacts such a policy. As with the optimal tariff argument, the desirability of such policies can be greatly altered when this assumption is relaxed. For example, with many countries paying export subsidies, the intended competitive advantage conferred on firms cancels out, and as a result all countries can be made worse off. Once more this is the familiar prisoners' dilemma argument. Individually it may be in the interests of countries to impose such policies, but collectively they are all made worse off. Whether free trade can be sustained as an equilibrium when governments repeatedly interact parallels many of the arguments presented above in connection with avoiding tariff wars.

EXERCISE 9.3

Find the subgame perfect Nash equilibrium output and subsidy levels for the Cournot duopoly model analysed previously under the assumption that both governments now pay the optimal export subsidy. Show that both countries are worse off compared to when neither government pays a subsidy.

Freedom of entry

Another assumption upon which the desirability or otherwise of strategic trade policy depends is the degree to which firms can enter the industry. The basic strategic argument for export subsidies is that it can shift economic rent from foreign to domestic firms. Economic rent will only persist, however, if there are significant barriers to entry. For example, firms will only continue to earn supernormal profits if other firms are prevented from entering the market. This will happen if there are significant barriers to entry such as high capital requirements, R&D requirements, or legal barriers. In the absence of such barriers other firms will enter the market and supernormal profits will disappear. With freedom of entry the benefits of export subsidies will typically be only short-lived. Indeed, once we introduce the possibility of entry, export subsidies can reduce national welfare. This may occur for a number of reasons. For example, entry into the industry is likely to be greater in countries paying an export subsidy. If this is true, the number of firms in such countries will expand. As the number of domestic firms increases, competition amongst domestic firms becomes excessive from the point of maximizing national welfare. (We are here assuming all output is exported, and so there is no beneficial increase in consumer surplus.) As argued above, with a greater number of domestic firms in the industry, the optimal policy is more likely to be an export tax, with an export subsidy reducing national welfare. Furthermore, the subsidy may induce excessive entry from the point of view of achieving optimal economies of scale. In this situation costs of production will rise more than would have been the case without the subsidy, and again national economic welfare is reduced.

These types of argument support the view that export subsidies, when there is freedom of entry, will at best only confer temporarily welfare gains to the country using them, and at worst may actually reduce national welfare. Venables (1985) has presented an alternative model where even with freedom of entry an export subsidy can have long-lasting benefits. Venables makes the important assumptions that domestic consumption occurs and the domestic and foreign markets are segmented in the sense that prices need not be equated between them. He also assumes that due to high fixed costs marginal costs are always falling. Suppose now that the domestic government introduces an export subsidy. Domestic firms will increase production and so their marginal costs will fall. Conversely, foreign firms will cut back on production and their marginal costs will rise. If domestic consumers buy proportionately more of the good from domestic firms rather than foreign firms, their welfare will increase as the price they pay for the good falls. Total domestic welfare increases because consumer surplus and government revenue increases and producers continue to earn normal profits due to entry and exit considerations. A variation on this model is where there are significant 'learning by doing' economies of scale. This is where production costs fall as firms gain greater experience. These economies can be obtained more quickly if the firm increases its rate of production. In this way, trade policy may enhance learning by doing economies, by stimulating domestic firms to increase their rate of production. This results in domestic production costs falling more quickly than production costs of foreign firms, and so may allow domestic firms to become dominant in the industry. This process can result in increased long-term profits for domestic firms and improved national welfare.

Related to the issue of freedom of entry is the idea that strategic trade policies can also be used to deter foreign firms entering an industry, and in this way improve the competitive position of domestic firms. If this policy is successful, it can limit the extent of foreign competition and so maintain supernormal profits of domestic firms. One simple model that illustrates this possibility is given by Laussel and Montet (1994). It is assumed there are two potential entrants into an industry, one domestic and one foreign. The following three-stage game is considered. In the first period the domestic government decides on the appropriate level of its trade policy. Here we only consider a subsidy paid to the domestic firm. In the second period the two firms decide whether or not to enter the market. If a firm does enter, it incurs a sunk cost equal to F. In the third period those firms that have entered compete against each other. The exact nature of the competition is not specified but profits are assumed to be negatively related to the number of firms in the industry. The pay-offs in terms of profits earned for the two firms are given in the normal form game shown in Fig. 9.6.

Foreign firm

		Enters	Stays out
Domestic firm	Enters	$\Pi(2)-F$, $\Pi(2)-F$	$\Pi(1)-F$, 0
	Stays out	0, $\Pi(1)-F$	0, 0

Fig. 9.6 Trade Policy and entry deterrence

Assuming that $\Pi(1) - F$ is non-negative, so that the industry can support at least one firm, Laussel and Montet consider the following two cases. The *first* is when $\Pi(2) - F < 0$. In this situation if both firms enter the industry, they each make a loss. With this condition there are two pure-strategy Nash equilibria for the final period of the game. These correspond to one firm entering and earning a positive profit, and the other firm staying out and breaking even. If the domestic firm could commit itself to entering the industry, it would do so, thus deterring the foreign firm from doing so. However, the mere threat of always entering the market is not credible, and so is not part of a subgame perfect Nash equilibrium for the entire game. Once more the government can ensure that the domestic firm always enters the industry by paying an appropriate subsidy. In this case the optimal lump-sum subsidy paid conditional on entry is equal to $F - \Pi(2)$. With this subsidy the domestic firm now has the (weakly) dominant strategy of always entering the industry. The foreign firm perceives this to be the case and so is deterred from entering. The domestic firm will earn profits equal to $\Pi(2) - \Pi(1) > 0$.

The *second* case considered is when $\Pi(2) - F \geq 0$. With this condition, entry dominates staying out of the industry for both firms, and so the Nash equilibrium is that both firms enter and make non-negative profits. Even so it may still be optimal for the domestic government to try and attempt to deter the foreign firm from entering industry thus securing monopoly power for the domestic firm. This will involve setting the domestic subsidy so that the foreign firm expects to make a loss if it enters the market. If this is possible, then the foreign firm will indeed stay out of the market, and the domestic firm will have a monopoly position.

From these two examples we see that strategic trade policy may be welfare-enhancing if it can effectively deter entry by foreign firms. This can be achieved by affecting either domestic firms' or foreign firms' entry conditions.

Factor prices

It has already been noted that increased economic rent earned by domestic firms as a result of strategic trade policy need not necessarily result in higher profits. For example, if the industry is dominated by strong unions, increased economic rent might be appropriated by workers in the form of higher wages. If this were merely a straight transfer from owners to employees, then it would leave net national welfare unchanged. However, if unions, or other institutions, do succeed in capturing some of the increased economic rent by forcing up costs, this will affect the competitive position of the firm. This will affect the equilibrium outcome of the underlying game. To the extent that costs are forced up, so the less effective is the export subsidy in improving the competitiveness of domestic firms, and so the smaller is the resulting welfare gain.

From a general equilibrium perspective, the consideration of factor prices can cause export subsidies, paid to certain targeted industries, to be detrimental to domestic welfare. Dixit and Grossman (1986), for example, consider the case where the subsidized industry uses a resource that is in fixed supply. They suggest that this might be either scientists or engineers. In this case, output can only expand in this industry if it contracts in another. For such a trade policy to be optimal the subsidy must be targeted on the industry capable of generating the greatest returns. If all industries have equal ability to capture foreign rents, then the optimal policy is one of non-intervention. If the government does not process sufficient information to compare relative returns, then there is the possibility that export subsidies will reduce national welfare.

Identifying industries to target

One final criticism that has been levied against the promotion of targeted industries via trade policies is the difficulty of identifying which industries to support. One aspect of this is the difficulty of measuring the economic rent earned by an industry. For example, in the entry deterrent arguments developed above, what is needed are reliable estimates of future industry returns. These are by their nature very difficult to obtain. Furthermore, the correct measure of economic rent earned in an industry needs to reflect the risk involved. Returns to R&D, for example, can be very large, but this often reflects the high degree of risk attached to such activities. For every successful R&D project there are many that fail to earn adequate returns. Just looking at the profits earned by the successful ventures overstates the amount of economic rent being earned because it ignores the returns to unsuccessful ventures. Such issues complicate the implementation of strategic trade issues when there is imperfect competition, and can be used to support the argument that such policies should be avoided as being too risky.

9.3 Conclusions

This chapter has analysed two ways that have been suggested for how a government might be able to increase national welfare, via international trade policy. The first was the optimal tariff argument. This suggests that a government can increase national welfare by exploiting the country's monopoly power in international markets. From a game theory perspective, this argument assumes that other countries do not impose import tariffs, which presupposes that they do not have any market power. In reality this assumption is unlikely to be met. With more than one country having some degree of market power in international trade, each of these countries will have an incentive to impose import tariffs. This raises the possibility that the final equilibrium will be Pareto inefficient, with all countries made worse off. In this situation countries will increase national welfare if they can co-ordinate on free trade, and set zero tariffs. This is clearly contrary to the optimal tariff argument. The problem with such co-ordination is how to prevent individual countries reneging on this commitment. Various ways suggested how this might be achieved include the possibility of punishing such behaviour, and the role of incomplete information. If these mechanisms are successful, individual countries will no longer have the incentive to set unilateral tariffs.

The second argument in favour of international trade policy is that such policies can, in the context of imperfect competition, be rent-shifting. This involves shifting economic rent from foreign to domestic firms, and hence increasing national welfare. These arguments have been developed using game theory models. As with the optimal tariff argument, however, any gains in national welfare are highly sensitive to the underlying assumptions of the model used. Issues such as retaliation by other governments, freedom of entry into international markets, the nature of competition between firms, and the role of incomplete information, can make otherwise beneficial trade policy detrimental to national welfare. The difficulty of identifying the nature and role of these factors in reality tends to undermine the usefulness of strategic trade policy in oligopolistic markets.

For both the optimal tariff argument, and the more recent policy prescriptions based on imperfect competition, game theory has greatly enhanced our understanding of when such trade policy will be effective in increasing national welfare. In general, game theory has highlighted the major difficulties that governments face when trying to implement optimal trade policy. These difficulties are largely due to interdependence between governments and competing firms. With such interdependence, and the adoption of 'beggar-my-neighbour' trade policies, the final equilibrium is likely to be Pareto inefficient. Based on these arguments many economists have recommended that governments forgo the use of strategic trade policies, and instead pursue free trade. This may involve countries giving up temporary benefits, but it is argued that in the long run all countries will be better off. The analysis of recent game theory models, as discussed in this chapter, has tended to support this view.

9.4 Solutions to Exercises

Exercise 9.1

In Fig. 9.7 only the domestic country has market power in international trade and so it has the same indifference and reaction curves as in Fig. 9.2. The foreign country has no market power which means if it sets any non-zero tariff its welfare will be reduced. Its indifference curves are therefore downward-sloping and its reaction function is along the horizontal axis. The Nash equilibrium involving international trade is at point N, which is the same as point A in Fig. 9.2. The traditional optimal tariff argument is therefore only justified as a Nash equilibrium when only one country enjoys market power. This is a Pareto-efficient outcome, as any other combination of tariffs must reduce the welfare of at least one country.

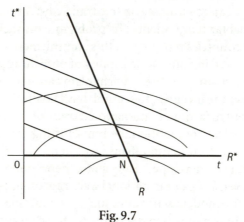

Fig. 9.7

Exercise 9.2

This two-period model can be solved using the principle of backward induction. In the second period, each firm simultaneously sets its output in order to maximize profits taking the subsidy paid to the domestic firm (s) and the output of its competitor as given, i.e.

$$\max \Pi = (a - q - q^* - c + s)\, q$$

$$\max \Pi^* = (a - q - q^* - c)\, q^*.$$

Differentiating these functions and setting them equal to zero gives us the first-order conditions for a maximum, and each firm's reaction functions.

$$\frac{d\Pi}{dq} = a - 2q - q^* - c + s = 0$$

$$\therefore \; q = \frac{a - q^* - c + s}{2}.$$

$$\frac{d\Pi^*}{dq} = a - q - 2q^* - c = 0$$

$$\therefore \ q^* = \frac{a - q - c}{2}.$$

A Nash equilibrium in the second period requires that each firm maximize its profits given the other firm's output. Setting the two reaction functions equal to each other yields

$$q = \frac{a - c + 2s}{3}$$

$$q^* = \frac{a - c - s}{3}.$$

These correspond to the Nash equilibrium output quantities, and significantly both firm's output decisions are conditional upon the level of the subsidy paid to the domestic firm. If $s = 0$, then each firm produces $(a - c)/3$ as shown by point N in Fig. 9.4. In the first period the domestic government sets the level of the subsidy so as to maximize domestic welfare, based upon its expectations of how firms will behave in the second period. It does this by maximizing the domestic firm's net of subsidy profit level, Π_N. (The government is concerned with net profits as the subsidy in itself is merely a transfer from the government to the firm, and so, assuming it yields the same value to both, it leaves domestic welfare unchanged.) The government sets the value of s so as to

$$\max \Pi_N = (a - q - q^* - c)\, q.$$

Substituting in for q and q^* derived in solving for the second period gives us

$$\Pi_N = \left(a - \frac{a - c - 2s}{3} - \frac{a - c - s}{3} - c \right) \cdot \frac{a - c - 2s}{3}.$$

This simplifies to

$$\Pi_N = 1/9 \left[(a - c)^2 + (a - c)\, s - 2s^2 \right].$$

The first-order condition for a maximum is therefore

$$\frac{d\Pi_N}{ds} = \frac{1}{9}[(a - c) - 4s] = 0$$

$$\therefore \ s = \frac{a - c}{4}.$$

This is the optimal level for the subsidy. Substituting this back into the previous equations for the two firms' conditional output levels gives us

$$q = \frac{a - c}{2}$$

$$q^* = \frac{a - c}{4}.$$

This confirms the values shown in Fig. 9.4 for point E, and corresponds to the Stackelberg equilibrium derived in Chapter 4. Finally, the monetary value of the increase in domestic welfare can be derived by calculating the difference in the domestic firm's net profits with and without the subsidy, $\Delta\Pi_N$.

$$\Delta\Pi_N = \tfrac{1}{9}[(a-c)^2 + (a-c)s - 2s^2] - \tfrac{1}{9}(a-c)^2 = \frac{(a-c)^2}{72} > 0.$$

This result shows that paying the subsidy does indeed increase national welfare, and so the domestic firm's profits rise by a greater amount than the subsidy it receives from the government.

Exercise 9.3

As with Exercise 9.2 this model is solved using the principle of backward induction. In the second period both firms determine their optimal output level given the subsidies paid by the domestic and foreign governments, s and s^* receptively, i.e.

$$\max \Pi = (a - q - q^* - c + s)\, q$$

$$\max \Pi^* = (a - q - q^* - c + s^*)\, q^*.$$

From the first-order conditions we derive the following reaction functions

$$q = \frac{a - q^* - c}{2}$$

$$q^* = \frac{a - q - c + s^*}{2}.$$

Setting these two reaction functions equal to each other we obtain the Nash equilibrium for the second period

$$q = \frac{a - c + 2s - s^*}{3}$$

$$q^* = \frac{a - c + 2s^* - s}{3}.$$

We can now solve the governments' optimization problem for determining the level of subsidy that maximizes each country's national welfare. As the two countries are symmetrical we need only derive s and then set this equal to s^*.

$$\max \Pi_N = (a - q - q^* - c)\, q.$$

Substituting in each firm's optimal output level conditional on the subsidies and rearranging gives

$$\Pi_N = 1/9\,[a - c - s^*) + (a - c - s^*)\, s - 2s^2].$$

Differentiating this and setting it equal to zero yields

$$\frac{d\Pi_N}{ds} = 1/9[(a - c - s^*) - 4s] = 0$$

$$\therefore\ s = \frac{(a - c - s^*)}{4}$$

$$\therefore\ s^* = \frac{(a - c - s)}{4}.$$

These are the governments' reaction functions for the optimal subsidies. Setting these equal to each other gives the Nash equilibrium for the first period.

$$s = \frac{a-c}{5}$$

$$s^* = \frac{a-c}{5}.$$

Substituting these optimal subsidies into the conditional output levels gives us

$$s = \frac{a-c}{5}$$

$$s^* = \frac{a-c}{5}.$$

To show that both countries are made worse off with both governments paying an optimal export subsidy we again calculate the difference in monetary value of each firm's net profits with and without subsidies. This is done explicitly for the domestic country.

$$\Delta\Pi_N = \Delta\Pi_N^* = 1/9[(a-c-s^*)+(a-c-s^*)s-2s^2]-1/9(a-c) = -\frac{7(a-c)^2}{225} < 0.$$

Further Reading

Bierman, H. S., and L. Fernandez (1993), *Game Theory with Economic Applications*, Reading, Mass.: Addison Wesley.

Dixit, A. (1987), 'Strategic Aspects of Trade Policy', in T. Bewley (ed.), *Advances in Economic Theory: Fifth World Congress*, New York: Cambridge University Press.

Krugman, P. R. (1989), 'Industrial Organization and International Trade', in R. Schmalensee and R. Willig (eds.), *Handbook of Industrial Organization*, ii, Elsevier Science Publishers.

Krugman, P. R. (1987), 'Is Free Trade Passé?' *Economic Perspectives*, 1: 131–44.

Krugman, P. R. (1986), *Strategic Trade Policy and the New International Economics*, Cambridge, Mass.: MIT Press.

Laussel, D., and C. Montet. (1994), 'Strategic Trade Policies', in D. Greenaway and L. A. Winters (eds.), *Surveys in International Trade*, Oxford: Blackwell.

10

Environmental Economics

I N recent decades there has been greater concern about environmental issues. This has primarily developed as we have become more aware of the detrimental effects of human activity on the environment. These range from local instances of environmental degradation to global issues such as climate change and ozone depletion. The predominant response of economists has been to highlight the underlying instances of market failure that often give rise to these problems. Three widely discussed types of market failure associated with man's interaction with his environment are externalities, common property resources, and public goods. Externalities occur when an individual's welfare is directly influenced by the actions of others. Pollution, for example, is a detrimental externality when a polluter's actions directly reduce the welfare of other individuals. Such interdependence is external to the market mechanism, and is a specific problem associated with incomplete markets. A common property resource is one where individuals have free access to a valuable asset. Examples include the atmosphere used for waste disposal, and ocean fishing. With individuals acting in their own self-interest such resources are likely to be overexploited. Finally, an environmental asset is a public good if one person's consumption does not reduce what is available for others to consume. An example of this is the value of biodiversity and carbon sequestration associated with the tropical rain forests. Such goods may represent instances of market failure due to the free-rider problem. Individuals have an incentive to avoid paying for such goods in the hope that others will do so. In equilibrium, therefore, public goods are likely to be undersupplied. Each of these instances of market failure implies that individuals are interdependent. These can also be used to justify and inform policy-makers on the need for remedial measures.

Much has been written on how authorities ought to respond to these instances of market failure when they occur within one country's borders. Here the government should intervene either to induce or force producers and/or consumers to act in a way that brings about the socially beneficial outcome. This, however, is not possible when market failure occurs in an international context. With international environmental problems there is, as yet, no supranational authority that can enforce the socially desirable outcome. Although there are organizations that seek to co-ordinate environmental policy between countries, such as the United Nations Environmental Programme, these do not have the authority to compel countries to forgo policies seen to be in their own self-interest. It is in this context that non-cooperative game theory makes a significant contribution to environmental economics. This chapter, therefore, focuses upon international and global environmental problems. The following topics are some of the international environmental problems for which non-cooperative game theory has proved particularly useful.

Transnational physical externalities

An obvious example of a physical externality between countries is pollution. It is often the case that pollution is not confined within national borders, but instead pollution generated in one country can adversely affect the welfare of individuals in other countries. Here we may distinguish the following three cases. First, there is *unidirectional pollution*. This is where pollution from one country adversely affects welfare in one or more other countries but this interdependence is not reversed. An example of unidirectional pollution is river pollution. Here upstream countries that pollute a river adversely affects the welfare of citizens in downstream countries. In Europe the river Rhine is such an example where German pollution adversely affects welfare in the Netherlands. On its own, unidirectional pollution does not give rise to mutual interdependence, and so there seems little scope for non-cooperative game theory. However, mutual interdependence can be introduced if downstream countries offer side payments to the upstream country. These are offered with the aim of inducing the upstream country to reduce its pollution levels. If there are several victims of such pollution, then we can observe once more the free-rider problem. Second, there can be *regional reciprocal pollution*. This is where a group of countries are both the source and victims of environmental pollution. An example of this is acid rain in European countries. Finally, there is *global pollution*. Here all countries in the world are affected. Examples of this type of pollution include global warming and ozone depletion. This type of pollution is very similar to regional reciprocal pollution, except now the region encompasses the whole world.

Non-physical externalities

With non-physical externalities interdependence is psychological rather than physical. This occurs, for example, if people are concerned about biodiversity and conservation of rare species. In this situation the destruction of tropical rain forests entails a negative externality. By its very nature such externalities are likely to have an international dimension, and affect many individuals in various countries.

International trade effects

Even if an environmental problem is limited to within individual countries, the response of government's to these problems can have effects on other countries via international trade. If, for example, government's require domestic industries to reduce their levels of pollution, this will, other things remaining equal, adversely affect the competitiveness of these industries in international trade. This additional economic cost of pollution abatement may provide national authorities with an incentive to relax their environmental standards. If all countries act on this incentive, environmental standards will be competitively bid down, and all countries will be made worse off.

International agreements

Due to the international dimension of environmental problems, it can often be in the interests of different countries to co-operate with each other to produce a Pareto-efficient outcome. As there is no supranational authority able to override national sovereignty international agreements must be self-enforcing. From the perspective of non-cooperative game theory a country will only be signatory to an international treaty or convention if it perceives it is acting in its own self-interest. Issues explored using non-cooperative game theory include analysing under what conditions countries will want to co-operate, and how countries can be induced to sign treaties not initially seen to be in their own self-interest.

To analyse some of these issues we will initially examine unidirectional and reciprocal environmental externalities in a two-country model. This is undertaken in section 10.1. With the aid of this model we examine the economic issues related to bilateral agreements, and specifically the role of side payments in overcoming international environmental problems. However, this two-country model is unable to capture certain important aspects of regional and global environmental problems. In section 6.2, therefore, we go on to examine a model with many countries. Using this multi-country model it is argued that groups of countries may have the incentive to form voluntary coalitions to overcome environmental problems. This possibility provides one explanation why countries voluntarily commit themselves to multilateral agreements. Finally, in this section we examine under what conditions such coalitions are likely to develop, and suggest ways they might be beneficially expanded.

10.1 Bilateral Agreements

In this section we will discuss how bilateral agreement between two countries can develop in order to overcome environmental problems associated with externalities. In the text we assume that the externality is unidirectional, whilst Exercise 10.1 assumes that it is reciprocal.

10.1.1 Unidirectional externalities

Consider the following two-country model, where each country is indexed by $i = 1, 2$. It is assumed that each country initially emits levels of a pollutant equal to E_i. Each country, however, is able to invest in a costly abatement technology which reduces its emissions of the pollutant. Levels of abatement are equal to A_i, and net emissions are equal to $E_i - A_i$. An externality is introduced by assuming that country 1's pollution is transported to country 2 via the environment. For example, the pollution may be either water- or air-borne, with country 1 being upstream or upwind, and country 2 being downstream or downwind. Country 1 is assumed to be adversely affected by its own emissions of the pollutant, while country 2 is adversely affected by both its own emissions and pollution transported to it from country 1. We make the simplifying assumption that all of country 1's pollution is transported to country 2.

With countries acting non-cooperatively the optimization problem for each country is to determine its level of emissions abatement that maximizes its own social welfare, V_i. Abatement has two effects on social welfare. First, increased abatement reduces net pollution and so raises welfare. Second, as abatement is assumed to be costly, increased abatement reduces the amount of resources available for other uses and so reduces welfare. If we let $F_i(.)$ be the social welfare function dependant upon levels of net pollution in country i, and $C_i(.)$ be the welfare function associated with the cost of emissions reduction, then total welfare for country 1 is given as

$$V_1 = F_1(A_1 - E_1) - C_1(A_1) \tag{10.1}$$

with dF_1/dA_1 and $dC_1/dA_1 > 0$.

Similarly total welfare for country 2 is equal to

$$V_2 = F_2(A_2 - E_2 + A_1 - E_1) - C_2(A_2) \tag{10.2}$$

with again dF_2/dA_2 and $dC_2/dA_2 > 0$.

Setting the differential of these total welfare functions with respect to each country's level of abatement equal to zero and rearranging gives us the following first-order conditions for the non-cooperative Nash equilibrium:

$$\frac{dF_1}{dA_1} = \frac{dC_1}{dA_1}$$
$$\frac{dF_2}{dA_2} = \frac{dC_2}{dA_2}. \tag{10.3}$$

In a non-cooperative Nash equilibrium each country sets its own marginal benefit of abatement, dF_1/dA_1, equal to its marginal cost, dC_1/dA_1. In particular it disregards any beneficial effect its own action might have for the other country. The Nash equilibrium for this simple game is illustrated in Fig. 10.1.

In the bottom half of the diagram we have drawn each country's marginal benefit, (MB_i), and marginal cost, (MC_i), curves of increased abatement. It is assumed that the marginal benefit of abatement rises, and marginal cost of abatement falls, the greater the level of pollution in each country. As pollution is negatively related to the level of abatement, the marginal benefit curve is downward-sloping, and the marginal cost curve upward-sloping. In the top left-hand quadrant of the diagram are drawn each

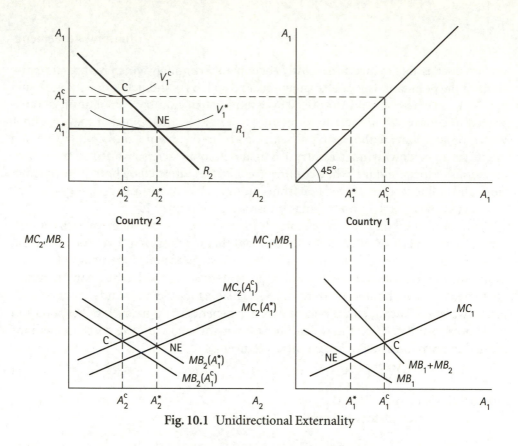

Fig. 10.1 Unidirectional Externality

country's reaction function. These show how each country's optimal level of abatement varies with respect to the other country's level of abatement.

Consider first the problem confronting country 1. As the externality is unidirectional country 1's marginal benefit and marginal cost curves are independent of pollution in country 2. These are shown as MB_1 and MC_1 respectively. Setting marginal benefit equal to marginal cost it is clear that country 1's optimal abatement level is also independent of country 2's actions. Its optimal level of abatement in this situation is equal to A_1^*. As its optimal level of abatement is independent of country 2's actions country 1's reaction function, R_1, is horizontal. This reaction curve corresponds to an indifference curve where social welfare for country 1 is maximized. Other indifference curves associated with lower welfare (not illustrated) are parallel to the reaction function. Any deviation away from the optimal level of abatement reduces social welfare in this country.

Now consider country 2's optimization problem. Due to the pollution externality country 2's marginal benefit and marginal cost curves are dependent on emissions in country 1. If country 1 reduces its emissions, then other things being equal there is less pollution in country 2. This will increase country 2's marginal costs of abatement, and reduce its marginal benefits. Taken together, this will induce country 2 to reduce its own level of abatement. Country 2's reaction function is therefore downward-sloping. Moving up this reaction function corresponds to higher levels of social welfare for country 2. This is shown in Fig. 10.1 by country 2 moving on to higher indifference curves associated with enhanced social welfare. Given that the optimal level of abatement in country 1 is A_1^*, the marginal benefit and marginal cost curves faced by country 2 are $MB_2(A_1^*)$ and $MC_2(A_1^*)$ respectively. Setting these equal to each other gives us country 2's optimal level of abatement as A_2^*. This corresponds to where the two countries' reaction functions intersect. The levels of abatement A_1^* and A_2^*, therefore, represent the non-cooperative Nash equilibrium. With these abatement levels, both countries are maximizing their individual social welfare dependent on their expectations of what the other country will do.

Despite the presence of a negative pollution externality it should be noted that the Nash equilibrium is Pareto efficient. This is illustrated by the fact that at the Nash equilibrium each country's indifference curves are tangent to each other. Any deviation away from this equilibrium will mean that at least one of the countries must be worse off. Any change in country 1's level of abatement from A_1^* will necessarily reduce its social welfare, while with this level of abatement, country 2 maximizes its social welfare by setting its abatement level equal to A_2^*. Country 2 would like country 1 to reduce its level of pollution even further, but it is not in the interests of country 1 to do this. Within the current game there is no incentive for country 1 to consider the detrimental effects it is having on country 2's welfare, and so there is no incentive for it to deviate from A_1^*.

Although the above Nash equilibrium is Pareto efficient it does not correspond to the *co-operative solution* to the game. In the co-operative solution each country sets its level of abatement so as to maximize joint social welfare, V. Aggregating over (10.1) and (10.2) we get that joint social welfare is equal to

$$V = F_1(A_1 - E_1) - C_1(A_1) + F_2(A_2 - E_2 + A_1 - E_1) - C_2(A_2). \qquad (10.4)$$

With countries seeking to maximize this function the first-order conditions are:

$$\frac{dF_1}{dA_1} + \frac{dF_2}{dA_1} = \frac{dC_1}{dA_1}$$

$$\frac{dF_2}{dA_2} = \frac{dC_2}{dA_2}. \qquad (10.5)$$

We can compare these optimality conditions with those derived when countries act non-cooperatively, as given in (10.3). The condition of optimality for country 2 remains unchanged. It is still required to set its own marginal benefit of abatement equal to marginal cost. This is because there is no externality associated with country 2's level of abatement . This, however, is not the case for country 1. Country 1's condition of optimality has now changed. To maximise joint welfare it needs to set the *sum of the marginal benefits*, $(dF_1/dA_1) + (dF_2/dA_1)$, equal to its marginal cost of abatement. To maximize joint welfare country 1 has to take into account the effect of its abatement policy on country 2. As the joint marginal benefits are greater than country 1's individual marginal benefit of abatement, the co-operative solution involves country 1 increasing its own level of abatement compared to the non-cooperative Nash equilibrium. This co-operative outcome is illustrated in Fig. 10.1 as point C. The optimal abatement levels are now A_1^C and A_2^C. This co-operative outcome is still on country 2's reaction curve, as its condition of optimality has not changed. However, it is off country 1's reaction function. Country 1 now abates more than when it acted in its own self-interest. In response to this change country 2 will decrease its level of abatement. This is because as pollution levels in that country fall its marginal costs of abatement will rise, and marginal benefits will fall. Its marginal benefit and marginal costs curves are now given by $MB(A_1^C)$ and $MC(A_1^C)$ respectively. Compared to the Nash equilibrium this co-operative outcome has made country 2 better off and country 1 worse off. However, as joint welfare is only now being maximized it must be the case that the gain to country 2 outweighs the loss incurred by country 1. This net gain in social welfare gives both countries the incentive to attempt to co-ordinate upon the co-operative solution, provided country 1 is compensated for its loss of welfare.

10.1.2 Side payments

One way of achieving the co-operative outcome, whilst maintaining the assumption that countries act in their own self-interest, is to introduce the possibility of *side payments* supported by binding contracts. By changing the nature of the game both countries can make themselves better off. Here we consider the effects of country 2 paying country 1 to reduce its level of pollution. With this financial inducement country 1 now has an incentive to increase its level of abatement. With appropriate inducement the co-operative outcome can be reproduced. With side payments allowed the social welfare functions for the two countries become

$$V_1 = F_1 (A_1 - E_1) - C_1 (A_1) + T(A_1).$$
$$V_2 = F_2 (A_2 - E_2 + A_1 - E_1) - C_2 (A_2) - T(A_1).$$

(10.6)

where $T(A_1)$ is the side payment transferred from country 2 to country 1. The amount of side payment depends on the level of pollution abatement undertaken by country 1. The first-order conditions under non-cooperation are given by the following two equations

$$\frac{dF_1}{dA_1} + \frac{dT}{dA_1} = \frac{dC_1}{dA_1}$$
$$\frac{dF_2}{dA_2} = \frac{dC_2}{dA_2}.$$

(10.7)

We can compare these conditions with those derived assuming co-operative behaviour, as given in (10.5). Clearly the conditions will be equivalent if $dT/dA_1 = dF_2/dA_1$. As $dF_2/dA_1 > 0$, so this condition implies that the side payment transferred from country 2 to country 1 must be positively related to the level of pollution abatement in country 1. In this way country 1 can be induced to reduce its level of pollution to the co-operative level and social welfare is maximized.

Using a two-country model we have shown that if there is either a unidirectional or reciprocal externality, then side payments can make both countries better off. Despite this result such transfers are rarely observed in practice. Here we discuss some criticisms levelled against the use of side payments, which may partially explain why they are rarely adopted.

EXERCISE 10.1

In the two-country model presented in the text it was assumed there was a unidirectional externality. The use of the environment by one country adversely affected the welfare of the other country. In this exercise we extend this model to analyse the effects of a reciprocal externality.

Assume there are two countries, indexed $i = 1, 2$. Both countries have free access to a shared common resource. This may, for example, be the atmosphere or shared open water. Each country uses the resource as a means of waste disposal. Social welfare in each country is dependent on the aggregate level of pollution of the shared environment. As in the text each country can invest in a costly abatement technology. Specifically, we assume that social welfare in each country is equal to $V_i = F(A_1 + A_2 - E) - C_i(A_i)$, where E is the initial aggregate rate of pollution, and other notation is as in the text. It is initially assumed that marginal benefit of abatement is positively related to aggregate pollution, whilst marginal cost is positively related to the level of abatement in each country.

(1) Find the first-order optimality conditions for each country given that they act non-cooperatively. Illustrate the reaction curves for these two countries and show the Nash equilibrium. Is this equilibrium Pareto efficient?

(2) Derive the optimality conditions if the countries work together co-operatively and seek to maximize joint social welfare. Compared to the results derived in (1) what does this co-operative solution imply about levels of abatement?

(3) Demonstrate that the two countries can be induced to replicate the co-operative outcome when the possibility of side payments is introduced into the model.

(4) What is the specific outcome for (3) when both countries are identical?

(5) What is the specific outcome for (3) when marginal costs of abatement are constant, but not necessarily the same in each country?

Polluter pays principle

In the previous models countries achieved the co-operative solution if the victim of pollution induces the polluter, via side payments, to reduce its emissions. A guiding principle, however, that is often adopted by countries when negotiating solutions to environmental problems is that it is the polluter, and not the victim, who should bear the costs of its actions. This is known as the polluter pays principle (PPP), and contrasts with the victim pays principle (VPP). For example, at the Stockholm Conference in 1972 the OECD countries declared that 'States have . . . responsibility to ensure that activities within their jurisdiction or control do not cause damage to the environment of other States or areas beyond the limits of national jurisdiction.' A strong argument in favour of this principle is that it accords with the notion of natural justice. This is based on the belief that individuals have the right to an unpolluted environment. One reason countries might be reluctant to use side payments in order to induce polluters to reduce their emissions is that it violates the polluter pays principle.

Indeterminacy

In order to induce the polluter country to reduce emissions to the co-operative level the *rate* of side payment must equal the marginal benefit of abatement for the other country. This maximizes the level of joint social welfare which can then be divided between the two countries. The exact distribution of social welfare, however, is not uniquely determined. There is in fact a range of varying levels of side payments that produce the co-operative outcome and make both countries better off. Because of this multiple equilibria the final outcome is indeterminant, and depends on bargaining between the two countries. This raises the possibility that the countries may not be able to reach a satisfactory agreement or that the costs of doing so outweigh the potential benefits. In either situation the two countries may again avoid using side payments.

Uncertainty

In the two-country model discussed above it was implicitly assumed that there was no uncertainty. If, however, there is incomplete or imperfect information, then countries may be unwilling to use side payments to offset environmental problems. Uncertainty may arise because countries marginal cost and marginal benefit functions of abatement are not common knowledge. In this situation countries have an incentive to lie about their cost or benefit functions in order to increase their share of the net gain in welfare. This may involve polluter countries overstating the true cost of abatement hoping to receive a greater level of side payment. Similarly victims of pollution may overstate the extent of environmental damage hoping to reduce the agreed level of side payment. Another instance of uncertainty is when the final level of abatement by the polluter country cannot be accurately measured and agreed upon by both countries. Again there is the incentive for countries to give false information. In situations such as these mechanisms will need to be instituted so as to induce countries to truthfully reveal their information. Such mechanisms, if they exist, may greatly increase the complexity of negotiations, and may cause countries to abandon the use of side payments.

More than two countries

The above result on the optimality of side payments was derived in only a two-country model. In reality environmental problems typically involve more than just two countries. Even in the case of a unidirectional externality there may be many countries polluting the environment and/or there may be many countries who are victims. These possibilities can change a country's incentive to make or receive side payments. For example, if there are many victims of one or more countries' pollution, then each victim has an incentive not to offer side payments in the hope that the other victims will do so. This free-rider problem, and how it may be avoided, is discussed more fully in the next section. Furthermore, even if one particular environmental problem is confined just to two countries, these countries may be involved in negotiations with other countries concerning separate though related issues. Here a country may be unwilling to adopt the victim pays principle associated with side payments so as not to appear a weak negotiator. In this way it hopes to develop a reputation for being a strong negotiator, and so improve its pay-off in the long run.

10.2 Multilateral Agreements

10.2.1 The free-rider problem

In the previous section we analysed the effects of an environmental externality in a two-country model. This model, however, can only be considered relevant to a small number of real world examples. Instances of bilateral environmental agreements include those made between the USA and Canada over acid rain, fishing rights, and management of the Great Lakes. Most environmental problems that confront the world today involve many countries. This is obviously true for global environmental problems such as ozone depletion and global warming. In order for there to be effective environmental control in these instances multilateral, rather than bilateral, agreements are needed. As in the two-country model the presence of environmental externalities and free access to common resources provides an incentive for all countries to co-ordinate their actions. When there are many countries, however, the free-rider problem becomes particularly severe. Here individual countries have the incentive not to co-ordinate their environmental policies with other countries. This is in the hope that other countries will address the environmental problem without them. In this way the free-rider country enjoys the benefits of the other countries environmental control, but incurs none of the associated costs. With all countries faced with this same incentive full co-operation between countries is not possible. Taking this game theory result on face value gives the pessimistic prediction that we should not expect to observe environmental co-operation between countries. Fortunately this prediction is not confirmed by reality. In practice we do observe countries co-ordinating their environmental policies for the common good. Examples of so-called international environmental agreements (IEAs) include the Helsinki Protocol (1985) on sulphur dioxide reduction and the Montreal Protocol (1987) on ozone depletion. This section explicitly considers how such IEAs can be sustained, and hence the free-rider problem overcome. This involves examining environmental policy when countries repeatedly interact and the possibility of groups of countries forming stable coalitions.

10.2.2 Repeated interaction

As considered in previous chapters allowing players repeatedly to interact can greatly alter the predicted outcome of a game. With continual interaction players can adopt punishment strategies in an attempt to induce other players to act in a certain way. This is most clearly illustrated in games where players are assumed to interact an infinite number of times. The most commonly quoted version of the Folk Theorem states that with infinite repetitions any feasible individually rational pay-off can be supported as a subgame perfect Nash equilibrium provided the players are sufficiently concerned with future pay-offs. By individually rational it is meant that each player gains at least its *maximin* level of welfare. This is the minimum pay-off a player can guarantee for itself provided they act rationally. A feasible outcome is merely one that can be obtained by some combination of players' strategies, not necessarily equilibrium ones. This result vastly increases the set of strategy combinations that can be supported as a credible equilibrium. In particular, given that countries adopt appropriate punishment strategies environmental co-operation can be sustained provided countries do not overly discount the future. In this way an IEA can be self-enforcing. A similar result can be obtained if interaction between countries is finite but indeterminant. Even if interaction ends after a finite period of time, an IEA may still be self-enforcing if there is incomplete information. In this situation there is uncertainty about another country's social welfare function. For example, it may not be completely known how strongly a country views a particular environmental problem. Here a country might on moral grounds credibly threaten severe retaliation against any country breaking an IEA. With this threat other countries may be deterred from deviating. Again all countries will be made better off, and the free-rider problem avoided.

As just discussed an IEA may be subgame perfect if countries adopt appropriate punishment strategies. One criticism often made of this approach is that it ignores the possibility of renegotiation. Specifically, the above mechanisms rely on countries adopting punishment strategies and pursuing them until the end of the game. However, with no international authority able to compel countries to act in this way, there is always the possibility that countries will seek to renegotiate an agreement. This can undermine the credibility of future punishment, and the basis of environmental co-operation. If, for example, one country breaks an environmental agreement, then according to the proposed punishment strategy it should be punished by the other countries. This may, however, involve the punishing countries themselves being made worse off compared to the co-operative solution. If this is the case, then they clearly have an incentive to let bygones be bygones and renegotiate the agreement. In this way it is hoped that co-operation can be restored, so that all countries can again be made better off. The problem with this reasoning is that if renegotiation is anticipated countries will not expect to be punished for breaking an agreement, and so countries are not deterred from doing so. Once again countries will be unable to co-ordinate on the co-operative outcome.

One way to incorporate the possibility of renegotiation is to require the initial equilibrium strategies to be *renegotiation proof*. With this refinement of Nash equilibrium the predicted outcome must be subgame perfect, and there must also be no incentive for players to renegotiate the agreement once deviation is observed. Conditions under which strategies are renegotiation proof have been given by Farrell and Maskin (1989). For a punishment strategy to be *weakly renegotiation proof* it must be the case that the punishing players are better off punishing the offender rather than letting bygones be bygones and returning to the co-operative outcome. A further requirement for a strategy to be *strongly renegotiation proof* is that the pay-offs during punishment must not be Pareto-dominated. As each of these refinements place further restrictions over the set of possible equilibrium strategies, it is no longer the case that the co-operative solution can be self-supporting. Barrett (1994) applies the strong renegotiation proof criteria to a multi-country model with a reciprocal environmental externality. In this model whether environmental co-operation is self-enforcing depends on specific parameter values. In particular, co-operation is only possible if the number of countries involved is below a critical number. This critical number of countries depends, in turn, on the marginal costs and benefits of environmental control. Barrett's conclusion is that when there are a large number of countries, IEAs are only self-supporting if the net benefits of co-operation are small. Significantly, if either the benefits or costs of co-operation are large, then the free-rider problem prevails, and full co-operation cannot be achieved. This yields the rather pessimistic conclusion that when co-operation is most needed it is least likely to be observed.

10.2.3 Stable coalitions

The free-rider problem discussed previously states that when all players in a game produce the fully co-operative outcome, some, if not all, players will seek to deviate from it. This implies that the fully co-operative solution is unstable. It can be noted, however, that the free-rider problem does not necessarily imply that all coalitions are unstable. It may well be the case that smaller coalitions, consisting of only a subset of players in the game, are stable. In this situation the players within the coalition seek to maximize their joint welfare, while other players maximize their individual welfare. The final outcome will be one of *partial co-operation*. Donsimoni *et al.* (1986) show that the existence of stable coalitions exists under fairly general conditions. This seems a potentially helpful insight in explaining the existence of IEAs, as indeed it is often only a subset of all nations who sign any agreement. In this context a coalition will be stable when two conditions are satisfied. (These conditions were initially developed by D'Aspremont and Gabszewicz (1986) in the context of oligopoly.) *First*, none of the signatories must have an incentive to leave the coalition unilaterally. This means that none of the signatories has an incentive to free-ride on the agreement. *Second*, none of the non-signatories, acting in self-interest, wants to join the coalition. When both of these conditions are satisfied, the number of signatories to an environmental agreement remains constant, and so the coalition is stable. The final outcome will lie somewhere between the fully co-operative outcome and the non-cooperative solution. The larger the number of countries forming the co-operative coalition the closer the final outcome will be to the fully

---

EXERCISE 10.2.*

In this exercise we determine the equilibrium number of countries that will sign an IEA which maximizes the joint welfare of signatories, for a specific multi-country model.

Assume there are n identical countries indexed $i = 1, \ldots, n$. Each country seeks to choose its optimal level of pollution abatement, A_i. Social welfare for country i (V_i) is given by

$$V_i = bA - \frac{c}{2} A_i^2$$

where A is the total level of pollution abatement across all countries, and b and c are positive constants. Assume that n^* countries sign an IEA to act co-operatively and maximize the joint welfare of the signatories nations. Non-signatories are assumed to act non-cooperatively, and maximize their individual welfare.

(1) Find expressions for the optimal levels of abatement for individual signatory and non-signatory countries.

(2) Determine the levels of welfare for individual signatory and non-signatory countries.

(3) Using your results from (2) specify the two conditions necessary for a coalition to be stable.

(4) Show that if there are five total countries, then a stable coalition comprising of three countries exists.

co-operative solution. In general the equilibrium number of countries wishing to sign an IEA will depend on the functional specification and parameters of the model being used.

One criticism of this approach is that the number of countries forming a stable coalition is often found to be small. This has led economists to seek ways that other countries can be induced to sign an IEA, and so enlarge the number of signatories. Here we consider three ways that have been suggested for how this might be achieved. These are the use of side payments when some countries are committed to environmental control, linking IEAs to other issues that countries are concerned about, and matching.

Side payments and commitment

One approach that has often been suggested how stable coalitions might be expanded is by again introducing the possibility of side payments. It is argued that because co-operating countries are made better off when the number of countries within the coalition increases there is an incentive for them to offer side payments to non-cooperating countries to induce them to become signatories. Carraro and Siniscalco (1995), however, have demonstrated that the resulting coalition is unstable. The reason for this is that with side payments on offer the incentive to be an original non-signatory is now greater. This induces some of the original signatories to leave the coalition. In equilibrium the number of countries joining the coalition is unchanged. One way to overcome this problem is to introduce some form of commitment by countries to remain part of the coalition. If this commitment exists, all countries can be made better off by inducing non-signatories to join the coalition via the use of side payments. Clearly the problem with this approach is that a country merely saying it is committed to an IEA is not credible. This is because the committed country could do better for itself if it free-rides on the agreement when other countries become signatories. In order for the coalition to be expanded current signatories need credibly to commit themselves to the agreement. One way to do this might be through overinvestment in abatement technology. This reduces the cost of future abatement, and makes it less likely that that country will leave the coalition. Alternatively, a country may try and develop a reputation for being co-operative, or morally committed to environmental control. This will only be possible if there is incomplete information about the true nature of signatories. To develop such a reputation it will need to undertake some action that is costly to itself. This might involve not breaking the conditions of an IEA even though this would increase its short-term welfare. Alternatively, it might increase its own pollution abatement above that required to maximize its own social welfare. In this way the country acts as a leader in overcoming international problems, and may lead to all countries being made eventually better off.

Linking IEAs to other issues

Another possible way of encouraging non-signatories to sign a multilateral environmental agreement is to link the agreement to other issues countries are concerned about. For example, continued free trade, financial aid, or co-operation on research and development might be made conditional on countries signing the environmental agreement. This carrot-and/or-stick approach will change the pay-offs faced by countries and may cause the stable coalition to be expanded. Carraro and Siniscalco (1995) demonstrate that this is indeed possible in a model where technological co-operation between countries is dependant on countries signing an IEA. In their model, enlarging environmental co-operation is desirable but on its own unstable. Technological co-operation, however, is both desirable and stable. By linking these issues all countries can be made better off. In effect the gains of free-riding on the IEA are now offset by the cost of reduced technological co-operation.

Related to this issue of linked agreements is the role of trade provisions within IEAs. The Montreal Protocol (1987), for example, bans the import and export of products containing chlorofluorocarbons (CFCs) from or to non-signatory nations. Although primarily designed to prevent non-signatories offsetting the pollution abatement of signatories, it also enhances the incentive for countries to sign the agreement. In this way the self-enforcing coalition is again expanded, and all countries are made better off.

Matching

As discussed above the equilibrium number of countries signing a self-enforcing IEA depends on the structure and parameter of the model. In particular it is dependent on the slope of the reaction functions of individual countries. If the reaction curves relating different countries abatement levels are negatively sloped, this means that if one country increases its level of abatement other countries will abate less. The more steeply sloped the reaction curves, the smaller the benefits of any one country reducing its emissions. This reduces the incentive to sign an IEA, and so other things being equal the smaller the resulting coalition. Conversely, the flatter the reaction curves, the larger the resulting coalition. One way in which reaction curves can be made flatter is for countries to adopt a matching rate of abatement. Here countries agree to match, at least to some extent, the abatement levels of other countries. This increases the benefits of any one country joining the coalition as now other signatories will match the increased abatement. This will increase the equilibrium number of countries within the coalition, and move the final outcome closer to the fully co-operative solution. Guttman (1978) has indeed shown, within a different context, that matching can under certain conditions, support the fully co-operative outcome.

10.3 Conclusions

This chapter has focused on international environmental problems. Specifically, we have analysed the incentives for countries to enter into international environmental agreements (IEAs). This was undertaken in the context of both bilateral and multilateral agreements. Of particular interest was the possible use of side payments between countries. It has been suggested that in bilateral agreements these can be used to internalize environmental externalities, and in multilateral agreements they can be used to expand the number of signatories. This chapter has, however, highlighted a number of theoretical and practical problems associated with side payments. These considerations reduce the likelihood that countries will use side payments to alleviate environmental problems. Instead, other mechanisms will have to be found for inducing countries to work co-operatively. These may include the use of punishment strategies directed against countries that break international agreements, the linking of IEAs to other issues, and the possibility of matching. By employing these and other strategies it is hoped countries will have the incentive to work together to improve our environment for the benefit of all.

10.4 Solutions to Exercises

Exercise 10.1

(1) Acting non-cooperatively each country maximizes its welfare taking the other country's level of abatement as given. Differentiating each country's welfare function with respect to its own level of abatement and setting this equal to zero yields the following first-order conditions.

$$\frac{dF}{dA_1} = \frac{dC_1}{dA_1}$$

$$\frac{dF}{dA_2} = \frac{dC_2}{dA_2}.$$

As each country's marginal benefit depends only on the aggregate level of pollution, and hence on the aggregate level of abatement, A, these conditions can be rewritten as

$$\frac{dF}{dA} = \frac{dC_1}{dA_1} = \frac{dC_2}{dA_2}.$$

In equilibrium each country determines its optimal level of abatement by setting its own marginal benefit equal to its own marginal cost. Assuming the equilibrium is not a corner solution marginal costs of abatement will be equal in both countries. This Nash equilibrium is illustrated as point NE in Fig. 10.2. At this point the indifference curves intersect and so this equilibrium is not Pareto efficient. Any point within the shaded lens shaped area will improve the welfare of both countries.

(2) Joint welfare of the two countries is given by

$$V = 2F(A_1 + A_2 - E) - C_1(A_1) - C_2(A_2).$$

Differentiating this function with respect to each country's level of abatement, we obtain the following optimality conditions.

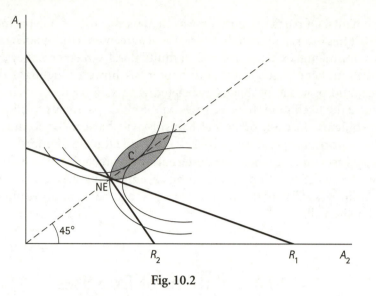

Fig. 10.2

$$2. \frac{\mathrm{d}F}{\mathrm{d}A} = \frac{\mathrm{d}C_1}{\mathrm{d}A_1} = \frac{\mathrm{d}C_2}{\mathrm{d}A_2}.$$

The first half of this expression states that countries will increase abatement until joint marginal benefit equals the marginal cost of doing so. Compared to the non-cooperative outcome this will entail a greater level of aggregate abatement as now each country considers the beneficial effects its environmental policy has on the other. Compared to the co-operative solution the Nash equilibrium entails excessive use of the common resource. This is an important game theory result that can be generalized. If individuals or countries have free access to a common resource and act non-cooperatively, then we can expect that resource to be overused, and the outcome to be Pareto inefficient. The second half of this condition again states that the marginal cost of abatement in equilibrium must be the same in each country. This guarantees that the aggregate level of abatement is produced at minimum cost. For efficiency to be achieved, not only must the socially desirable level of abatement be achieved, but also the costs of doing so must be optimally shared between countries. These conditions can be replicated if the two countries adopt appropriate side payments dependent on the other country's level of abatement. This is demonstrated in (3).

(3) With the possibility of side payments between countries dependent upon levels of abatement each country's welfare function is given as

$$V_1 = F(A_1 + A_2 - E) - C_1(A_1) + T_2(A_1) - T_1(A_2)$$

and

$$V_2 = F(A_1 + A_2 - E) - C_2(A_2) + T_1(A_2) - T_2(A_1).$$

where $T_i(A_{-i})$ is the amount country i transfers to the other country $(-i)$, dependent upon the other country's level of abatement. Differentiating each function with respect to that country's level of abatement and setting these equal to zero yields the following first-order conditions.

$$\frac{dF}{dA_1} + \frac{dT_2}{dA_1} = \frac{dC_1}{dA_1}$$

$$\frac{dF}{dA_2} + \frac{dT_1}{dA_2} = \frac{dC_2}{dA_2}.$$

With the marginal rates of transfer payments set equal to the marginal benefit of abatement we obtain the co-operative solution. Here each country is induced to increase its own optimal level of abatement due to the financial incentive provided by the other country.

(4) If both countries are identical, then each country will abate pollution by the same amount. In the diagram given in answer to (1) this is given as point C. This point is Pareto efficient as the two countries' indifference curves are tangential, and on the 45° line. It seems reasonable to assume that with identical countries the gains of co-ordinating upon this outcome will be divided evenly. If this is true, each country will receive the same level of transfer payment from the other. If only *net* side payments are actually transferred, then there will be no payments made. The co-operative solution is derived from instrumentally rational behaviour supported by side payments even though in equilibrium no side payments are ever made! The reason for this paradoxical result is that there is now an effective punishment if either country deviates from the 'co-operative' outcome. Without the possibility of side payments each country will reduce its level of abatement. However, with side payments this means that any deviating country will pay a net side payment to the other country. It is this extra cost of deviating from the co-operative solution that induces countries to maintain the optimal abatement levels.

(5) If marginal costs are constant, either we obtain the result explained in (4), or only one country abates its pollution. This first result occurs when the countries have the same constant marginal cost of abatement, and so the two countries are identical. The second result occurs when the countries have different constant marginal costs. In this situation the requirement that in equilibrium marginal costs are equal cannot be satisfied, and so we have a corner solution. In order for aggregate abatement to be produced at least cost the more efficient country will undertake all the required abatement. In this situation only the abating country receives any side payment, and pays nothing to the other country.

Exercise 10.2

(1) Non-signatories to the IEA seek to maximize $V_i^{NS} = bA - (c/2)A_i^2$. By differentiating with respect to A_i we can derive that non-signatories will set their level of abatement equal to $A_i^{NS} = b/c$. Signatories to the IEA, however, seek to maximize their joint welfare

$$V^S = n^* bA - \sum_{i=1}^{N^*} \frac{c}{2} A_i^2.$$

From the first-order condition for a maximum we obtain that signatories set their abatement levels equal to $A_i^S = n^* b/c$.

(2) From (1) total abatement, A, is equal to $(n^* - n)(b/c) + n^*((n^*b)/c)$. Substituting this into each country's welfare function and simplifying gives us the following levels of welfare for signatories and non-signatories:

$$V_i^S(n^*) = \frac{b^2(n^{*2} - 2n^* + 2n)}{2c}.$$

$$V_i^{NS}(n^*) = \frac{b^2(2n^{*2} - 2n^* + 2n - 1)}{2c}.$$

(3) The first condition for an equilibrium is that signatories must have no incentive to leave the coalition unilaterally. This implies that $V_i^S(n^*) \geq V_i^{NS}(n^* - 1)$. From the answer to (2) this means that in equilibrium

$$V_i^S(n^*) = \frac{b^2(n^{*2} - 2n^* + 2n)}{2c} \geq \frac{b^2[2(n^* - 1)^2 - 2(n^* - 1) + 2n - 1]}{2c} = V_i^{NS}(n^* - 1).$$

The second equilibrium condition is that non-signatories have no incentive to become signatories. This implies that $V_i^{NS}(n^*) \geq V_i^S(n^* + 1)$. This can be written as

$$V_i^S(n^*) = \frac{b^2(n^{*2} - 2n^* + 2n - 1)}{2c} \geq \frac{b^2[(n^* + 1)^2 - 2(n^* + 1) + 2n]}{2c} = V_i^S(n^* + 1).$$

(4) When $n = 5$ and $n^* = 3$ it can be confirmed that the first of the above equilibrium conditions is just satisfied, while the second condition is met by an inequality. This means that the signatories are indifferent to becoming non-signatories, but non-signatories strictly prefer not joining the coalition. With both conditions being jointly satisfied the coalition of three countries is confirmed to be a stable equilibrium.

Further Reading

Barrett, S. (1990), 'The Problem of Global Environmental Protection', *Oxford Review of Economic Policy*, 6: 68–79; repr. in D. Helm (1991), *Economic Policy Towards the Environment*, Oxford: Blackwell; also in T. Jenkinson (1996), *Readings in Microeconomics*, New York: Oxford University Press.

Field, B. (1994), *Environmental Economics: An Introduction*, New York: McGraw-Hill.

Hanley, N., J. F. Shogren, and B. White (1997), *Environmental Economics: In Theory and Practice*, London: Macmillan.

Mäler, G-M. (1991), 'International Environmental Problems', in D. Helm (ed.), *Economic Policy Towards the Environment*, Oxford: Blackwell.

Pearce, D. W., and R. K. Turner (1990), *Economics of Natural Resources and the Environment*, Hemel Hempstead: Harvester Wheatsheaf.

Perman, R., Y. Ma, and J. McGilvray (1996), *Natural Resources and Environmental Economics*, London: Longman.

11
Experimental Economics

PREVIOUS chapters have largely focused on the theoretical implications of applying game theory concepts to various areas of economics. Part of economics, however, has been concerned with testing whether the predictions of game theory are confirmed by individuals' making interdependent decisions in a controlled environment. This is part of the rapidly expanding area of experimental economics. In this chapter we review a number of experiments that have directly sought to test some of the more important game theory concepts used in previous chapters.

In section 11.1 the fundamental concept of Nash equilibrium is examined. Here we present experiments where individuals played both one-off and repeated prisoners' dilemma games. Observations from such experiments can then be used to test the predictions of Nash equilibrium and subgame perfect Nash equilibrium. A typical finding in these experiments is that the cooperative outcome is observed much more frequently than is suggested by these equilibrium concepts. This section also outlines possible explanations for why this might be so. One common interpretation of why individuals are observed to be more co-operative than predicted is that, in the games being played, there is incomplete information. With this type of uncertainty one relevant refinement of Nash equilibrium is that of sequential equilibrium. Given the widespread use of sequential equilibrium, section 11.2 reviews a number of experiments that set out to test its predictions against observed behaviour.

In many games the predictions of game theory are highly specific and can be directly tested against experimental evidence. This is true for the decision-making problems used in experiments reviewed in the first two sections of this chapter. In other games, however, the predictions of game theory are less precise. This occurs, for example, when there are multiple equilibria. In such games there is the possibility of co-ordination failure. This occurs when players fail to co-ordinate on a Pareto-dominant equilibrium. Section 11.3 reviews experiments that examine how individuals make decisions when there is this possibility of co-ordination failure.

11.1 Nash Equilibrium

A number of experiments have sought to test the predictions of game theory about how rational individuals will play certain games. For example, there have been an enormous number of experiments concerned with how people play prisoners' dilemma games. If players view each game as a one-off event, then observed behaviour can be used to test the prediction that individuals determine their optimal strategy based on Nash equilibrium reasoning or strict-dominance arguments. Alternatively, if individuals perceive they are playing a finite number of repetitions of the prisoners' dilemma game, then observed behaviour can be used to test the prediction that individuals determine their chosen strategy based on the principle of backward induction, which yields the subgame perfect Nash equilibrium. Before examining some of the experimental evidence conducted on prisoners' dilemma games it should be remembered that the concepts of Nash equilibrium and subgame perfection are based on the combination of two fundamental assumptions. The *first* is that individuals are instrumentally rational, whilst the *second* is that this is common knowledge. At best, experimental evidence can only test the joint hypothesis formed by these two assumptions. If the experimental evidence contradicts the predictions of either Nash equilibrium or subgame perfection, it will not, in general, be clear which of these two underlying assumptions has been violated.

Rather than attempt to review the now hundreds of experiments undertaken to examine how individuals play one-off and repeated prisoners' dilemma games, we restrict ourselves to reporting two recent and fairly typical experiments. The first is by Cooper *et al.* (1991) and is concerned with how individuals play a series of one-off prisoners' dilemma games. The second by Selten and Stoecker (1986) examines the effects when such games are finitely repeated.

In the Cooper *et al.* (1991) experiment individuals played a prisoners' dilemma game twenty times against different players. The reason why players were not paired together more than once was to encourage subjects to view each game as a one-off rather than as a single round of a repeated game. Players made their moves simultaneously without communicating with their opponent. The actual game played is shown in Fig. 11.1.

The pay-offs shown, however, do not correspond to monetary payments but rather to points a player could earn. The greater the number of points a player obtains, the greater the probability that he or she will win a monetary prize in a subsequent lottery. The incentive behind this mechanism is to offset differences in risk preference. In contrast, if the pay-offs in Fig. 11.1 corresponded directly to monetary payments, and players perceived their opponent was playing a mixed strategy, then their optimal strategy would depend on risk preference. The lottery mechanism, therefore, seeks to induce individuals to maximize the number of points earned irrespective of their risk preference.

With individuals seeking to maximize the number of points earned the unique Nash equilibrium for this game is that both players should play non-cooperatively and adopt

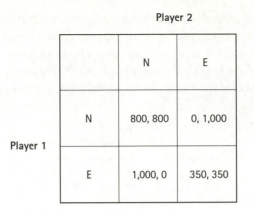

Fig. 11.1 The Prisoners' Dilemma Game used by Cooper *et al.* (1991)

the pure strategy, E. As this is a prisoners' dilemma game this is also the solution based on strict dominance. If, however, both players play co-operatively, that is N, then both are made better off. Finally, the preferred outcome for a player is for that player to deviate from co-operation, E, whilst the other player co-operates, N. The results of how subjects played this game are shown in Table 11.1.

Table 11.1 Results from Cooper *et al.* (1991)

Matchings	Percentage of co-operative choices (N)
1–5	43%
6–10	33%
11–15	25%
16–20	20%

As can be seen from Table 11.1 subjects played the co-operative solution a significant proportion of the time even though this is strictly dominated by the strategy of always playing non-cooperatively. However, as the subjects gain greater experience of the game the rate of co-operation falls. For the first five matchings co-operation was observed 43 per cent of the time. For the last five matchings this fell to only 20 per cent. From these observations it seems that individuals need some experience of the game before they tend towards the Nash equilibrium. However, even after many repetitions of the game some individuals continued to play the dominated strategy at least some of the time. These results are fairly typical of other experiments conducted on one-off prisoners' dilemma games. In conclusion, the prediction that the outcome of the game played between rational individuals will be the Nash equilibrium receives only limited support. Similar conclusions are derived by Selten and Stoecker (1986).

In Selten and Stoecker's experiment individuals played a 10-period repeated prisoners' dilemma 'supergame' game, which was itself repeated twenty-five times. Within each 'supergame' subjects played against the same opponent, but they played different opponents in different 'supergames'. Subjects did not know whom they were playing against. The outcome of each individual prisoners' dilemma game was announced to the players at the end of each period. Apart from this there was no communication between players. The actual stage game played by subjects in this experiment is shown in Fig. 11.2.

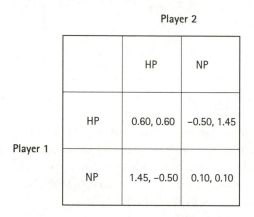

Fig. 11.2 The Prisoners' Dilemma Game used by Selten and Stoecker (1986)

In this experiment the pay-offs were monetary payments denominated in German Marks. Although subjects played the same prisoners' dilemma game repeatedly against the same opponent the subgame perfect equilibrium is that the Nash equilibrium for this stage game (NP/NP) will be played in every period. This can be confirmed by applying the principle of backward induction to each 'supergame'.

The main finding of this experiment was that subjects again co-operated much more than predicted on the basis of (subgame perfect) Nash equilibrium. Once subjects had gained sufficient experience of the game the following pattern of behaviour typically emerged. At the start of each 'supergame' both players would initially co-operate, (HP), until one of them defected, (NP). Once defection was observed both players would then play non-cooperatively until the end of that 'supergame'. Based on observed behaviour and written statements by the players Selten and Stoecker estimated the intended period of deviation for each player within each 'supergame'. The mean and standard deviation of these estimates over all subjects are plotted in Fig. 11.3 for the final twelve 'supergames'. In calculating these statistics Selten and Stoecker only included 'supergames' which were classified as an 'end-effect play'. This was defined as a game where at least four periods of co-operation were observed followed firstly by defection by one player and then the Nash equilibrium thereafter. If a player intended to co-operate for the entire 'supergame', their intended period of deviation was set equal to 11.

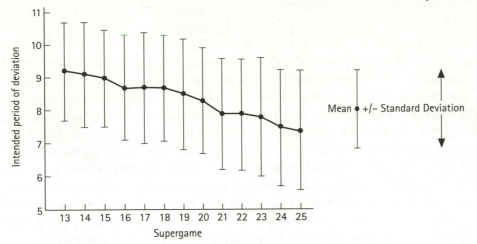

Fig. 11.3 Mean and Standard Deviation of the Intended Period of Deviation in 'End-Effect Plays' for Final 12 'Supergames' (Selten and Stoecker 1986)

As can be seen from Fig. 11.3 players experienced with this 'supergame' intended to co-operate, on average, for at least the first seven periods. It is also clear that on average players intended to deviate earlier in later 'supergames'. It appears that having initially learnt to co-operate, players then learnt to deviate earlier in the hope of being the first player to do so and so earn a higher pay-off. It is not clear, however, if this subsequent unravelling process would have continued with extended repetitions until subjects ceased to co-operate in any period. Despite this possibility the subgame perfect Nash equilibrium is not a good predictor of how subjects actually played this finitely repeated prisoners' dilemma game. This finding has again been confirmed by many other experiments analysing how individuals play repeated prisoners' dilemma games.

From the experiments reported by Cooper *et al.* (1991), Selten and Stoecker (1986), and others, the predictions of game theory based on the dual assumptions that individuals are instrumentally rational and common knowledge of rationality can only be said to have received limited support. In general individuals are more likely to act co-operatively than is predicted on the basis of these assumptions. This evidence indicates that the predictions of game theory based on these assumptions do not give us the complete picture, and that important aspects of how individuals make decisions have been ignored. Partly as a result of these experimental findings economists and non-economists have attempted to identify what some of these missing aspects might be. Here we review five suggested explanations for why individuals are observed to be more co-operative than the predictions of Nash equilibrium and subgame perfect Nash equilibrium when confronted with prisoners' dilemma games.

11.1.1 Altruism

One common interpretation of the above experimental evidence is that not all individuals are solely motivated by monetary rewards. Instead it is often argued that some individuals receive additional utility when they act altruistically. Andreoni and Miller (1993) present three different ways in which altruism might affect an individual's utility within a prisoners' dilemma game. The first is called *pure altruism*. In this situation a player is not only concerned with his or her own pay-off but also with the utility of the other player. Here an individual receives additional utility the greater the pay-off gained by the other player. The second model of altruism they call *duty*. Here the individual feels a certain moral obligation to act co-operatively rather than competitively. In this case an individual receives additional utility when he or she acts co-operatively. Finally, an individual's utility may be affected by *reciprocal altruism*. In this case an individual receives extra utility if *both* players act co-operatively. This model has also been called the 'warm glow' effect as it is supposes that players receive particular pleasure when there is mutual co-operation.

The significant effect of each of these types of altruism is that individuals' pay-offs from playing a game such as the prisoners' dilemma need no longer be the same as those explicitly set by the experimenter. With a different pay-off function it may cease to be true that competition dominates co-operation. With this interpretation individuals observed to co-operate may still be maximizing their pay-off functions, but that these can no longer be directly observed. Furthermore as the pay-off functions are no longer directly observed this means that the game actually being played is one of incomplete information. Each player can be assumed to know their own pay-off function but is unsure of the pay-off function of the opponent. This clearly increases the uncertainty each player experiences when playing the game. This uncertainty raises the possibility that in repeated prisoners' dilemma games players may seek to develop a reputation for being altruistic by playing co-operatively. As discussed below each of these considerations of uncertainty and reputation have been further used to explain experimental results observed with prisoners' dilemma games.

11.1.2 Learning

Another interpretation of the experimental results obtained from prisoners' dilemma games concerns the role of learning when individuals are boundedly rational. One suggestion is that individuals do not determine which strategy to play on the basis of explicit maximization, but rather on the basis of trial and error. This approach has replicated work undertaken by biologists seeking to explain the evolution of animal behaviour. In consequence games incorporating these learning dynamics are known as *evolutionary games*. In these games individuals initially choose an arbitrary strategy, and then adjust their strategy in the light of experience. If a strategy is seen to be successful, it is more

EXERCISE 11.1

In the text it was argued that individuals may choose to play co-operatively within a prisoners' dilemma game if they are sufficiently altruistic. This exercise demonstrates this proposition using each of the three models of altruism discussed previously. Assume that in a hypothetical experiment subjects are asked to play the following one-off prisoners' dilemma game against a randomly assigned anonymous opponent.

Player 2

		C	D
Player 1	C	10, 10	6, 12
	D	12, 6	8, 8

Assume there are a large number of individuals, indexed $i = 1, \ldots, n$, all of whom seek to maximize *expected utility*. Predict the proportion of subjects that will play co-operatively under the following scenarios.

(1) Duty
Individual i's utility (V_i) is given by the equation $V_i = \Pi_i + \alpha_i$, where Π_i is the pay-off as given by the game itself, while α_i is the extra utility the person obtains if he or she plays co-operatively, (C). Individuals only know their own value of α and that within the subject population this variable is uniformly distributed over the range of 0 to 8 inclusive.

(2) Reciprocal altruism
Again an individual's utility is given by $V_i = \Pi_i + \alpha_i$, but this time α_i refers to the extra utility gained if *both* players co-operate (C). Other assumptions are the same as those given in (1).

(3) Pure altruism
This time an individual i's utility is given as $V_i = \Pi_i + \alpha_i \Pi_{-i}$, where Π_{-i} is the pay-off gained by the other person, and α_i the weight an individual attaches to other people's welfare. Individuals only know their own value of α and that within the subject population this variable is uniformly distributed over the range 0 to 1 inclusive.

Hint: For each model let *Prob* equal the probability that an individual's opponent will play co-operatively, and then calculate the expected levels of utility associated with playing either C or D. From these equations calculate the critical value of α_i, α^*, so that individual's with $\alpha_i > \alpha^*$ will play co-operatively. Finally *Prob* can be determined from the equation $Prob(\alpha_i > \alpha^*) = (\alpha_{max} - \alpha^*)/\alpha_{max}$, where α_{max} is the maximum possible value of α.

likely to be adopted in the future rounds. If seen to be unsuccessful, then it is less likely to be adopted in the future. This adjustment process may be viewed in one of two ways. The first is to imagine that a number of individuals change their adopted pure strategy to more successful strategies. The second justification is that individuals initially play a mixed strategy and subsequently adjust the probability mix over their pure strategies. Here the probability of an individual playing a successful strategy increases. In either situation the result is the same. Successful strategies are played more frequently in the future. With either process an equilibrium occurs when the economy reaches a steady state, and by definition the probability distribution over alternative strategies remains unchanged. Such an equilibrium may be either stable or unstable. An equilibrium is stable if, when disturbed by small changes in players' strategies, possibly due to players making mistakes, players eventually return to their original strategies . In this case the equilibrium is known as an *evolutionarily stable strategy*. If the dynamics of the system lead away from the original equilibrium, it is said to be unstable. Significantly an evolutionarily stable strategy must be a Nash equilibrium. However, not all Nash equilibria are evolutionarily stable. Furthermore whilst learning is still taking place out-of-quilibrium strategies will be played. To illustrate some of these ideas we apply a particular learning process to the prisoners' dilemma game used in the experiment by Cooper *et al.* (1991).

We assume that a large number of individuals play this one-off game a number of times against different randomly selected opponents. It is assumed that the learning process adopted by individuals can be represented by the following dynamic equation

$$\frac{\mathrm{d}Prob}{\mathrm{d}t} = Prob(\Pi(\mathrm{E}) - \overline{\Pi}) \tag{11.1}$$

where *Prob* is the probability that a player will play strategy E, $\Pi(\mathrm{E})$ is the expected pay-off from playing this strategy, and $\overline{\Pi}$ is the average pay-off over all individuals. This equation states that the change in the probability of players playing strategy E is proportional to its current probability multiplied by the difference between its expected pay-off and the average pay-off. If the strategy's expected pay-off is greater than the average pay-off received by players, then the probability of this strategy being played increases over time.

Using the game represented in Fig. 11.1 we can calculate the expected pay-off for an individual playing either N or E. The expected pay-off of playing N is

$$\Pi(\mathrm{N}) = 800(1 - Prob) + 0\ Prob = 800 - 800\ Prob \tag{11.2}$$

and the expected pay-off of playing E is

$$\Pi(\mathrm{E}) = 1{,}000(1 - Prob) + 350\ Prob = 1{,}000 - 650\ Prob \tag{11.3}$$

From these equations we can calculate the average pay-off over all individuals.

$$\overline{\Pi}\ Prob\ \Pi(\mathrm{E}) + (1 - Prob)\ \Pi(\mathrm{N})$$

$$= 150\,Prob^2 - 600\,Prob + 800. \tag{11.4}$$

Substituting (11.3) and (11.4) into (11.1) and rearranging gives us the following dynamic equation

$$\frac{\mathrm{d}Prob}{\mathrm{d}t} = Prob(\Pi(\mathrm{E}) - \overline{\Pi}) \tag{11.5}$$

Fig. 11.4 plots this equation over the permitted range of *Prob* between 0 and 1 inclusive. From this so-called phase diagram two steady-state equilibria can be identified.

EXERCISE 11.2

In a hypothetical experiment assume that subjects are asked to play one of the two following symmetric games a number of times against different anonymous opponents. For successive repetitions of the game individuals are randomly paired together from a large subject pool. For each of the one-off games identify the pure and mixed-strategy Nash equilibria. Finally, assuming that individuals are boundedly rational, determine the evolutionary stable strategy when subjects adopt the following learning process

$$\frac{\mathrm{d}Prob}{\mathrm{d}t} = Prob(\,\Pi(\mathrm{A}) - \overline{\Pi}\,)$$

where *Prob* is the probability that an individual will play strategy A, $\Pi(\mathrm{A})$ is the expected pay-off from playing strategy A, and $\overline{\Pi}$ is the average pay-off over all individuals.

(1) Co-ordination game

Player 2

		A	B
Player 1	A	20, 20	10, 0
	B	0, 10	30, 30

(2) Chicken

Player 2

		A	B
Player 1	A	30, 30	20, 40
	B	40, 20	10, 10

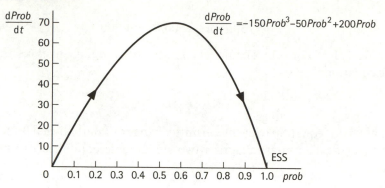

Fig. 11.4 An Evolutionarily Stable Strategy (ESS)

These occur when $dProb/dt = 0$ and so the probabilities $Prob = 0$ and $Prob = 1$ both correspond to steady-state equilibria. With any other initial probability distribution it must be true that $dProb/dt > 0$. This implies that out of equilibrium the probability of individuals playing strategy E will increase over time. (This is illustrated by the directional arrows in the phase diagram.) This result generally conforms to the observations made by Cooper *et al.* (1991) that the percentage of subjects playing the co-operative strategy (N) declined over the course of the experiment. This learning approach predicts, however, that this process should eventually converge upon the equilibrium where all players play the non-cooperative strategy all the time. This equilibrium is the unique evolutionarily stable strategy, and corresponds to the Nash equilibrium of this prisoners' dilemma game.

The above analysis has demonstrated how a dynamic learning process can be used to analyse a series of symmetrical one-off games. Exercise 11.2 provides two further examples of this type of game. This approach can also be extended to analyse more complex repeated games. Indeed Selten and Stoecker (1986) develop a learning model to interpret the results observed from their repeated prisoners' dilemma experiment. Specifically, the period in which individuals intend to deviate to the non-cooperative strategy is related to the outcome in the previous 'supergame'. They demonstrate that based on parameter estimates derived from the first twenty 'supergames' they can successfully predict individual's strategies in the last five 'supergames'.

11.1.3 Uncertainty

The prisoners' dilemma game has not only been of interest to economists but also to many psychologists. Shafir and Tversky (1992), for example, use experiments on a prisoners' dilemma game to examine how subjects make decisions in the presence of uncertainty. In their experiment they compare the rates of co-operation in the normal one-off prisoners' dilemma game with co-operation rates when one of the players is informed of the other player's initial move. In the sequential move game 16 per cent of subjects played co-operatively when they knew their opponent had initially played co-operatively. In contrast only 3 per cent of subjects played co-operatively when they knew their opponent had played non-cooperatively. On its own this evidence tends to support the model of reciprocal altruism discussed above. However, the most significant result of this paper is that in the simultaneous game 37 per cent of subjects were observed to play co-operatively. Shafir and Tversky argue that this result cannot be solely attributed to players being altruistic, as this would imply subjects being most co-operative when they knew their opponent had played co-operatively. Instead they attribute some of the high rates of co-operation in the normal prisoners' dilemma game to the inherent uncertainty of the game. Thus they write 'uncertainty promotes a tendency to co-operate, which disappears once the other player's decision has been determined. It appears that many subjects did not appropriately evaluate each possible outcome and its implications.' With this interpretation individuals attempt to maximize their utility but are unable fully to evaluate outcomes when their consequences are unclear. It is again this limited rationality that causes individuals to act co-operatively.

11.1.4 Reputation

The above explanations of why individuals co-operate in prisoners' dilemma games have essentially focused on the psychological factors of altruism, learning, and bounded rationality. Interestingly Kreps *et al.* (1982) have demonstrated that if, due to these reasons, players perceive there is a small probability that their opponent will play co-operatively, then within a finitely repeated prisoners' dilemma game it can be rational for players to co-operate in early periods of the game. In this way player's develop a reputation for being co-operative, and this maximizes their pay-off over the entire game. This explanation states that due to incomplete information a relevant equilibrium concept used to predict the behaviour of individuals playing such a game is that of sequential equilibrium. Typically the profile of an individual's play in such an equilibrium involves three stages. Initially rational players play co-operatively. In the second phase players adopt a mixed strategy where they assign positive probabilities over co-operation and deviation. In this stage non-deviation will enhance the individual's reputation for being co-operative. Eventually, in the third stage a rational player, if he or she has not already done so, will certainly deviate from co-operation. It may be noted that such an equilibrium fits well with the observed behaviour of experienced players in Selten and Stoecker's (1986) repeated game experiment. Indeed, even the unravelling process, whereby individuals having learnt to co-operate then learnt to deviate earlier in the game, can be explained as part of a sequential equilibrium. This is done by assuming that, as the players gain more experience of the game, they revise downwards the probability that other players are 'irrational'. If there were no 'irrational' players in the subject population, this process would continue until the sequential equilibrium converged on the subgame perfect equilibrium.

11.1.5 Group reputation

In the sequential equilibrium described above individuals may seek to establish a reputation of being co-operative. This can only occur in the context of a *repeated* game with incomplete information. In a series of one-off prisoners' dilemma games against different anonymous opponents there is no possibility of an individual developing such a reputation. Kandori (1992), however, demonstrates that if the number of subjects is not too large, then players may adopt strategies whereby the group as a whole builds and maintains a reputation for being co-operative.

In Kandori's example a number of individuals play a series of one-off prisoners' dilemma games. It is supposed that the players are randomly and anonymously matched from the group population. It is further assumed that there is no communication between players, and that they can only observe the outcome of the games in which they are directly involved. In this context Kandori demonstrates that co-operation can be maintained if players adopt 'contagious punishments'. With players adopting this strategy reputation is related to the group as a whole and not individuals. If a player has never observed any of their opponents playing non-cooperatively, then he will perceive that the group as a whole is co-operative. If, however, a player observes one of his opponents deviating, then he ceases to view the group as co-operative. In a contagious equilibrium an individual will play co-operatively in early repetitions of the game if he perceives the group is co-operative. If he views the group as being non-cooperative, he will also play non-cooperatively. With all players adopting this strategy once any player defects from co-operation deviation spreads like an epidemic throughout the entire population. This continues until co-operation within the whole group breaks down. It is this collapse of co-operation that effectively deters individuals from initially deviating in early repetitions of the game. Once more co-operation can be part of rational equilibrium behaviour, and so may partly explain the observed experimental evidence of individuals playing a series of one-off prisoners' dilemma games.

11.2 Sequential Equilibrium

As discussed in the previous section one possible way of explaining experimental results on how individuals play repeated prisoners' dilemma games has been to assume there is incomplete information. With this assumption it can be rational for individuals to co-operate so as to develop a reputation for such behaviour. Given the prominence of sequential equilibrium in explaining experimental evidence, and also its use in many economic models, it is not surprising that experimental economists have explicitly sought to test this hypothesis. In this section we review four recently conducted experiments.

Andreoni and Miller (1993)

In an extension to previous experiments Andreoni and Miller (1993) contrast the behaviour of individuals playing a series of one-off prisoners' dilemma games against those playing the game repeatedly. The intention here is to test whether observed behaviour is consistent with the sequential equilibrium hypothesis that rational individuals will seek to build a reputation for being co-operative. This constitutes a direct test of the model proposed by Kreps *et al.* (1982). Specifically Andreoni and Miller contrast the rates of co-operation between players who play a one-off prisoners' dilemma game 200 times against 'strangers', with those who play a ten-period repeated version of the stage game twenty times against 'partners'. In the repeated game subjects are paired with the same individual for each ten-period game but with different individuals for different 'supergames'. Clearly only players involved in the repeated version of the game can develop individual reputations for being co-operative. This means that according to the sequential equilibrium hypothesis individuals playing against 'partners' should be observed to be more co-operative in early rounds than those playing against 'strangers'. The results of this experiment are shown in Fig. 11.5.

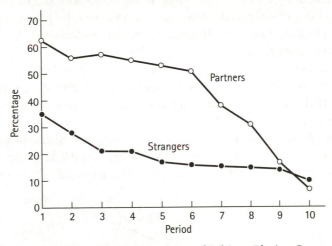

Fig. 11.5 Andreoni and Miller (1993): Percentage of Subjects Playing Co-operatively by Period

This diagram shows the percentage of subjects playing co-operatively over the ten periods. As indicated the results are generally consistent with the sequential equilibrium hypothesis. In particular, the 'partners' are observed to be significantly more co-operative than strangers (at the 0.1 per cent level). Furthermore, 'partners' are found to be significantly more co-operative in the first five rounds compared to the final five rounds. This was not found to be true for the 'strangers'. Andreoni and Miller also note that the rates of co-operation in the final period are virtually identical for the two groups. All these feature of the data are consistent with the sequential equilibrium hypothesis. Regarding the behaviour of those playing the one-off game in isolation

Experimental Economics

Andreoni and Miller argue that persistent co-operation observed by some of their subjects indicates that a significant number of individuals are altruistic. Based on their observations they estimate that the prior probability that an opponent will play co-operatively in these one-off games was approximately 20 per cent. This interpretation that some players are indeed altruistic further justifies the assumption of incomplete information. As Andreoni and Miller point out in a strict interpretation of the sequential equilibrium hypothesis no altruistic or irrational players need exist. Instead, it need only be assumed that players *believe* such players exist. With this assumption all players may be viewed as *acting* rationally. This, however, implies that players' beliefs are wrong. A more reasonable assumption would seem to be that rational players believe other players are altruistic or irrational, because some of them actually are. Andreoni and Miller's observations indicate that such beliefs are justified.

Camerer and Weigelt (1988)

In each of the experiments previously discussed incomplete information may be inferred from the behaviour of individuals playing the game. In contrast the experiment undertaken by Camerer and Weigelt explicitly introduces such uncertainty. Observations from this experiment are again used to test the predictions of sequential equilibrium. The basic nature of the game resembles the decisions faced by a lender and a borrower. The inherent uncertainty within the game is that the lender does not know for certain whether the borrower will repay a loan or default. If the perceived probability that the borrower will renege on the loan is high, the loan will be withheld. One stylized version of the stage game that subjects were asked to play in this experiment is shown in Fig. 11.6.

In this game there are two possible types of borrower. Which type actually plays the game is represented as being determined by 'Nature'. Type Y, according to the pay-offs of the game, never has the incentive to default. (This is because they receive a pay-off of

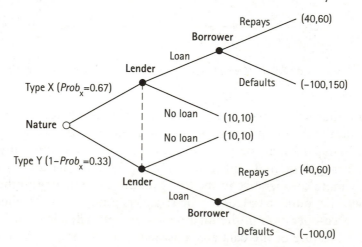

Fig. 11.6 One Version of the Extensive Form Game used by Camerer and Weigelt (1988)

242

60 if they repay the loan, but nothing if they default.) Type X, however, does have such an incentive. (Here they receive a pay-off of 150 if they default.) The probability that a borrower is type X, $Prob_X$, is 0.67, while the probability they are type Y, $1 - Prob_X$, is 0.33. All subjects were informed of these probabilities but the lender is initially unclear what type of borrower she faces. In order for there to be a sequential equilibrium this one-off game was repeated eight times between the same players. Each subject then repeated this game a number of times against different opponents. Alternative versions of the game were derived by changing two parameters, the proportion of X- and Y-type borrowers, and the pay-offs to the lender.

Camerer and Weigelt demonstrate that for each version of their repeated games there is a unique sequential equilibrium. This equilibrium is characterized by three successive phases. In the first phase a type-X borrower will not wish to reveal his true identity, and so he always repay the loan. The lender anticipates this behaviour and is therefore prepared to offer the loan. In this phase loans are always made and repaid irrespective of the type of borrower. In the second phase, an X-type borrower will play a mixed strategy, with the probability of repayment decreasing over successive periods of the game. If repayment was observed in the previous period, then the loan is made in the current period. If the loan was not repaid in the previous period, then the lender knows the borrower is type-X, and so no further loans are made. In the final phase of the game a type-X borrower will definitely default on the loan. For the parameter values used by Camerer and Weigelt this corresponds to the final period of the game. The predicted probabilities of defaulting on the loan for different periods of the game are shown in Fig. 11.7.

These probabilities are calculated for X-type borrowers, assuming they have not previously defaulted, and the parameters are as shown in Fig. 11.6. Fig. 11.7 also depicts the actual proportions of experienced type-X borrowers initially defaulting in each period.

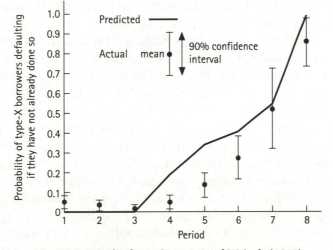

Fig. 11.7 Results from Camerer and Weigelt (1988)

(In early plays of the game subjects' behaviour was highly erratic, with individuals presumably still learning the nature of the game.)

As can be seen from Fig. 11.7 there is strong evidence of reputation-building, with the majority of type-X borrowers repaying the loan in early periods. However, as can be seen from the diagram the actual proportion of subjects defaulting in each period of the game was generally lower than those predicted by the sequential equilibrium hypothesis. As the 90 per cent confidence intervals indicate, such discrepancies, except for period 7, cannot be merely dismissed as chance. Camerer and Weigelt attribute these high levels of repayment to the presence of 'homemade priors' which increase individual's subjective probability that borrowers are of type Y. This is based on the belief that other players will seek to play co-operatively for altruistic reasons. In this game playing co-operatively corresponds to offering the loan and not defaulting. From their empirical evidence Camerer and Weigelt estimate that the home-made prior probability that potential X-type player will play as a Y-type player is approximately 0.17. This estimate was derived under the twin assumptions that the home-made prior is common knowledge, and that individuals adopt strategies in accordance with the sequential equilibrium hypothesis. To test these assumptions Camerer and Weigelt compare the estimated home-made prior across different experiments of this and alternative versions of the game. They report that the resulting estimates are generally consistent. This can be interpreted as providing further support for sequential equilibrium hypothesis. Camerer and Weigelt (1988) conclude that once subjects were familiar with the game they were playing, and after home-made priors had been introduced, the predictions of sequential equilibrium fitted the data reasonably well. This positive conclusion has, however, been challenged by further experimental evidence provided by Neral and Ochs (1992).

Neral and Ochs (1992)

In this experiment Neral and Ochs initially asked subjects to play the game presented in Fig. 11.6. Despite slight modifications, such as in this experiment in which the repeated game consisted of six, rather than eight, periods, their results are not substantially different from those obtained by Camerer and Weigelt (1988). In fact less out-of-equilibrium behaviour was observed this time compared to the initial experiment. Having replicated Camerer and Weigelt's results Neral and Ochs asked a different set of subjects to play a slightly modified version of the previous game. The only difference between the two games was that now the pay-off to a type-X borrower if he defaulted was reduced from 150 to 100. All other parameters of the game remained unchanged. This parameter change was selected because the predictions based on sequential equilibrium are extremely counter-intuitive. The sequential equilibrium hypothesis predicts that when the pay-off for defaulting is reduced, then the borrower's behaviour will remain unchanged, but the lender will reduce her probability of offering the loan during the mixed strategy phase of the sequential equilibrium. (This result is illustrated in Exercise 11.3.) In contrast, the intuitive prediction is that reneging on the loan will be less likely, because the pay-off from doing so is smaller, and as a result the lender will be more likely to offer the loan. If subjects are observed to play counter-intuitively in line with the game theory prediction, this would be strong evidence in favour of the sequential equilibrium hypothesis. Subjects, however, were not observed to play according to the predictions of sequential equilibrium. The relevant results from Neral and Ochs are presented in Table 11.2.

Table 11.2 Results from Neral and Ochs (1992)

	Probability of loan being made				Probability of initial default by type-X borrower			
Period	Original experiment	Modified experiment	Chi-square statistic	Significance/ exact probability	Original experiment	Modified experiment	Chi-square statistic	Significance/ exact probability
1	1.000	0.979	2.231	0.135	0.983	1.000	0.832	0.362
2	0.989	0.996	0.059	0.809	0.966	0.994	1.577	0.209
3	0.878	1.000	27.571	0.000	0.636	0.968	46.924	0.000
4	0.600	0.873	31.722	0.000	0.515	0.690	2.818	0.093
5	0.698	0.667	0.065	0.800	0.546	0.468	0.022	0.882
6	0.875	0.192	40.471	0.000	0.000	0.375	–	0.209

In this table the observed probabilities of a loan being made and a type-X borrower initially defaulting over different periods are reported for both sets of experiments. To test whether the change in pay-offs has had any significant effect on subjects' behaviour the chi-square statistic is calculated. Finally, the exact probability of observing the reported differences is presented for each of the two hypotheses. If this figure is less than 0.01 then we can state that the reported difference is significant at the 1 per cent level. We first consider the behaviour of the lenders. From the table it can be seen that for three out of five periods for which a mixed strategy is predicated (periods 2–6) the lenders *increase* the probability of offering a loan. This is contrary to the sequential equilibrium hypothesis. Furthermore, this increase in the propensity to lend is significant for periods 3 and 4. Neral and Ochs therefore reject the null hypothesis that the parameter change will *reduce* the probability of loans being offered. We now consider the behaviour of type-X borrowers. Again it can be seen that the observed probability of initial default has risen in all periods except period 5. This increase is significant for period 3. Once more Neral and Ochs reject the null hypothesis that the parameter change will have no effect on borrower behaviour.

The results from Neral and Ochs experiment are therefore mixed. As with Camerer and Weigelt (1988) there is strong evidence that subjects seek to develop favourable reputations. This is consistent with the sequential equilibrium hypothesis. However, subjects' behaviour is inconsistent with the predictions of sequential equilibrium following a specific parameter change. Neral and Ochs do not offer an explanation why subjects responded to the parameter change in the way they did. However, they do note that such finding cannot be explained merely by introducing home-made priors similar to those used by Camerer and Weigelt. As with previous experimental results the predictions of game theory do not tell us the whole story. What some of the missing factors might be is suggested by an experiment by McKelvey and Palfrey (1992).

McKelvey and Palfrey (1992)

In this test of sequential equilibrium subjects played a modified version of Rosenthal's (1981) centipede game. The extensive form of this modified game was initially presented in Appendix 3.2. This game is reproduced in Fig. 11.8. (McKelvey and Palfrey also asked subjects to play a six-period version of this game. We do not report the results from this experiment as they were similar to those derived from this four-period game.)

EXERCISE 11.3.*

Both Camerer and Weigelt (1988) and Neral and Ochs (1992) use a repeated version of the game depicted in Fig. 11.6. Experimental observations were then used to test the predictions of the sequential equilibrium hypothesis. In particular Neral and Ochs examine whether subjects playing this game follow the counter-intuitive sequential equilibrium prediction that if the pay-off for a type-X borrower reneging on a loan falls, then the probability of default remains unchanged but the probability of the lender offering a loan decreases. In this exercise we illustrate these predictions for a two-period version of this game. Initially we examine the subgame perfect Nash equilibrium if the game is played only once.

(1) Using the principle of backward induction derive the subgame perfect Nash equilibrium if the game illustrated in Fig. 11.6 is played only once, with the modification that $Prob_X = 0.25$. Explain why this predicted outcome is Pareto inefficient.

(2) Derive the characteristics of the sequential equilibrium if the game in Fig. 11.6 is played twice and $Prob_X = 0.25$. Based on these equilibrium predictions calculate each player's expected pay-off at the beginning of the game.

(3) Derive the sequential equilibrium comparative static predictions if the pay-off for a type-X borrower defaulting falls from 150 to 100. Assume all other aspects of the game remain the same as for (2). Based on these equilibrium predictions calculate each player's expected pay-off at the beginning of this modified game.

In Appendix 3.2 we derived the predictions for a rational player based on the common knowledge assumption that 5 per cent of players are altruistic in that they always play across. From these predictions we are able to calculate the implied probabilities of the game reaching each of the five possible outcomes. These predictions are shown in the second column of Table 11.3. For example, the final outcome corresponding to both players twice playing across (AAAA) will only be achieved, according to the sequential

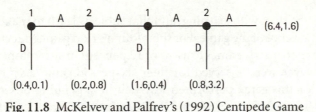

Fig. 11.8 McKelvey and Palfrey's (1992) Centipede Game

equilibrium hypothesis, if each player is altruistic. The probability of this occurring is $0.05 \times 0.05 = 0.0025$

In McKelvey and Palfrey's experiment subjects were asked to play this game up to ten times against different opponents. Each subject remained either player 1 or player 2 in successive repetitions of the game. In total this game was played 281 times between different pairings of twenty-nine subjects. The proportion of these games reaching each of the possible final outcomes is shown in the third column of Table 11.3. Clearly there is again strong evidence of reputation-building, with only 7 per cent of games played ending with player 1 initially moving down. However, as can be seen from comparing columns 2 and 3 of this table the sequential equilibrium hypothesis is unable to explain all the features of the observed results. For example, the outcome AD is observed significantly less frequently than that predicted by the sequential equilibrium hypothesis.

Table 11.3 Results from McKelvey and Palfrey (1992)

Outcome	Sequential equilibrium	Actual	Learning/Errors
D	0.0000	0.071	0.097
AD	0.6498	0.356	0.333
AAD	0.3001	0.370	0.324
AAAD	0.0476	0.153	0.218
AAAA	0.0025	0.049	0.028

McKelvey and Palfrey argue that what is missing from the sequential equilibrium hypothesis is the possibility that individuals make errors in their intended actions, and have errors in their beliefs about their opponents. To test these possible explanations they estimate an econometric model based on sequential equilibrium hypothesis using maximum-likelihood methods. This model incorporates the possibility of both errors in action and errors in belief. The predictions using this econometric model are shown in column 4 of Table 3.2. Clearly these predictions are much closer to those actually observed than produced by sequential equilibrium alone. Based on this econometric model they estimate that approximately 5 per cent of the population may be considered altruistic. (This justifies the sequential equilibrium predictions given in column 2.) Furthermore they conclude that there is significant evidence of subjects making errors in action and having errors in beliefs. Concerning errors in action they conclude that their model is consistent with learning, and that subjects learn to make fewer errors the greater their experience of the game. For their four-period game the error rate falls from a high of 18 per cent in early games to a low of 12 per cent in latter games. (Much smaller error rates, however, were observed for their six-period game. As a result the econometric model for this game performed less well in explaining observed behaviour.) Regarding errors in belief, McKelvey and Palfrey reject the hypothesis that subjects have common beliefs regarding the proportion of altruists in the population. They cannot, however, reject the rational expectations hypothesis which states that beliefs are correct on average. McKelvey and Palfrey conclude that the sequential equilibrium hypothesis, after allowing for the presence of altruists, errors in actions, and errors in beliefs is able to account for the main features of their data.

Reviewing the studies reported in this and the previous section we may conclude that game theory predictions derived on the assumptions that individuals always act rationally, and that this is common knowledge, are not confirmed by experimental evidence. This inconsistency can be interpreted in one of two ways. Either the theory is wrong or the experimental evidence is unreliable. Indeed, various reasons can be suggested why evidence derived from controlled experiments must be interpreted with care. Some of these reasons are discussed in the conclusion to this chapter. Despite these provisos it would seem reasonable to conclude, given the extent of the experimental evidence, that game theory models based on common knowledge of rationality need to be modified, and alternative assumptions employed. This could include allowing a proportion of individuals to be altruistic so that they are not solely motivated by monetary payments. Rather than undermining recent game theory models this supports the emphasis given to studying games based on incomplete information. However, as experiments discussed in this section suggest, even this departure from complete rationality may be insufficient to fully explain individuals' behaviour. Other factors suggested by the experimental evidence include the necessity of modelling how individuals learn over time and respond when confronted with genuine uncertainty. Each of these factors would seem to provide promising areas for future research. (These issues are discussed more fully in Chapter 12, where theoretical criticisms of recent game theory models are evaluated.)

11.3 Multiple Equilibria

All the games so far considered in this chapter have the property that there is a unique equilibrium strategy. In games with multiple equilibria this is no longer true. In such games players have the increased difficulty of trying to predict how other rational players will play the game. Without such co-ordination the final outcome will not be a Nash equilibrium. Even if the final outcome is an equilibrium this need not be the Pareto-dominant equilibrium. In either case we can say there has been co-ordination failure.

Given the prominence of multiple equilibria, especially in recent macroeconomics games, it is clearly of interest to examine how individuals respond to this situation. A number of questions readily come to mind. Are individuals able to co-ordinate upon one of the many equilibria? Will this be the Pareto-efficient equilibrium? What factors influence how individuals select one equilibrium from many? Does the possibility of pre-play communication between players help them to avoid co-ordination failure? In this section we review a number of experiments that have attempted to provide answers to these and other questions.

Van Huyck, Battalio, and Beil (1990)

In a series of experiments Van Huyck, Battalio, and Beil (1990) asked subjects to play a game that exhibited Pareto-ranked Nash equilibria. The intention of these experiments was to determine whether individuals playing such a game could co-ordinate upon an equilibrium, and if so whether this would be the Pareto-dominant equilibrium. In one of the experiments individuals were placed in groups of between fourteen and sixteen people. Each player in the group was then asked to select an integer between 1 and 7 inclusive, in the knowledge that their pay-off would be determined by his or her own choice, and the minimum value chosen by the group. The exact pay-offs are shown in Table 11.4.

Table 11.4 Pay-off Matrix for Van Huyck *et al.* (1990)

		Smallest integer chosen						
		7	6	5	4	3	2	1
	7	1.30	1.10	0.90	0.70	0.50	0.30	0.10
Individual	6	—	1.20	1.00	0.80	0.60	0.40	0.20
i's	5	—	—	1.10	0.90	0.70	0.50	0.30
choice	4	—	—	—	1.00	0.80	0.60	0.40
of	3	—	—	—	—	0.90	0.70	0.50
integer	2	—	—	—	—	—	0.80	0.60
	1	—	—	—	—	—	—	0.70

From these pay-offs each player has an incentive to try and ensure a high minimum value. However, each player is penalized for choosing a number greater than the minimum. There are seven Pareto-ranked Nash equilibria for this game, one corresponding to each symmetrical outcome. The Pareto-dominant equilibrium is where all players select the number 7. Players played this game ten times within the same group, with no possibility of communication between members. The minimum value of each round was reported to the members of that group before the next round was played. In total 107 subjects played this game divided into seven groups. Results for the first group, made up of sixteen individuals, are shown in Fig. 11.9.

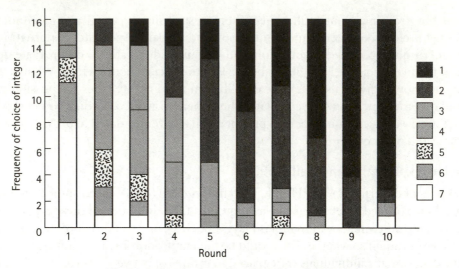

Fig. 11.9 Results from Van Huyck *et al.* (1990)

The vertical axis of Fig. 11.9 gives the frequency a particular integer was chosen. The horizontal axis shows how these frequencies vary over the ten successive rounds of the game. For example, in the first round eight out of sixteen subjects chose the value 7, three chose 6, two chose 5, and the values 4, 3 and 2 were chosen by only one subject. A typical result observed across all groups was that subjects quickly learnt to select smaller numbers. In Fig. 11.9 this is clearly indicated by the dramatic rise in the number of individuals choosing the minimum value of 1. Significantly, the vast majority of subjects (72 per cent) chose the value 1 in the final round of the game. Indeed, this was the minimum value chosen over all groups from the fourth round onwards. This may be interpreted as evidence that the groups were converging on the Nash equilibrium where all individuals simultaneously choose the value 1. Indeed, with extended play of this and a modified game some groups were indeed observed to converge on this Nash equilibrium. The results from this experiment illustrate the possibility of co-ordination failure. This contradicts the view sometimes made by theorists that if there are Pareto-ranked Nash equilibria, players will co-ordinate upon the Pareto-efficient equilibrium as this acts as a focal point.

One factor that might be supposed to influence whether co-ordination failure occurs is the number of players in the game. Van Huyck, Battalio, and Bell test this supposition by asking a proportion of subjects to play the previous game against only one other opponent. The pairs were formed in one of two ways. In the first version players were permanently paired together and asked to play a series of games against each other. In the alternative version subjects played a series of one-off games against randomly matched opponents.

With fixed pairings the results were quite different from those derived from the large groups. In particular, most pairs were able to quickly converge on the Pareto-dominant equilibrium. For example ten out of the fourteen fixed pairings co-ordinated on this equilibrium after only four rounds of this game. This was despite the fact that only one of these pairs initially played this equilibrium. Once a pair had co-ordinated upon the Pareto-dominant equilibrium they remained there for all subsequent repetitions of the game. With random pairings, however, there was no convergence upon any of the equilibria. These results illustrate the importance of both repeated play and the number of players in the game. Repeated interaction between a small number of players seems able to reduce the occurrence of co-ordination failure.

Cooper, DeJong, Forsythe, and Ross. (1990)

In another series of experiments Cooper *et al.* (1990) seek to test three separate hypotheses in games with multiple Nash equilibria. The first two hypotheses are the same as for Van Huyck, Battalio, and Bell (1990). These are firstly that subjects will co-ordinate upon a Nash equilibrium, and secondly that a Pareto-dominant equilibrium will be selected. The third hypothesis is that equilibrium selection should not be influenced by other dominated strategies. This final hypothesis conforms with the common assumption in game theory that dominated strategies are ignored when players choose their optimal strategies. To test these hypotheses Cooper *et al.* asked subjects to play a series of one-off co-ordination games against different anonymous opponents. Two such games are shown in Fig. 11.10. Again, so as to avoid the effects of differences in risk preferences, these pay-offs are not monetary payments but rather points. These points then determine the probability of winning a subsequent lottery. Both games shown in Fig. 11.10 have two pure-strategy Nash equilibria. One corresponds to both players adopting strategy 1. The other is when both play strategy 2. These equilibria are Pareto ranked, with the outcome corresponding to both players choosing strategy 2 Pareto dominant.

Game 1 — Player 2

	1	2	3
1	350, 350	350, 250	700, 0
2	250, 350	550, 550	0, 0
3	0, 700	0, 0	600, 600

Game 2 — Player 2

	1	2	3
1	350, 350	350, 250	700, 0
2	250, 350	550, 550	1,000, 0
3	0, 700	0, 1,000	600, 600

Fig. 11.10 Co-ordination Games from Cooper *et al.* (1990)

Experimental Economics

The only difference between the two games is the pay-off for each player choosing strategy 2 while their opponent chooses strategy 3. In Game 1 this pay-off is 0, in Game 2 it is 1,000. However, it should be noticed that strategy 3 is strictly dominated by strategy 1. This means that strategy 1 always gives a higher pay-off compared to strategy 3 irrespective of what the other player does. The implication of this is that the changed pay-off between the two games should be irrelevant if the other player is assumed never to play a dominated strategy. This hypothesis, however, is not confirmed by observation. The results given by Cooper *et al.* of subjects playing these two games are shown in Fig. 11.11.

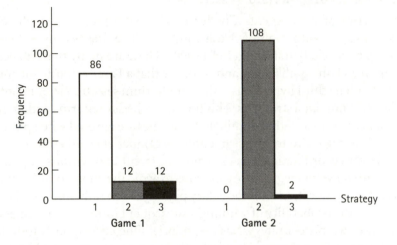

Fig. 11.11 Results from Cooper *et al.* (1990)

These results have been derived by aggregating over 110 repetitions of the two games played between experienced subjects. As can be seen, players overwhelmingly selected a single strategy in each of these games. For Game 1 this was strategy 1, and for Game 2 it was strategy 2. These findings are consistent with the prediction that players will select a strategy consistent with a Nash equilibrium. However, as subjects tended to co-ordinate on strategy 1 in the first game, the prediction that the Pareto-dominant equilibrium will act as a focal point must be rejected. In Game 1 subjects co-ordinated on a Pareto-inefficient outcome and experienced co-ordination failure. Furthermore, as the changed behaviour must be attributed to the parameter change, the final hypothesis must also be rejected. Although players do not, in general, select a dominated strategy, it seems that such a strategy can influence which Nash equilibrium players co-ordinate upon. Contrary to the practice adopted in many game theory models it seems that dominated strategies can have an effect on players' behaviour. In the above experiment the change in pay-offs alter which of the possible equilibria is focal. This is despite the fact that the changed pay-off can only be considered relevant if there is some possibility that the other player will act irrationally and play strategy 3. Given this possibility, however, it is easy to see why a rational player may switch strategies as a result of the parameter change. Once again the assumption of common knowledge of rationality appears to be violated.

Cooper, DeJong, Forsythe, and Ross (1989)

The above experiments involving games with multiple equilibria have demonstrated that co-ordination failure is a distinct possibility. Factors determining whether co-ordination failure occurs have included the number of players in the game, the nature of repeated play, and the pay-offs associated with out-of-equilibrium play. To conclude this section we discuss an experiment undertaken by Cooper *et al.* (1991). The purpose of this experiment was to investigate the role of pre-play communication in avoiding the possibility of co-ordination failure. In particular it seeks to determine whether costless, non-binding, and pay-off-irrelevant communication can help players co-ordinate their actions on a Pareto-efficient outcome. This type of communication is often referred to as 'cheap-talk'. Subjects were asked to play a version of the battle of the sexes game shown in Fig. 11.12.

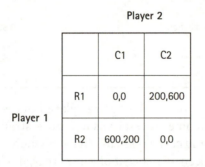

Fig. 11.12 The Battle of the Sexes Game used by Cooper *et al.* (1989)

Again the pay-offs represent points which then determine the probability of players winning a lottery. Individuals played this one-off game a number of times against different, anonymous opponents. This game has three Nash equilibria. The first two correspond to the two pure-strategy equilibria (R1, C2) and (R2, C1). The third equilibrium is where the players adopt mixed strategies. In this equilibrium player 1 plays strategy R1 with probability 0.25 and strategy R2 with probability 0.75. Similarly player 2 plays C1 with probability 0.75 and C2 with probability 0.25. Given players adopt these mixed strategies the probability that the final outcome will be one of the pure-strategy Nash equilibrium is 0.375. With these strategies the probability of *ex post* co-ordination failure is, therefore, 0.625.

In order to investigate the effects of pre-play co-ordination Cooper *et al.* divided the subject population into various groups and allocated to each group an alternative communication structure. In the experiment four different communication structures were allowed. In the first group no pre-play communication was allowed. In the second group one round of one-way communication was allowed. In this group player 1 was initially allowed to state her intended strategy before both players simultaneously chose their actions. Alternatively player 1 could, if she so desired, choose not to send any message, or even lie about her intentions. In the third group one round of two-way communication was allowed. Here both players were allowed to state their intended strategy before play began. In the final group players were allowed three rounds of two-way communication. This involves players sending and receiving up to three messages about their possible intentions. The results from these different communication structures are shown in Table 11.5.

Table 11.5 Results from Cooper *et al.* (1989)

Type of pre-play communication	Proportion of hits
No communication	0.48
One-way communication (One round)	0.95
Two-way communication (One round)	0.55
Two-way communication (Three rounds)	0.63

In this table we report the proportion of games played under each communication structure where the final outcome corresponds to a pure-strategy Nash equilibrium. These are referred to as 'hits' and correspond to instances where communication failure has been avoided. As can be seen 48 per cent of games played with no communication resulted in *ex post* equilibrium. This is significantly higher than the prediction based on players adopting the Nash equilibrium with mixed strategies. None the less *ex post* co-ordination failure is still the most likely outcome, with *ex post* disequilibrium occurring 52 per cent of the time. This rate of disequilibrium is greatly reduced when one-way communication is allowed. With this type of communication the proportion of hits was observed to be 95 per cent. In the vast majority of these games player 1 sent the message that she intended to play R2. This was typically believed by player 2 who then responded with C1. Clearly this type of communication has a major impact on reducing the occurrence of co-ordination failure. In contrast, two-way communication was less effective in reducing the incidence of such failure. With one round of two-way communication the proportion of hits only increased to 55 per cent, while with three rounds it increased to 63 per cent. Whilst two-way communication does help players co-ordinate their actions, there is a greater likelihood of conflict compared to one-way communication. Cooper *et al.* conclude that the type of communication structure faced by players can greatly influence the outcome of co-ordination games. This is true even when communication is restricted to non-binding announcements.

11.4 Conclusions

This chapter has reviewed a number of experiments undertaken to examine how individuals play various games when their decisions are interdependent. These observations have been compared with the predictions of game theory. From these studies it is clear that game theory predictions are not always confirmed by experimental evidence. However, before we can confidently reject certain elements of game theory as being unrealistic great care needs to be taken in interpreting the experimental evidence. In some of the experiments undertaken to test the full rationality of individuals the experimenters may be viewed as a*gent provocateurs*. Subjects are often placed in situations where intuitive reasoning alone will cause them to commit the crime of not acting in accordance with the principles of complete rationality. The experimenters then declare that such evidence proves beyond reasonable doubt that individuals are irrational. In assessing such evidence, however, the context from which it is amassed must be taken into consideration. Subjects are, in effect, asked to play contrived games, in artificial settings, where the predictions of the relevant hypothesis are often counterintuitive. In these circumstances it does not seem entirely surprising that individuals are observed to act in ways not entirely consistent with full rationality. This is true even when individuals have had prolonged experience of the game they are asked to play.

There are indeed several problems in attempting to generalize experimental results to the choices individuals make when confronted with everyday decisions. For example, individuals typically have a much greater familiarity with the decisions they are required to make in everyday life compared to the problems devised by experimental economists. This is especially true when it is realized that most experiments are presented in purely abstract terms with little or no perceived relevance to real-life decisions. This enhanced familiarity with real-life problems is due to repeated experience of the same problem, as well as the ability of individuals to make links with other related problems of which they have experience. Furthermore, such learning will typically take place over a much longer time-period. This will enable individuals to more fully evaluate their decisions and revise future strategies. With little time to reflect upon decisions it may be necessary for individuals to rely on their intuition. This may be the case even though such intuition was developed in contexts where it was more appropriate.

Another problem in generalizing some of the findings discussed above is that, contrary to the nature of many experiments, individuals are rarely required to solve complex decision problems in isolation. Instead, real world decisions are often encountered within a social context. Again, such social interaction is likely to enhance the learning process, and cause individuals to modify their intended strategies. Allowing individuals more time and social interaction also introduces the possibility that they will seek further information before deciding on a particular course of action. This may involve seeking the advice of so-called experts, with the explicit intention of helping individuals to reach a more rational decision. Each of these considerations raises questions about the relevance of experimental evidence. Indeed, given the diverse nature of experimental and real-world decisions, it is perhaps surprising how often observed behaviour fits with the predictions derived from full rationality.

The above arguments have stressed the difficulty of generalizing experimental evidence to real-life decision-making. None the less two broad conclusions would appear warranted by such evidence. *First*, it seems reasonable to conclude that not all individuals act according to instrumental rationality all of the time. This may be due to bounded rationality, altruism, or how individuals respond when faced with genuine uncertainty. In part this conclusion would seem to validate the importance of modelling incomplete information, and the use of sequential equilibrium in economics. However, it seems undoubtedly true that greater insight is needed into how individuals make complex decisions. These insights can then inform economists on how to improve the predictions of game theory. *Second*, when individuals are confronted with unfamiliar decision problems considerable learning is often required. From this perspective the predictions of game theory may only be considered relevant once such learning has taken place. This conclusion would seem to validate the use of evolutionarily stable strategies, especially when there are multiple equilibria. Again it seems that in the areas of learning and avoiding co-ordination failure further experimental evidence is required. Only then will economists be able to devise and test theories about how individuals learn to be rational and co-ordinate their optimal strategies.

11.5 Solutions to Exercises

Exercise 11.1

(1) *Duty*

With *Prob* equal to the probability that an opponent will play co-operatively the expected level of utility for subject i playing C is

$$EV_i(\text{C}) = Prob(10 + \alpha_i) + (1 - Prob)(6 + \alpha_i)$$

$$= 6 + 4\,Prob + \alpha i.$$

Similarly the expected level of utility of playing D is

$$EV_i(\text{D}) = Prob(12) + (1 - Prob)8$$

$$= 8 + 4\,Prob.$$

Individual i will therefore maximize expected utility by playing co-operatively if

$$6 + 4\,Prob + \alpha_i > 8 + 4\,Prob$$

$$\therefore \alpha_i > 2.$$

The critical value of α_i is therefore 2. From the assumed distribution of α over the population we can predict that 75 per cent of subjects will play co-operatively.

(2) *Reciprocal altruism*

Following the same methodology as in (1) we can obtain the following expressions for expected utility from playing C or D.

$$EV_i(C) = Prob(10 + \alpha_i) + (1 - Prob)6$$

$$= 6 + 4\,Prob + \alpha_i\,Prob.$$

and

$$EV_i(D) = Prob(12) + (1 - Prob)\,8$$

$$= 8 + 4\,Prob.$$

This time individual i will play co-operatively if

$$6 + 4\,Prob + \alpha_i\,Prob > 8 + 4\,Prob$$

$$\therefore \alpha_i > 2/Prob.$$

From the equation $Prob\,(\alpha_i > \alpha^\star) = (\alpha_{max} - \alpha^\star)/\alpha_{max}$, where $\alpha^\star = 2/Prob$, we can derive the result that $Prob = 0.5$. In this example it is predicted that 50 per cent of subjects will play co-operatively.

(3) *Pure altruism*

With individual i's utility function as given we can derive the following expressions

$$EV_i(C) = Prob(10 + \alpha_i 10) + (1 - Prob)(6 + \alpha_i 12)$$

$$= 6 + 4\,Prob + 12\,\alpha_i - 2\,\alpha_i\,Prob$$

and

$$EV_i(D) = Prob(12 + \alpha_i) + (1 - Prob)(8 + \alpha_i 8)$$

$$= 8 + 4\,Prob + 8\,\alpha_i - 2\,\alpha_i\,Prob.$$

With these expected levels of utility subject i will play co-operatively if

$$6 + 4\,Prob + 12\,\alpha_i - 2\,\alpha_i\,Prob > 8 + 4\,Prob + 8\,\alpha_i - 2\,\alpha_i\,Prob$$

$$\alpha_i > 1/2.$$

Once more it is predicted that 50 per cent of subjects will play co-operatively.

Exercise 11.2

(1) *Co-ordination game*

Using the two-stage procedure for identifying pure-strategy Nash equilibria developed in Chapter 2 it can be confirmed that there are two such equilibria for this game. One is where both players play strategy A, and the other is where they both play strategy B. In the mixed strategy equilibrium the expected return from each of these two strategies must be equal to each other. Letting *Prob* equal to the probability that players adopt strategy A the expected pay-off of strategy A is

$$\Pi(A) = 20\,Prob + 10(1 - Prob) = 10 + 10\,Prob.$$

Similarly the expected pay-off of strategy B is

$$\Pi(B) = 0\,Prob + 30(1 - Prob) = 30 - 30\,Prob.$$

Setting these expected pay-offs equal to each other and solving for *Prob* gives us the mixed-strategy Nash equilibrium where each player sets $Prob = 0.5$. In this equilibrium players set the probability of playing each strategy equal to 0.5, and their expected pay-off is 15. These equilibria are Pareto ranked. The game is called co-ordination, as players would ideally like to co-ordinate on the Pareto-efficient equilibrium. Any other outcome represents a co-ordination failure.

The average pay-off, given the value of *Prob*, over all individuals is

$$\bar{\Pi} = Prob\,\Pi(A) + (1 - Prob)\,\Pi(B)$$

$$= 40\,Prob^2 - 50\,Prob + 30.$$

Substituting the values for $\Pi(A)$ and $\bar{\Pi}$ into the dynamic-learning equation gives us the following expression

$$\frac{dProb}{dt} = -40\,Prob^3 - 60\,Prob^2 + 20\,Prob.$$

This equation is plotted in the phase drawn in Fig. 11.13. As can be seen from this diagram there is a steady-state equilibrium corresponding to each of the three previously identified Nash equilibria. However, as indicated by the directional arrows, the mixed-strategy equilibrium is unstable, while the other two equilibrium are stable. These two pure-strategy Nash equilibria are the evolutionarily stable strategies. In this evolutionary game players either converge upon always playing strategy A or always playing strategy B. Which equilibrium players co-ordinate upon depends on the initial probability distribution over the two strategies. If initially $Prob > 0.5$, then they converge on strategy A. If $Prob < 0.5$, then they converge on strategy B. If any point on this unit interval is equally likely, then the players will converge on the Pareto-dominated equilibrium with probability 0.5.

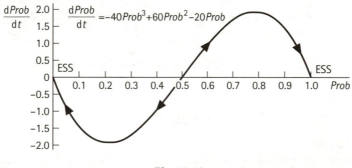

Fig. 11.13

(2) *Chicken*

This game is traditionally called chicken for the following reason. The two players represent motorists speeding towards each other. Each has the choice of either swerving to avoid a collision, or driving straight on. If both drivers swerve then a crash is avoided and both players receive a pay-off of 30. If neither swerve there is a head-on collision and players receive the smaller pay-off of 10. Finally, if one player swerves but the other drives straight on, the crash is again avoided. This time, however, the driver who was 'chicken' receives only 20 due to loss of face, while the other receives 40 on account of his or her bravery.

Using the same methodology used in the previous co-ordination game we can identify three Nash equilibria. Two of these are pure-strategy Nash equilibria where players adopt the same strategy. The third is where players adopt a mixed strategy of playing strategy A with a probability 0.25, and strategy B with probability 0.75. Deriving the relevant equations for $\Pi(A)$ and $\overline{\Pi}$ and substituting these into the dynamic learning equation yields the following expression

$$\frac{\mathrm{d}Prob}{\mathrm{d}t} = -40Prob^3 - 50Prob^2 + 10Prob.$$

Again this equation is plotted in Fig. 11.14. Once more there is a steady-state equilibrium corresponding to each of the three Nash equilibria. This time, however, only the mixed-strategy Nash equilibrium is stable and so this corresponds to the evolutionarily stable strategy.

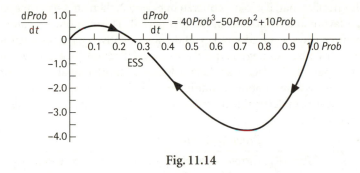

Fig. 11.14

Exercise 11.3

(1) Using the principle of backward induction we can state that if a loan has been made then this will only be repaid if the borrower is of type Y ($60 > 0$). If the borrower is type X, the loan will not be repaid ($60 < 150$). Moving back to the lender's decision, a loan will only be offered if the expected net pay-off from doing so is greater than or equal to zero. With common knowledge of the proportion of X- and Y-type borrowers this expected net gain is equal to

$$-100(Prob_X) + 40(1 - Prob_X) - 10 = 30 - 140Prob_X = -5 < 0.$$

With the expected net pay-off of making a loan negative no loan will be offered. The subgame perfect Nash equilibrium is, therefore, no loan will be made by the lender and each player will receive a pay-off of 10.

This solution is clearly Pareto inefficient. If the borrower could precommit himself to repaying the loan, then both players would be better off. In this situation the lender would receive a pay-off of 40, and the borrower a pay-off of 60. This corresponds to the co-operative solution. Without precommitment, however, this outcome is not credible. If the borrower is type X, there is a clear incentive to default on the loan. This is demonstrated by noting that the co-operative solution does not comprise a Nash equilibrium for the sub-game beginning at the borrower's decision node if he is type X. For this reason the co-operative solution is not subgame perfect.

(2) To solve for the sequential equilibrium we again use the principle of backward induction. This involves solving for the second and last period first, conditional on what has occurred in the first period of the game.

In the final period we know that if a loan has been made a type-Y borrower will certainly repay it and a type-X borrower will certainly default. Let $Prob_{Y2}$ be the probability assessment by the lender that the borrower is type Y at the beginning of the second period. This corresponds to the borrower's reputation for being type Y. With this reputation the lender will only offer a loan if the net expected pay-off of doing so is greater or equal to zero. A loan will therefore only be made in period 2 if

$$-100(1 - Prob_{Y2}) + 40\, Prob_{Y2} - 10 \geq 0.$$

This implies that a loan will only be made if the borrower's reputation, $Prob_{Y2}$, is greater than or equal to 0.785. As this is greater than the initial prior probability that a borrower is of type Y, this implies that, if a loan is offered in period 2, then an X-type player must have invested in a favourable reputation in the first period. This can only occur, however, if a type-X borrower plays a mixed strategy and subsequently repays the loan in period 1. Specifically, with a mixed strategy a type-X borrower will set the probability of repaying the loan in the first period, $Prob(R_{X1})$, so that the lender is indifferent about offering a loan in period 2. This means that the above condition must hold as an equality and $Prob_{Y2} = 0.785$. Using Bayes' rule we can determine the value of $Prob(R_{X1})$ so that this requirement is satisfied. Thus we can write

$$Prob_{Y2} = 0.785 = \frac{Prob(R_{Y1}).Prob_Y}{Prob(R_{Y1}).Prob_Y + Prob(R_{X1}).Prob_X} = \frac{1(0.75)}{1(0.75) + Prob(R_{X1})0.25}.$$

From this equation we derive the prediction that if a loan is made to an X-type borrower in the first period, it will be repaid with probability 0.821, and reneged upon with probability 0.179. With these probabilities the expected net pay-off for the lender making a loan in the first period equals

$$40[0.75 + 0.25(0.821)] - 100[0.25(0.179)] = 23.735 > 0.$$

As this is positive the lender will certainly make the loan in the first period. If this is repaid, then the lender will also play a mixed strategy in the second period so as to cause the borrower to be indifferent between repaying and defaulting in the first period. (If the borrower were not indifferent between repaying and defaulting in the first period, then he would cease to play a mixed strategy.) This will happen when the borrower's total expected pay-off from both periods is independent of $Prob(R_{X1})$. Letting $Prob(L_2)$ be the probability that a loan is made in the second period, a type-X borrower's total expected pay-off equals

$$Prob(R_{X1})[60 + 150\, Prob(L_2) + 10(1 - Prob(L_2))] + [1 - Prob(R_{X1})](150 + 10).$$

From this equation it can be calculated that the lender must set $Prob(L_2) = 0.643$.

We can now summarize the predictions made by the sequential equilibrium hypothesis. In the first period the loan is made with certainty. If the borrower is type Y, this is repaid. If the borrower is type X, it will be repaid with probability 0.821. If the borrower defaults in this period, then no loan will be made in the next period, as the lender will know the borrower is type X. If, however, the first period loan is repaid, then the lender will offer the loan with probability 0.643. If made, this will be repaid if the borrower is type Y, but will not be repaid if the borrower is type X.

The expected pay-offs at the beginning of the game can be calculated as follows
X-type borrower:

$$Prob(R_{X1})[60 + 150 \, Prob(L_2) + 10(1 - Prob(L_2))] + [1 - Prob(R_{X1})](150 + 10) = 160.$$

Y-type borrower:

$$60 + 60.Prob(L_2) + 10[1 - Prob(L_2)] = 102.15.$$

Lender:

$$40 \{Prob_Y + Prob_X.Prob(R_{X1})\} + 10 \{Prob_X.(1 - Prob(R_{X1}))\}$$

$$+ Prob(L_2)\{40.Prob_Y - 100.Prob_X\} + 10.\{1 - Prob(L_2)\} = 45.53.$$

(3) The only effects of a reduction in the pay-off for a type-X borrower defaulting are to reduce the probability of the lender offering a loan in the final period, and to change the expected pay-offs for players. In particular, the equilibrium strategies of the borrowers remain unchanged. This can be confirmed by noting that the modified pay-off did not enter any of the calculations determining the borrower's equilibrium strategies in (2). The first occurrence of this pay-off was when determining the probability that the lender will offer a loan in the second period. This was calculated so that an X-type borrower would be indifferent between repaying or defaulting on his first period loan. The modified equation now becomes

$$Prob(R_{X1})[60 + 100 \, Prob(L_2) + 10(1 - Prob(L_2))] + [1 - Prob(R_{X1})](100 + 10).$$

From this equation it can be predicted that the lender will now set $Prob(L_2) = 0.444$.

Substituting this revised probability into the expected pay-offs for the players at the beginning of the game gives us the following values.
X-type borrower:

$$Prob(R_{X1})[60 + 100 \, Prob(L_2) + 10(1 - Prob(L_2))] + [1 - Prob(R_{X1})](100 + 10) = 110.$$

Y-type borrower:

$$60 + 60.Prob(L_2) + 10[1 - Prob(L_2)] = 92.20.$$

Lender:

$$40 \{Prob_Y + Prob_X.Prob(R_{X1})\} + 10 \{Prob_X.(1 - Prob(R_{X1}))\}$$

$$+ Prob(L_2)\{40.Prob_Y - 100.Prob_X\} + 10.\{1 - Prob(L_2)\} = 46.44.$$

Comparing these pay-offs with those derived in (2), the lender is now expected to be better off, while the borrower is worse off, irrespective of his type.

Further Reading

Davis, D. D., and C. A. Holt (1993), *Experimental Economics*, Princeton: Princeton University Press.

Coleman, A. M. (1983), *Game Theory and Experimental Games*, Oxford: Pergamon Press.

Hey, J. (1991), *Experiments In Economics*, Oxford: Blackwell.

Kagel, J. H., and A. E. Roth (1995), *The Handbook of Experimental Economics*, Princeton: Princeton University Press.

Poundstone, W. (1992), *Prisoner's Dilemma*, New York: Doubleday.

12
Criticisms of Game Theory

IN Chapter 1 we defined game theory as being concerned with how rational individuals make decisions when they are mutually interdependent. In subsequent chapters we have presented various game theory concepts and examined how these have been applied to a diverse range of economic issues. Each of these chapters has illustrated how the use of game theory has helped economists to developed important insights and challenged previous theories. None the less a number of criticisms have been levelled against recent game theory models and their application to economics. In particular, the use of instrumental rationality has been severely challenged on both empirical and theoretical grounds. Some of these empirical inconsistencies were discussed in Chapter 11 on Experimental Economics. There we concluded that although the predictions of game theory often perform remarkably well, they are not all confirmed by the experimental evidence. As a consequence it was argued that greater research is needed on how individuals solve complex decisions under uncertainty, and how they seek to learn and co-ordinate their actions over time. In this chapter we will argue that similar conclusions are justified on the basis of theoretical criticisms of recent game theory models. In particular we illustrate with reference to games analysed in previous chapters, three broad reasons why the widely used assumptions of instrumental rationality, and common knowledge of such rationality, have been viewed as unsatisfactory. The *first* argument is that the use of instrumental rationality by individuals can be self-defeating. This means that individuals may actually serve their own self-interest better if they act in ways not considered instrumentally rational. The *second* criticism is that often the solution to a game based on instrumental rationality is indeterminant. When this occurs non-rational considerations must be introduced to provide a unique prediction. *Finally*, it is argued that these assumptions yield logical contradictions when the predicted outcome is based on arguments about what happens out of equilibrium. In response to each of these criticisms we suggest alternative assumptions that might be adopted. These form the basis of ongoing research within game theory.

12.1 Instrumental Rationality can be Self-defeating

Instrumental rationality states that individuals are solely interested in satisfying their own preferences or desires. That is, individuals are assumed to act in their own self-interest. If an agent is observed to act in a way not consistent with satisfying his desires he is considered irrational. Such irrationality presupposes that the individual holds some false belief. At its simplest level this false belief is that the observed action was the best way of satisfying the individual's desires. It is this false belief, rather than the act itself, that is considered irrational. One problem with such a means–end view of rationality is that it can be self-defeating. This means that in certain circumstances a person might be able to best satisfy his desires if he rejects the prescriptions of instrumental rationality. An obvious example of such an occurrence is when two players are confronted with a prisoners' dilemma game. According to instrumental rationality each player should play non-cooperatively. If, however, both players co-operate, then they are each made better off. Given that co-operation leads to a Pareto improvement some economists have argued that such behaviour should not be classified as irrational. Instead it is often proposed that an alternative definition of rationality needs to be adopted.

One alternative definition of rationality that is often discussed is based on the work of Kant (1788). According to Kant individuals behave rationally if they act according to *categorical imperatives*. These are laws that prescribe a certain type of behaviour derived from reason alone. Furthermore, as all individuals can use their reasoning to formulate the same imperatives, rationality will only dictate behaviour all individuals can undertake. If it is not possible for all individuals to undertake an action, then that action is said to be irrational. For example, consider an employee considering the choice between working hard or shirking. According to instrumental rationality such a decision depends purely on which course of action best satisfies that individual's self-interest. In Chapter 7 such factors as the probability and costs of being caught shirking were used to develop an efficiency wage model. In this model involuntary unemployment was caused by firms setting the wage rate above the market-clearing level in order to induce employees to work hard. According to Kantian rationality, however, the categorical imperative is for employees to work hard. The reason for this is that not all employees would choose to shirk as this would cause the firm to go bankrupt. Given this moral imperative a worker observed to be shirking is considered irrational. With decisions now being based on moral reasoning rather than self-interest the final outcome can be very different. In this example there is no efficiency wage, and in equilibrium there is no unemployment. This is because firms no longer have to induce their employees to work hard. Similar arguments have been used to argue how it can be rational for individuals to co-operate in a prisoners' dilemma game.

Although Kantian rationality may be considered an extreme alternative to instrumental rationality other, less radical, definitions may generate similar results. One less extreme conception of rationality is bounded rationality. This is primarily associated with Simon (1982). According to this concept of rationality individuals have limited computational ability. As a result of these limitations individuals may well adopt procedures, or rules of behaviour, that help them to achieve satisfactory outcomes. Again this view of rationality may be used to avoid the self-defeating nature of instrumental rationality in certain situations. An interesting illustration of how simple rules of thumb can out perform more complex decision rules has been provided by an experiment undertaken by Axelrod (1980).

In this experiment Axelrod invited game theorists to submit computer programs on how best to play a repeated prisoners' dilemma game. The programs were then randomly paired in a round-robin tournament against one another. Within each pairing a prisoners' dilemma game was repeated 200 times. This process itself was repeated five times and average pay-offs calculated. Initially there were fourteen entrants. The most successful strategy was tit-for-tat submitted by Anatol Rapoport. Under this strategy the program starts with co-operation, and then does whatever its opponent did in the previous period. Not only was this the most successful strategy but it was also the simplest. Commenting on this result Rapoport (1987) notes that 'Tit-for-tat did not "beat" a single strategy against which it was pitted.' However, this strategy was most successful because other programs 'designed to beat their opponents, reduced each other's scores when pitted against each other, including themselves.' In this way the simplest strategy outperformed more complex strategies explicitly designed to win the tournament. On the basis of such evidence we may conclude that it is sometimes rational to act irrationally. Alternatively, so as to avoid this contradictory statement, we may wish to alter our definition of what it means to be rational.

12.2 Indeterminacy

A second criticism often made against game theory models is that instrumental rationality often fails to prescribe a unique course of action. This occurs when there are multiple equilibria. The prime example of this occurs in co-ordination games. An example of such a game is illustrated in Fig. 12.1.

In this game there are three Nash equilibria. Two of these equilibria are with pure strategies. These correspond to both players adopting the same strategy. The other equilibrium involves mixed strategies. Here both players adopt each strategy with a probability of 0.5. On the basis of instrumental rationality there is no unique prescription of how either player should play the game. Even with the strong assumption of common knowledge of rationality the optimal strategy remains indeterminant. What a player should do depends on his or her expectations of what the other player will do. In such a situation the choice of which equilibrium strategy to play must be dependent on non-rational considerations. For example, following the work of Schelling (1960), it is

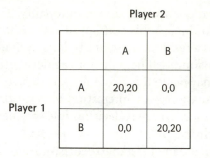

Fig. 12.1 A Co-ordination Game

often argued that agents will co-ordinate upon the focal point. The argument here is that agents use some salient feature of the game they are playing to co-ordinate their actions so that the final outcome is an equilibrium. Significantly these salient features cannot be determined by rationality alone, for otherwise there would be no problem of indeterminacy. Instead it will often be the case that what individuals consider salient is conditioned by their culture, previous experience, and the way the game has been presented to them. The implication of this is that when game theorists appeal to the concept of salience they are using something other than instrumental rationality. In order for economists to fully understand why agents co-ordinate upon one particular outcome rather than another it would seem that greater emphasis needs to be given to such factors as the institutional, cultural, and historical context within which decisions are made. In doing this economists will increasingly move away from models based solely on instrumental rationality and introduce additional considerations specific to the problem under consideration.

Another criticism of recent game theory models is directed against the use of a mixed-strategy Nash equilibrium. As discussed in Chapter 2 this is a weak equilibrium concept. This is because if a player expects others to play according to the mixed-strategy Nash equilibrium, then he or she is indifferent over the pure strategy components of their mixed-strategy equilibrium. This feature has led economists to question why individual players should persist with the mixed strategy. Even if the mixed-strategy equilibrium is unique, it is consistent with instrumental rationality for players to play *any* probabilistic combination of their pure-strategy components. Once more there is a basic indeterminacy. One interpretation of mixed strategies that tries to overcome this problem is associated with Aumann (1987). In this interpretation the probability distribution over pure strategies does not correspond to what players will do, but rather to their *subjective beliefs* about what other players will do. Equilibrium requires, therefore, that these beliefs are consistent. Aumann then appeals to the *Harsanyi doctrine* that states that if rational players have the same information, then they must necessarily hold the same beliefs. If this is true, then the problem of indeterminacy disappears, as beliefs will only be consistently aligned at the mixed-strategy Nash equilibrium. The problem with this argument is that it is not clear that rational individuals with the same information always reach identical conclusions. For example, if such beliefs are under-determined then it seems likely that different individuals will interpret available information in different ways. In this situation the problem of indeterminacy remains. To resolve such issues greater attention needs to be given to how individuals determine their initial beliefs.

12.3 Inconsistency

A third broad criticism of game theory has been directed at the concept of subgame perfection. This criticism was first presented by Binmore (1987, 1988) and illustrated with reference to Rosenthal's centipede game. This game was initially discussed in Chapter 3, and its extensive form is reproduced in Fig. 12.2.

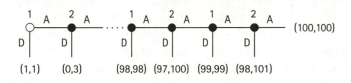

Fig. 12.2 Rosenthal's Centipede Game

Using the principle of backward induction it can be confirmed that the subgame perfect Nash equilibrium for this game is for player 1 to play down at the initial node. Binmore argues, however, that such reasoning is based on the use of counterfactuals that are inconsistent with the assumption of common knowledge of rationality. To understand this criticism consider the final decision node. Here we consider what player 2 will do if the game has continued this far. From the pay-offs it seems reasonable to suppose that player 2 will play down. With common knowledge of rationality backward induction applies similar logic to all preceding decision nodes, and at each one the same prediction is generated. The problem with such reasoning is that common knowledge of rationality predicts that the game will end at the first node. It is therefore inconsistent with this assumption to ask what a player will do if a subsequent node is reached. According to instrumental rationality these nodes will never be reached and so any argument based on this reasoning is spurious. An alternative way of appreciating this argument is to consider what player 2 should believe about player 1 if she has not initially played down. Player 2 now has clear evidence that player 1 is 'irrational' but this contradicts his certain knowledge, by assumption, that player 1 is rational. No possible belief is able to reconcile these two facts. Once more there is a logical contradiction.

Seen from this perspective the problem with assuming common knowledge of rationality is that it imposes a false certainty into a game where there is inherent uncertainty.

It rules out the possibility of any player ever playing across even though this is a legitimate choice. A number of ways have been suggested for how the resulting inconsistencies might be avoided. The first, as proposed by Selten (1975), involves assuming that players may make random mistakes when carrying out their intentions. With this so-called trembling-hand assumption a player may play across without violating the assumption of rationality. The resulting equilibrium is then known as trembling-hand perfection. Although errors of this kind might be considered justified in certain contexts, it does not seem appropriate for all games.

A more radical departure from subgame perfection is to allow agents to *believe* that other players might be irrational. It was this assumption, often referred to as common belief of rationality, that Kreps and Wilson (1982*b*) used in their development of sequential equilibrium. In their model this belief was held even though all agents were assumed rational. As argued in Chapter 11, a more reasonable assumption seems to be that some agents are in fact 'irrational'. Whichever approach is adopted players are now justified in considering the possibility of out-of-equilibrium behaviour.

Despite these proposals Binmore argues that to resolve the problem an alternative definition of rationality is needed. In particular Binmore agues for a type of procedural rationality. This is introduced so as to avoid the infinite regress arguments needed to determine a player's optimal strategy. These arguments are of the type 'I believe, that you believe, that I believe . . .' and so on. To avoid such continual reflection players must adopt an arbitrary stopping rule. With different agents adopting different stopping rules deviations from subgame perfection need not be inconsistent with procedural rationality. The conclusion of this argument is that perfect rationality is an impossibility. This is because it implies a never-ending reasoning process. Instead there are different types of procedural rationality, each differentiated by an alternative stopping rule.

12.4 Conclusions

This chapter has presented three broad criticisms directed against recent game theory models. In particular we argued that in certain situations the assumptions that all individuals are instrumentally rational, and that this is common knowledge, are unsatisfactory. This is because they are either self-defeating, incomplete, or involve inconsistencies. These theoretical criticisms reinforce those made in Chapter 11 where we observed that not all game theory predictions are supported by empirical evidence. However, rather than viewing these criticisms as being purely destructive, they can be seen as providing a stimulus for further research. Indeed, this is an ongoing process. In recent years game theorists have developed many alternative conceptions of rationality and equilibrium, some of which have been discussed in this book. Areas which offer the greatest potential for yielding further insights and results are expected to derive from models based on modifications to instrumental rationality and common knowledge.

This will involve a re-evaluation of what is meant by rationality, so as to incorporate factors such as learning, uncertainty, morality as well as computational limitations. Furthermore, it would appear that greater emphasis will need to be given to considerations such as the role of institutions, culture, and history. It is predicted that game theory and its application to economics will be at the forefront of these advances.

Further Reading

Bianchi, M., and H. Moulin (1991), 'Strategic Interactions in Economics: The Game Theory Alternative', in N. De Marchi and M. Blaug (eds.), *Appraising Economic Theories*, Aldershot: Edward Elgar.

Binmore, K. (1992), *Fun and Games: A Text on Game Theory*, Lexington, Mass.: Heath.

Binmore, K. (1987), 'Modeling Rational Players: Part I', *Economics and Philosophy*, 3: 179–214; repr. in K. Binmore (1990), *Essays on the Foundations of Game Theory*, Oxford: Blackwell.

Binmore, K. (1988), 'Modeling Rational Players: Part II', *Economics and Philosophy*, 4: 9–55; repr. in K. Binmore (1990), *Essays on the Foundations of Game Theory*, Oxford: Blackwell.

Gerrard, B. (1993), *The Economics of Rationality*, London: Routledge.

Hargreaves Heap, S. (1989), *Rationality in Economics*, Oxford: Blackwell.

Hargreaves Heap, S., and Y. Varoufakis (1995), *Game Theory: A Critical Introduction*, London: Routledge.

Sugden, R. (1991), 'Rational Choice: A Survey of Contributions from Economics and Philosophy', *Economic Journal*, 101: 751–85.

BIBLIOGRAPHY

Abreu, D. (1986), 'Extremal Equilibria of Oligopolistic Supergames', *Journal of Economic Theory*, 39: 191–235.

Akerlof, G. A., and J. L. Yellen (1985), 'A Near-Rational Model of the Business Cycle, with Wage and Price Inertia', *Quarterly Journal of Economics*, 100: 823–38; repr. in N. G. Mankiw and D. Romer (1991), *New Keynesian Economics*, i, Cambridge, Mass.: MIT Press.

—— —— (1986), *Efficiency Wage Models of the Labour Market*, Cambridge, Mass.: Cambridge University Press.

Alvi, E. (1993), 'Near Rationality/Menu Costs, Strategic Complementarity and Real Rigidity', *Journal of Macroeconomics*, 15: 619–25.

Andreoni, J., and J. H. Miller (1993), 'Rational Cooperation in the Finitely Repeated Prisoner's Dilemma: Experimental Evidence', *Economic Journal*, 103: 570–85.

Aumann, R. J. (1987), 'Correlated Equilibrium as an Expression of Bayesian Ignorance', *Econometrica*, 55: 1–18.

Aumann, R., and S. Hart (1992), *Handbook of Game Theory with Economic Applications*, New York: North-Holland.

Axelrod, R. (1980), 'The Emergence of Cooperation Among Egoists', *American Political Science Review*, 75: 306–18.

Backus, D., and J. Driffel (1985), 'Inflation and Reputation', *American Economic Review*, 75: 530–8.

Bain, J. (1956), *Barriers To New Competition*, Cambridge, Mass.: Harvard University Press.

Ball, L., N. K. Mankiw, and D. Romer (1988), 'The New Keynesian Economic and the Output-Inflation Trade-off', *Brookings Papers on Economic Activity*, 1: 1–65; repr. in N. G. Mankiw and D. Romer (1991), *New Keynesian Economics*, i, Cambridge, Mass.: MIT Press.

—— and D. Romer (1990), 'Real Rigidities and the Non-Neutrality of Money', *Review of Economic Studies*, 57: 183–203; repr. in N. G. Mankiw and D. Romer (1991), *New Keynesian Economics*, i, Cambridge, Mass.: MIT Press.

—— —— (1991), 'Sticky Prices as Coordination Failure', *American Economic Review*, 81: 939–52.

Barrett, S. (1990), 'The Problem of Global Environmental Protection', *Oxford Review of Economic Policy*, 6: 68-79; repr. in D. Helm (1991), *Economic Policy Towards the Environment*, Oxford: Blackwell. Also in T. Jenkinson (1996), *Readings in Microeconomics*, New York: Oxford University Press.

—— (1994), 'Self-Enforcing International Environmental Agreements', *Oxford Economic Papers*, 46: 878–94.

Barro, R. J. (1986), 'Reputation in a Model of Monetary Policy', *Journal of Monetary Economics*, 17: 3–20.

—— and D. A. Gordon (1983), 'Rules, Discretion and Reputation in a Model of Monetary Policy', *Journal of Political Economy*, 17: 101–22.

Baumol, W., J. Panzer, and R. Willig (1982), *Contestable Markets and the Theory of Industry Structure*, New York: Harcourt Brace Jovanovich.

Benoit, J. P., and V. Krishna (1985), 'Finitely Repeated Games', *Econometrica*, 53: 890-904.

—— —— (1987), 'Dynamic Duopoly: Prices and Quantities', *Review of Economic Studies*, 54: 23–36.

Bianchi, M., and H. Moulin (1991), '*Strategic Interactions in Economics: The Game Theory Alternative*', in N. De Marchi and M Blaug (eds.), *Appraising Economic Theories*, Aldershot: Edward Elgar.

Bierman, H. S., and L. Fernandez (1993), *Game Theory with Economic Applications*, Reading, Mass.: Addison Wesley.

Binmore, K. (1987), 'Modeling Rational Players: Part I', *Economics and Philosophy*, 3: 179–214; repr. in K. Binmore (1990), *Essays on the Foundations of Game Theory*, Oxford: Blackwell.

—— (1988), 'Modeling Rational Players: Part II', *Economics and Philosophy*, 4: 9–55; repr. in K. Binmore (1990), *Essays on the Foundations of Game Theory*, Oxford: Blackwell.

—— (1992), *Fun and Games: A Text on Game Theory*, Lexington, Mass.: Heath.

Blackburn, K. (1992), 'Credibility and Time Consistency in Monetary Policy', in K. Dowd and M. K. Lewis (eds.), *Current Issues in Financial and Monetary Economics*, London: Macmillan.

Bladen-Hovell, R. C. (1992), 'International Monetary Policy', in K. Dowd and M. K. Lewis (eds.), *Current Issues in Financial and Monetary Economics*, London: Macmillan.

Blanchard, O. J. (1983), 'Price Asychronization and Price Level Inertia', in R. Dornbusch and M. Simonsen (eds.), *Inflation, Debt, and Indexation*, Cambridge, Mass.: MIT Press; repr. in N. G. Mankiw and D. Romer (1991), *New Keynesian Economics*, i, Cambridge, Mass.: MIT Press.

—— and N. Kiyotaki (1987), 'Monopolistic Competition and the Effects of Aggregate Demand', *American Economic Review*, 77: 647–66; repr. in N. G. Mankiw and D. Romer (1991), *New Keynesian Economics*, i, Cambridge, Mass.: MIT Press.

Brander, J. A., and B. J. Spencer (1983), 'International R&D Rivalry and Industrial Strategy', *Review of Economic Studies*, 50: 707–22.

—— —— (1984), 'Tariff Protection and Imperfect Competition', in H. Kierzkowski (ed.), *Monopolistic Competition and International Trade*, New York: Oxford University Press.

—— —— (1985), 'Export Subsidies and International Market Share Rivalry', *Journal of International Economics*, 18: 83–100.

Bresnahan, T. F. (1981), 'Duopoly Models with Consistent Conjectures', *American Economic Review*, 71: 934–45.

Buiter, W. H., and R. C. Marston (1985), *International Economic Policy Coordination*, Cambridge, Mass.: Cambridge University Press.

Camerer, C., and K. Weigelt (1988), 'Experimental Tests of the Sequential Equilibrium Reputation Model', *Econometrica*, 56: 1–36.

Canzoneri, M. B., and P. Minford (1986), 'When Policy Coordination Matters: An Empirical Analysis', *CEPR Discussion Paper* No. 119.

Carraro, C., and D. Siniscalco (1995), 'Policy Coordination for Sustainability: Commitments, Transfers, and Linked Negotiations', in I. Goldin and L. A. Winters (eds.), *The Economics of Sustainable Development*, Cambridge: Cambridge University Press.

Chamberlain, E. H. (1933), *The Theory of Monopolistic Competition*, Cambridge, Mass.: Harvard University Press.

Coleman, A. M. (1983), *Game Theory and Experimental Games*, Oxford: Pergamon Press.

Bibliography

Cooper, R. W., D. V. DeJong, R. Forsythe, and T. W. Ross. (1989), 'Communication in the Battle of the Sexes Game: Some Experimental Results', *Rand Journal of Economics*, 20: 568–87.

—— —— —— and T. W. Ross (1990), 'Selection Criteria in Coordination Games: Some Experimental Results', *American Economic Review*, 80: 218–33.

—— —— —— —— (1991), 'Cooperation without Reputation', Working Paper, University of Iowa.

—— and A. John (1988), 'Coordinating Coordination Failures in Keynesian Models', *Quarterly Journal of Economics*, 103: 441–63; repr. in N. G. Mankiw and D. Romer (1991), *New Keynesian Economics Vol. 2*, Cambridge, Mass.: MIT Press.

Cournot, A. (1838), *Recherches sur les Principes Mathematiques de la Theorie des Richesses*, English edn.: N. Bacon (ed.), *Researches into the Mathematical Principles of the Theory of Wealth*, New York: Macmillan 1897.

Currie, D. A. (1990), 'International Policy Coordination', in D. T. Llewellyn and C. Milner (eds.), *Current Issues in International Monetary Economics*, London: Macmillan.

Currie, D. A., and P. Levine (1985), 'Macroeconomic Policy Design in an Interdependent World', in W. H. Buiter and R. C. Marston (eds.), *International Economic Policy Coordination*, Cambridge and New York: Cambridge University Press.

—— —— (1991), 'International Policy Coordination—A Survey', in C. J. Green and D. T. Llewellyn (eds.), *Surveys in Monetary Economics*, i, Oxford: Basil Blackwell; repr. in D. Currie and P. Levine (1993), *Rules, Reputation and Macroeconomic Policy*, Cambridge and New York: Cambridge University Press.

—— —— and N. Vidalis (1987), 'International Cooperation and Reputation in an Empirical Two-Bloc Model', in R. Bryant and R. Portes (eds.), *Global Macroeconomic Policy Conflict and Cooperation*, London: Macmillan.

D'Aspremont, C. A., and J. J. Gabszewicz (1986), 'On the Stability of Collusion', in G. F. Matthewson and J. E. Stiglitz, *New Developments in the Analysis of Market Structure*, New York: Macmillan.

Davis, D. D., and C. A. Holt (1993), *Experimental Economics*, Princeton: Princeton University Press.

Diamond, P. A. (1982), 'Aggregate Demand Management in Search Equilibrium', *Journal of Political Economy*, 90: 881–94; repr. in N. G. Mankiw and D. Romer (1991), *New Keynesian Economics*, ii, Cambridge, Mass.: MIT Press.

Dixit, A. (1981), 'The Role of Investment in Entry Deterrence', *Economic Journal*, 90: 95–106.

—— (1987), 'Strategic Aspects of Trade Policy', in T. Bewley (ed.), *Advances in Economic Theory: Fifth World Congress*, New York: Cambridge University Press.

—— and G. M. Grossman (1986), 'Targeted Export Promotion with Several Oligopolistic Industries', *Journal of International Economics*, 21: 233–49.

—— and B. J. Nalebuff (1991), *Thinking Strategically: The Competitive Edge in Business, Politics, and Everyday Life*, New York: Norton.

Donsimoni, M. P., N. S. Economides, and H. M. Polemarchakis (1986), 'Stable Cartels', *International Economic Review*, 27: 317–27.

Durlauf, S. N. (1989), 'Locally Interacting Systems, Coordination Failure, and the Behavior of Aggregate Activity', Stanford University, mimeo.

Eaton, J., and G. Grossman (1986), 'Optimal Trade and Industrial Policy under Oligopoly', *Quarterly Journal of Economics*, 101: 383–406.

Eatwell, J., M. Milgate, and P. Newman (1989), *The New Palgrave: Game Theory*, New York: W. W. Norton.

Farrell, J., and E. Maskin (1989), 'Renegotiation in Repeated Games', *Games and Economic Behaviour*, 1: 327–60.

Field, B. (1994), *Environmental Economics: An Introduction*, New York: McGraw-Hill.

Fischer, S. (1977), 'Long Term Contracts, Rational Expectations and the Optimal Money Supply Rule', *Journal of Political Economy*, 85: 191–205; repr. in N. G. Mankiw and D. Romer (1991), *New Keynesian Economics*, i, Cambridge, Mass.: MIT Press.

Frenkel J. A., and K. R. Rockett (1988), 'International Macroeconomic Policy Coordination When Policymakers Do Not Agree on the True Model', *American Economic Review*, 78: 318–40.

Friedman, J. (1971), 'A Non-cooperative Equilibrium for Supergames', *Review of Economic Studies*, 38: 1–12.

—— (1977), *Oligopoly and the Theory of Games*, Amsterdam: North-Holland.

—— (1986), *Game Theory with Applications to Economics*, Oxford: Oxford University Press.

Friedman, M. (1953), 'The Methodology of Positive Economics', in M. Friedman, *Essays in Positive Economics*, Chicago: University of Chicago Press; repr. in B. Caldwell (1984), *Appraisal and Criticism in Economics: A Book of Readings*, Boston: Allen & Unwin.

—— (1968), 'The Role of Monetary Policy', *American Economic Review*, 58: 1–17.

Fudenberg, D., and E. Maskin (1986), 'The Folk Theorem in Repeated Games with Discounting or with Incomplete Information', *Econometrica*, 54: 533–56.

—— and Tirole, J. (1986), *Dynamic Models of Oligopoly*, New York: Harwood.

Gerrard, B. (1993), *The Economics of Rationality*, London: Routledge.

Ghosh, A. R., and P. Masson (1988), 'International Policy Coordination in a World with Model Uncertainty', *International Monetary Fund Staff Papers*, 35: 230–58.

Gibbons, R. (1992), *Game Theory for Applied Economists*, Princeton: Princeton University Press.

Gilbert, R. J. (1989), 'Mobility Barriers and the Value of Incumbency', in R. Schmalensee and R. D. Willig (eds.), *Handbook of Industrial Organization*, i, Elsevier Science Publishers.

Gordon, R. J. (1981) 'Output Fluctuations and Gradual Price Adjustment', *Journal of Economic Literature*, 19: 493–530.

—— (1990), 'What is New-Keynesian Economics?' *Journal of Economic Literature*, 28: 1115–71.

Gravelle, H., and R. Rees (1992), *Microeconomics*, London: Longman.

Gray, J. (1976), 'Wage Indexation: A Macroeconomic Approach', *Journal of Monetary Economics*, 2: 221–35.

Green, E., and R. Porter (1984), 'Noncooperative Collusion under Imperfect Price Information', *Econometrica*, 52: 87–100.

Guttman, J. M. (1978), 'Understanding Collective Action: Matching Behaviour', *American Economic Review Papers and Proceedings*, 68: 251–5.

Hallwood, C. P., and R. MacDonald (1994), *International Money and Finance*, Oxford: Blackwell.

Hamada, K. (1974), 'Alternative Exchange Rate Systems and the Interdependence of Monetary Policies', in R. Z. Aliber (ed.), *National Monetary Policies and the International Financial System*, Chicago: University of Chicago Press.

—— (1976), 'A Strategic Analysis of Monetary Interdependence', *Journal of Political Economy*, 86: 677–700.

Bibliography

Hamada, K. (1979), 'Macroeconomic Strategy and Coordination under Alternative Exchange Rates', in R. Dornbusch and J. A. Frenkel (eds.), *International Economic Policy: Theory and Evidence*, Baltimore: John Hopkins University Press.

Hanley, N., J. F. Shogren, and B. White (1997), *Environmental Economics: In Theory and Practice*, London: Macmillan.

Hargreaves Heap, S. (1989), *Rationality in Economics*, Oxford: Blackwell.

—— (1992), *The New Keynesian Macroeconomics: Time, Belief and Social Interdependence*, Aldershot: Edward Elgar.

—— and Y. Varoufakis (1995), *Game Theory: A Critical Introduction*, London: Routledge.

Harsanyi, J. (1967, 1968), 'Games with Incomplete Information Played by Bayesian Players I, II and III', *Management Science*, 14: 159–82, 302–34, and 486–503.

Hey, J. (1991), *Experiments In Economics*, Oxford: Blackwell.

Hicks, J. R. (1937), 'Mr. Keynes and the 'Classics': A Suggested Interpretation', *Econometrica*, 5: 147–59.

Hoover, K. D. (1988), *The New Classical Macroeconomics*, Oxford: Blackwell.

Howitt, P. (1981), 'Activist Monetary Policy under Rational Expectations', *Journal of Political Economy*, 89: 249–69.

—— and R. P. McAfee (1988), 'Stability of Equilibria with Externalities', *Quarterly Journal of Economics*, 103: 261–78.

Hughes Hallet, A. J. (1987), 'The Impact of Interdependence on Economic Policy Design: The Case of the US, EEC, and Japan', *Economic Modelling*, 10: 377–96.

—— (1989), 'Macroeconomic Interdependence and the Coordination of Economic Policy', in D. Greenaway (ed.), *Current Issues in Macroeconomics*, London: Macmillan.

Jacquemin, A., and M. E. Slade (1989), 'Cartels, Collusion, and Horizontal Merger', in R. Schmalensee and R. D. Willig (eds.), *Handbook of Industrial Organization*, i, Elsevier Science Publishers.

Johnson, H. G. (1954), 'Optimum Tariffs and Retaliation', *Review of Economic Studies*, 21: 142–53.

Kagel, J. H., and A. E. Roth (1995), *The Handbook of Experimental Economics*, Princeton: Princeton University Press.

Kandori, M. (1992), 'Social Norms and Community Enforcement', *Review of Economic Studies*, 59: 63–80.

Kant, I. (1788), *Critique of Practical Reason*, trans. and ed. L. W. Beck, *Critique of Practical Reason and Other Writings in Moral Philosophy*, Cambridge: Cambridge University Press.

Kennan, J., and R. Riezman (1988), 'Do Big Countries Win Tariff Wars?' *International Economic Review*, 29: 81–5.

Keynes, J. M. (1936), *General Theory of Employment, Interest and Money*, London: Macmillan.

Kiyotaki, N. (1988), 'Multiple Expectational Equilibria under Monopolistic Competition', *Quarterly Journal of Economics*, 102: 695–714.

Kreps, D. (1990a), *A Course in Microeconomic Theory*, New York: Harvester Wheatsheaf.

—— (1990b), *Game Theory and Economic Modelling*, Oxford: Clarendon Press.

—— P. Milgrom, J. Roberts, and R. Wilson (1982), 'Rational Cooperation in the Finitely Repeated Prisoners' Dilemma Game', *Journal of Economic Theory*, 27: 245–52.

—— and R. Wilson (1982a), 'Reputation and Imperfect Information', *Journal of Economic Theory*, 27: 253–79.

—— —— (1982b), 'Sequential Equilibria', *Econometrica*, 50: 863–94.

Krugman, P. R. (1986), *Strategic Trade Policy and the New International Economics*, Cambridge, Mass.: MIT Press.

—— (1987), 'Is Free Trade Passé?' *Economic Perspectives*, 1: 131–44.

—— (1989), 'Industrial Organization and International Trade', in R. Schmalensee and R. Willig (eds.), *Handbook of Industrial Organization*, ii, Elsevier Science Publishers.

Kuga, K. (1973), 'Tariff Retaliation and Policy Equilibrium', *Journal of International Economics*, 3: 351–66.

Laussel, D., and C. Montet (1994), 'Strategic Trade Policies', in D. Greenaway and L. A. Winters (eds.), *Surveys in International Trade*, Oxford: Blackwell.

Leslie, D. (1993), *Advanced Macroeconomics*, London: McGraw-Hill.

Levine. P. (1990), 'Monetary Policy and Credibility', in T. Bandyopadhyay and S. Clutah (eds.), *Current Issues in Monetary Economics*, London: Macmillan.

—— and D. Currie (1987), 'Does International Macroeconomic Policy Coordination Pay and is it Sustainable? A Two Country Analysis', *Oxford Economic Papers*, 39: 38–74.

Lucas, R. E. (1972), 'Expectations and the Neutrality of Money', *Journal of Economic Theory*, 4: 103–24.

—— (1980), *The Death of Keynesian Economics: Issues and Ideas*, Chicago: University of Chicago Press.

Lyons, B., and Y. Varoufakis (1989), 'Game Theory, Oligopoly and Bargaining', in J. D. Hey (ed.), *Current Issues in Microeconomics*, London: Macmillan.

McKelvey, R. D., and T. R. Palfrey (1992), 'An Experimental Study of the Centipede Game', *Econometrica*, 60: 802–36.

Mäler, G-M. (1991), 'International Environmental Problems', in D. Helm (ed.), *Economic Policy Towards the Environment*, Oxford: Blackwell.

Mankiw, N. G. (1985), 'Small Menu Costs and Large Business Cycles: A Macroeconomic Model of Monopoly', *Quarterly Journal of Economics*, 100: 529–37; repr. in N. G. Mankiw and D. Romer (1991), *New Keynesian Economics*, i, Cambridge, Mass.: MIT Press.

—— (1992), *Macroeconomics*, New York: Worth Publishers.

Martin, S. (1992), *Advanced Industrial Economics*, Oxford: Blackwell.

Mayer, W. (1981), 'Theoretical Considerations on Negotiated Tariff Adjustments', *Oxford Economic Papers*, 33: 135–53.

Milgrom, P., and J. Roberts. (1982a), 'Limit Pricing and Entry Under Incomplete Information: An Equilibrium Analysis', *Econometrica*, 50: 443–59.

—— —— (1982b), 'Predation, Reputation and Entry Deterrence', *Journal of Economic Theory*, 27: 280–312.

Miller, M., and M. Salmon (1985), Policy Coordination and the Time Inconsistency of Optimal Policy in Open Economies', *Economic Journal*, Supplement: 124–35.

Minford, P., and M. B. Canzoneri (1987), 'Policy Interdependence: Does Strategic Behaviour Pay?' *CEPR Discussion Paper*, No. 201.

Modigliani, F. (1958), 'New Developments on the Oligopoly Front', *Journal of Political Economy*, 66: 215–32.

Murphy K. J., A. Shleifer, and R. Vishny (1989a), 'Income Distribution, Market Size, and Industrialization', *Quarterly Journal of Economics*, 104: 537–64.

—— —— —— (1989b), 'Industrialization and the Big Push', *Journal of Political Economy*, 96: 1221–31.

Bibliography

Muth, J. F. (1961), 'Rational Expectations and the Theory of Price Movements', *Econometrica*, 29: 315–35.

Nash, J. (1951), 'Non-Cooperative Games', *Annals of Mathematics*, 54: 286–95.

Neral, J., and J. Ochs (1992), 'The Sequential Equilibrium Theory of Reputation Building: A Further Test', *Econometrica*, 60: 1151–69.

Nordhaus, W. (1975), 'The Political Business Cycle', *Review of Economic Studies*, 42: 169–90.

Okun, A. M. (1975), 'Inflation: Its Mechanics and Welfare Costs', *Brookings Papers on Economic Activity*, 2: 351–401; repr. in N. G. Mankiw and D. Romer (1991), *New Keynesian Economics*, ii, Cambridge, Mass.: MIT Press.

—— (1981), *Prices and Quantities: A Macroeconomic Analysis*, Oxford: Blackwell.

Ordover, J. A., and G. Saloner (1989), 'Predation, Monopolization, and Antitrust', in R. Schmalensee and R. D. Willig (eds.), *Handbook of Industrial Organization*, i, Elsevier Science Publishers.

Oudiz, G., and J. Sachs (1984), 'Macroeconomic Policy Coordination Among the Industrial Economies', *Brookings Papers on Economic Activity*, 1: 1–64.

—— —— (1985), 'International Policy Coordination in Dynamic Macroeconomic Models', in W. H. Buiter and R. C. Marston (eds.), *International Economic Policy Coordination*, Cambridge and New York: Cambridge University Press.

Parkin, M. (1986), 'The Output-Inflation Trade-off when Prices are Costly to Change', *Journal of Political Economy*, 94: 200–24.

Peel, D. (1989), 'New Classical Macroeconomics', in D. Greenaway (ed.), *Current Issues in Macroeconomics*, London: Macmillan.

Perman, R., Y. Ma, and J. McGilvray (1996), *Natural Resources and Environmental Economics*, London: Longman.

Phelps, E. S. (1992), 'Expectations in Macroeconomics and the Rational Expectations Debate', in A. Vercelli and N. Dimitri (eds.), *Macroeconomics: A Survey of Research Strategies*, Oxford: Oxford University Press.

—— and J. Taylor (1977), 'Stabilizing Powers of Monetary Policy with Rational Expectations', *Journal of Political Economy*, 85: 163–90.

Phlips, L. (1995), *Competition Policy: A Game Theoretic Perspective*, Cambridge, Cambridge University Press.

Porter, R. (1983), 'Optimal Cartel Trigger-Price Strategies', *Journal of Economic Theory*, 29: 313–38.

Poundstone, W. (1992), *Prisoner's Dilemma*, New York: Doubleday.

Radner, R. (1980), 'Collusive Behavior in Oligopolies with Long but Finite Lives', *Journal of Economic Theory*, 22: 136–56.

Rasmusen, E. (1993), *Games and Information*, Oxford: Blackwell.

Rapoport, A. (1987), 'Prisoner's Dilemma', in J. Eatwell, M. Milgate and P. Newman (eds.), *The New Palgrave Game Theory*, New York: W. W. Norton & Co.

Rees, R. (1993), 'Tacit Collusion', *Oxford Review of Economic Policy*, 9: 27–40; repr. in T. Jenkinson (1996), *Readings in Microeconomics*, New York: Oxford University Press.

Rogoff, K. (1985), 'Can International Monetary Policy Coordination be Counter-Productive?' *Journal of International Economics*, 18: 199–217.

Romer, D. (1996), *Advanced Macroeconomics*, New York: McGraw-Hill.

Rosenthal, R. (1981), 'Games of Perfect Information, Predatory Pricing, and the Chain-store Paradox', *Journal of Mathematical Psychology*, 25: 92–100.

Rotemberg, J., and G. Saloner (1986), 'A Supergame-Theoretic Model of Price Wars during Booms', *American Economic Review*, 76: 390–407; repr. in N. G. Mankiw and D. Romer (1991), *New Keynesian Economics*, ii, Cambridge, Mass.: MIT Press.

—— —— (1987), 'The Relative Rigidity of Monopoly Pricing', *American Economic Review*, 77: 917–26.

—— and M. Woodford (1991), 'Markups and the Business Cycle', *NBER Macroeconomics Annual.*

Salop, S. C. (1979), 'A Model of the Natural Rate of Unemployment', *American Economic Review*, 69: 117–25.

Sargent, T. J. (1973), 'Rational Expectations, the Real Rate of Interest, and the Natural Rate of Unemployment', *Brookings Papers on Economic Activity*, 2: 429–72.

—— and N. Wallace (1975), 'Rational Expectations, the Optimal Monetary Instrument and the Optimal Money Supply Rule', *Journal of Political Economy*, 83: 241–54.

Schaling, E. (1995), *Institutions and Monetary Policy*, Aldershot: Edward Elgar.

Schelling, T. (1960), *The Strategy of Conflict*, Cambridge, Mass.: Harvard University Press.

Selten, R. (1975), 'Re-examination of the Perfectless Concept for Equilibrium Points in Extensive Games', *International Journal of Game Theory*, 4: 22–55.

—— and R. Stoecker (1986), 'End Behavior in Sequences of Finite Prisoner's Dilemma Supergames', *Journal of Economic Behavior and Organization*, 7: 47–70.

Shafir, E., and A. Tversky (1992), 'Thinking Through Uncertainty: Nonconsequential Reasoning and Choice', *Cognitive Psychology*, 24: 449–74.

Shapiro, C. (1989), 'Theories of Oligopoly Behavior', in R. Schmalensee and R. D. Willig (eds.), *Handbook of Industrial Organization*, i, Elsevier Science Publishers.

Shapiro, N., and J. Stiglitz (1984), 'Equilibrium Unemployment as a Discipline Device', *American Economic Review*, 74: 433–44; repr. in N. G. Mankiw and D. Romer (1991), *New Keynesian Economics*, ii, Cambridge, Mass.: MIT Press.

Shleifer, A. (1986), 'Implementation Cycles', *Journal of Political Economy*, 94: 1163–90; repr. in N. G. Mankiw and D. Romer (1991), *New Keynesian Economics*, ii, Cambridge, Mass.: MIT Press.

—— and R. W. Vishny (1988), 'The Efficiency of Investment in the Presence of Aggregate Demand Spillovers', *Journal of Political Economy*, 96: 1221–31.

Simon H. A. (1982), *Models of Bounded Rationality*, Cambridge, Mass.: MIT Press.

Snowdon, B., H. Vane, and P. Wynarczyk (1994), *A Modern Guide to Macroeconomics: An Introduction to Competing Schools of Thought*, Aldershot: Edward Elgar.

Stiglitz, J. E. (1984), 'Price Rigidities and Market Structure', *American Economic Review*, 74: 350–55; repr. in N. G. Mankiw and D. Romer (1991), *New Keynesian Economics*, ii, Cambridge, Mass.: MIT Press.

—— (1987), 'The Causes and Consequences of the Dependency of Quality on Price', *Journal of Economic Literature*, 25: 1–48.

Sugden, R. (1991), 'Rational Choice: A Survey of Contributions from Economics and Philosophy', *Economic Journal*, 101: 751–85.

Sylos-Labini, P. (1962), *Oligopoly and Technical Progress*, Cambridge, Mass.: Harvard University Press.

Taylor, J. B. (1985), 'International Coordination in the Design of Macroeconomic Policy Rules', *European Economic Review*, 28: 53–82.

Bibliography

Tinbergen, J. (1952), *On The Theory of Economic Policy*, Amsterdam: North-Holland.

Tirole, J.(1988), *The Theory of Industrial Organisation*, Cambridge, Mass.: MIT Press.

Thursby, M., and R. Jensen (1983), 'A Conjectural Variations Approach to Strategic Tariff Equilibria', *Journal of International Economics*, 14: 145–61.

Van Huyck, J. B., R. C. Battalio, and R. O. Beil (1990), 'Tacit Coordination Games, Strategic Uncertainty, and Coordination Failure', *American Economic Review*, 80: 234–48.

Varian, H. (1992), *Microeconomic Analysis*, New York: Norton.

Venables, A. (1985), 'Trade and Trade Policy with Imperfect Competition: The Case of Identical Products and Free Entry', *Journal of International Economics*, 19: 1–19.

Vickers, J. (1985), 'Strategic Competition among the Few—Some Recent Developments in the Economics of Industry', *Oxford Review of Economic Policy*, 1: 39–62; repr. in T. Jenkinson (1996), *Readings in Microeconomics*, New York: Oxford University Press.

Weiss, A. (1980), 'Job Queues and Layoffs in Labour Markets with Flexible Wages', *Journal of Political Economy*, 88: 526–38.

—— (1991), *Efficiency Wages: Models of Unemployment, Layoffs and Wage Dispersion*, Oxford: Clarendon Press.

Wilson, R. (1992), 'Strategic Models of Entry Deterrence', in R. J. Aumann and S. Hart (eds.), *Handbook of Game Theory with Economic Applications*, New York: North-Holland.

INDEX

Index

Index

Index